The CIA,
Fidel Castro,
the Bogotazo
and the
New World Order

Other works by Servando Gonzalez

BOOKS

Arte: realismo o realidad
Historia de las artes visuales (con Armando Ledón)
Historia herética de la revolución fidelista
(published in México as *Fidel Castro para herejes y otros invertebrados*)
Observando
The Secret Fidel Castro: Deconstructing the Symbol
The Nuclear Deception: Nikita Khrushchev and the Cuban Missile Crisis
La madre de todas las conspiraciones
Psychological Warfare and the New World Order
La CIA, Fidel Castro, el Bogotazo y el Nuevo Orden Mundial
OBAMANIA: The New Puppet and His Masters
American Inventors
The Swastika and the Nazis
Partners in Crime
Coronavirus for Dunces
Coronavirus y Nuevo Orden Mundial
2024: El Gran Comienzo

MULTIMEDIA

Real History of "The Horse" : A HyperComic
How to Create Your Own Personal Intelligence Agency
The Riddle of the Swastika: A Study in Symbolism
Popol Vuh: An Interactive Educational Game
Hypertext for Beginners

DOCUMENTARIES

Treason in America: The Council on Foreign Relations
Partners in Treason: The CFR-CIA-Castro Connection

Servando Gonzalez

The CIA,
Fidel Castro,
the Bogotazo
and the
New World Order

Psychological Warfare
Against Latin America

Spooks Books
Hayward, California

ISBN-9780932367310

To the memory of the thousands of Colombians who died as the result of the Bogotazo and the Violence it unleashed.

Contents

Epilogue 193

Appendix 196

Notes 203

Foreword

> It seems "conspiracy theory" is now nothing more than
> a synonym for truths that cannot be told.
>   —Gore Vidal.

This book is about a conspiracy. Although it is centered on the events
of April 1948 in Bogota, Colombia, which later came to be called
the Bogotazo, as we shall see, these events were only a small part of
a vast conspiracy that marked the first steps in establishing what is
now known as the New World Order.

The globalist conspirators pushing this NWO are a relatively
small group of sociopaths and psychopaths, composed primarily of
international bankers, oil tycoons and top executives of transnational
corporations. Although this criminal group maintains alliances with
both the Fascist right and the Communist left —in fact they have
created both ideologies[1]— the themselves lack a coherent ideology,
and only use existing ideologies to gain maximum power and control.

In order to carry out their plans, this group of sociopathic conspirators does not hesitate to resort to lies, coercion, extortion, usury
and theft, as well as torture, murder and death on a large scale. To
execute these evil plans they have made use of a large number of
criminal psychopaths they have managed to recruit.[2] Their ultimate
goal is to destroy the established order, especially the democratic
sovereign republics, and to establish a totalitarian Communo-Fascist world society under their total control —a society they have
euphemistically call the New World Order.

This small group of conspirators focuses primarily on various
organizations they have created for their own benefit, such as the
Council on Foreign Relations, the United Nations, the Trilateral
Commission, the World Bank, the International Monetary Fund and,
more recently, globalist organizations such as the Bilderberg Group
and the World Economic Forum.

The efforts of this group of conspirators to gain total control
over the American continent began in 1898 with the blowing up of
the battleship USS Maine in Havana Bay and intensified during the
presidency of Woodrow Wilson. However, it was not until the end of
World War II that they became a secret psychological war of immense proportions against the peoples of North, Central and South
America. Important elements in this struggle are the U.S. State De-

partment, the National Security Council, and the Central Intelligence Agency.

Key figures in this psychological warfare have been Nelson and David Rockefeller, Allen and John Foster Dulles, George Marshall, Fidel Castro, Henry Kissinger, Zbigniew Brzezinski and Hillary Clinton. Although most American presidents have been under the control of these conspirators, lately they have all been an active part of this conspiracy. These have been the cases of Jimmy Carter, Bush Sr. and Jr., Bill Clinton and, most recently, Barack Obama and Joe Biden.

It was this group of oil tycoons and Wall Street bankers who conspired in the shadows to artificially create the Russian "revolution" that created the Soviet Union, the Nazi movement that brought Hitler to power in Germany, and the "revolutions" that allowed Mao tse-Tung and Fidel Castro to take power in China and Cuba respectively. These are the same people who have fomented the "revolutions" in the Middle East known as the "Arab Spring" and the overthrow of a legitimate government in the Ukraine.

This vast conspiracy, ignored by most of the American and Latin American people because it is never mentioned in the officialist press, resembles a gigantic jigsaw puzzle, in which some of the pieces are missing or have been intentionally placed out of place in an effort to confuse. This explains why most of those who have studied the phenomenon have not been able to find the real cause of the problem.

One of the most interesting features of intelligence and espionage work is that sometimes a seemingly irrelevant piece of information serves to connect a multitude of facts which provide a coherent whole. In fact, all criminal investigative work comes down to trying to find a connection, a link between the crime and the criminal. According to some intelligence officers if one succeeds in finding this link, one could rewrite history from a very different point of view than is commonly accepted.

Although I had long suspected the official story about the Bogotazo was not true,[3] the information which allowed me to arrange most of the pieces of the puzzle into a coherent whole was a secret meeting that took place in early 1948 in a mansion in the Biltmore, a millionaire's suburb on the western outskirts of Havana.

1. Conspiracies and Conspiracy Theories

I am sure some of the polemical theses I will express in this book will contribute to my being permanently labeled as a promoter of "conspiracy theory" on my lapel, which, in the end, I do not mind.

However, historical facts are extremely rich and complex, and cannot be fully explained by labels alone. But my major objection is not that someone says I study "conspiracy theory", but the use of the word "theory" to denote the kind of knowledge I have tried to unravel in this book. The problem stems from the use of the word "theory."

A scientific theory is nothing but a temporary explanation of the causes of a phenomenon for which we do not have all the information. Therefore, based on only a few verifiable data and a large percentage of logical conclusions, initially in the form of a hypothesis, a theory is eventually formulated. With the passage of time, and after many attempts to verify its veracity, the theory is either discarded or, on the contrary, accepted by the scientific community as a proven fact —which does not indicate it is accepted as ultimate and absolute truth, but as another temporary explanation which, although more substantiated, could also eventually be denied.

In fact, the cornerstone of the scientific method is that there is a possibility that any theory can be scientifically denied. If this possibility does not exist, the theory is automatically considered to fall outside the field of study of science. This does not mean a theory is true or false, but simply that (Western) science lacks the methodological elements to study it. A typical example: since it is scientifically impossible to deny or prove the existence of God, or that Picassos paintings are superior to Matisse's, or that rock is superior to country music, these discussions fall outside the field of science.

In the case of conspiracies, most people, consciously or unconsciously, seem to follow the postulate of what is known as "Shallit's Razor." According to this postulate, what can simply be explained as the result of stupidity or incompetence should not be considered a conspiracy.

Nevertheless, year after year, most of the people I mention in this book as part of this conspiracy have acted on multiple occasions against the interests of the American people and the peoples of Latin America. Therefore, as former U.S. Secretary of Defense James Forrestal stated, "Those people who have conspired in this book have acted against the interests of the American people and the peoples of Latin America on multiple occasions,

Those people who have conspired time and again to destroy your country are neither stupid nor incompetent, but on the contrary, they are extremely skillful and intelligent. If they were only stupid, they would have occasionally made mistakes, some of them in our favor, but they have never done so. On the contrary, they systematically work to destroy our country and its freedoms.[4]

Therefore, it is not unreasonable to conclude that what most people see as mistakes and failures are actually successes. The cause of this confusion is because the conspirators are not what they say they are.

So, to Shallit's Razor, I oppose my Corollary to Shallit's Razor: What can simply be explained as the result of a conspiracy should not be considered stupidity or incompetence. Moreover, I would like to express my own Law of Conspiracies:

> Certain types of events caused by human beings, which are repeated over and over again, particularly those that result to the detriment of broad segments of the population, but to the benefit of a small, but powerful group, are most likely not the product of chance, stupidity or incompetence, but the result of the activities of a well-organized group of conspirators.

A few years ago I was captivated and kept awake until after 2:00 a.m. by a radio program I happened to discover late at night: Coast to Coast AM . This particular program dealt with secret societies, and was composed of a panel of specialists in the field: Linda Moulton Howe, Alex Jones, Steve Quayle and Jim Marrs, well known researchers in the field of conspiracy theory.

One of the things they mentioned on the program that piqued my curiosity was a report produced by the Project for the New American Century (PNAC), an organization formed by the so-called "neocons" [neoconservatives] who supported President Bush. The 90-page report, entitled "Rebuilding America's Defenses: Strategy, Forces and Resources For a New Century", had been published in September 2000.

The Report called for a new era of naked and unabashed U.S. imperialism based on brute military force that no one could oppose. Because of the cynicism and the overt manner in which the writers informed the world of the course of action the conspirators were going to follow to carry out their plans for world domination, some of the panelists on the program compared the PNAC *Report* to Adolf Hitler's *My Struggle* manifesto.

Being rather skeptical of such things, I did not rely solely on the words of the panelists and, the next day, I located on the Internet and read the Report in its entirety. There I confirmed that the paragraph quoted by the panelists existed in the Report and that it had been quoted verbatim and in context with the rest of the publication.

With extraordinary cynicism, the authors of the Report mention that, in order to radically transform the United States and prepare the American people for the military challenges they will face,

> This process of transformation, even if it entails revolu-
> tionary changes, will be slow and long-term, *unless there
> is a catastrophic event that serves as a catalyst – such as
> a new Pearl Harbor*. [Emphasis added.][5]

It should be remembered that this PNAC Report was published in September 2000, exactly one year before the events of September 11, 2001, which was the catastrophic event that served as a pretext for them to leap forward in implementing the revolutionary changes they planned. However, as other panel participants expressed, the conspirators have become so confident and arrogant, or so convinced that the rest of the people are nothing more than a bunch of ignorant fools who lack the ability to think for themselves, that they are no longer afraid to speak openly about their evil plans.

As I continued my research on the Internet in search of critical opinions about the Project, I found a number of interesting articles, including a rather revealing one written by Alex Callinicos, a professor at the University of York, UK, entitled "The Grand Strategy of the American Empire."[6] In his article, Callinicos, who describes himself as a "Marxist", after making a detailed analysis of American foreign policy since 9/11, 2011, concludes that "the Marxist theory of imperialism is the best tool for understanding the present American war-mongering impulse." This is the same Marxist theoretical tool used by Professor James Petras in a recently published book.[7]

However, just a cursory analysis of Callinicos' article and Petras' book shows that, contrary to his conclusions, Marxist theory is not the appropriate methodological tool to understand what is happening in this chaotic post-September 11, 2011 world.[8] The reason for this is not only because Marxism is a biased and crude tool of theoretical analysis, but also because it was created by the conspirators themselves —Moses Mordecai Marx Levi, aka Karl Marx, was one of their secret agents— as a key element of disinformation to mislead their critics and capture the minds of the gullible.

The fact explains why American universities are filled with Marxist professors who fight against the evils of capitalism and imperialism —Noam Chomsky is one of the most notorious— while receiving financial support from foundations controlled and funded by the very imperialist conspirators these professors criticize. This also explains why, although Marxist theory is widely studied in American universities, Conspiracy Theory, considered a legitimate field of study by large sectors of the population, is totally absent from the curricula, and is mentioned only to ridicule those who study the subject, calling them fools and madmen.

However, despite what Marx and Lenin (another agent of the conspirators) claimed, the real engine of society has never been class struggle or capitalist greed, but the various oligarchies and secret groups conspiring in the shadows and fighting each other for control of the world.

It is a widely held view that forensic science is only about crime, autopsies or something like that. But, like Yahoo, Google, and other search tools on the Internet, forensic science is mostly about connections or links that connect one thing to another. The basic principle of forensic science, as stated by Dr. Edmond Locard, one of the great experts in the field, is very simple: Every contact leaves a trace.[9] Forensic science is primarily about finding these traces at a crime scene and, through them, establishing the contacts between the crime and the criminal.

Once a criminal commits a crime, the first thing he does is to try to hide, erase or destroy all physical evidence that connects him to the crime. This ranges from wiping all polished surfaces with a napkin in order to erase his fingerprints, or even sending someone to a party pretending to be him, in order to use him later as an alibi, confirmed by some eyewitnesses, that he was somewhere else when the crime was committed.

Forensic science has concrete applications beyond the field of law. Forensic science and history merge at the edges, and where one ends the other begins. In fact, conspiracy theory is an important tool in the field of historical forensics. The job of the historical forensic investigator is precisely to uncover these hidden links and reveal the connections between the criminal and the crime.

Some of the investigators who have been interested in unraveling the events of the Bogotazo and the assassination of Gaitán suspect the CIA had a hand in the events. However, their attitude mostly consists of waiting for the CIA to voluntarily declassify its secret documents and, as if by magic, documentary evidence of this involvement will appear.

But the work of the intelligence analyst differs from that of the historian in that he cannot wait for the documents to appear because, in the case of top secret operations, these documents will never be made public or simply do not exist because the orders were transmitted verbally precisely so as not to leave compromising evidence.

The investigators who patiently wait for the documentary evidence to appear are apparently unaware that one of the essential characteristics of intelligence analysis work is that one must work with incomplete or misleading sources. Unlike historians, intelligence analysts fill the information gaps with their intuition, experience and knowledge of the subject matter, as well as by using a special methodology they have developed for the evaluation of information. (See, Appendix, The Assessment of Information).

If intelligence analysts were to wait for all the documentary evidence to appear, their work would be reduced to zero, and they would produce their intelligence reports when the information was already totally irrelevant. On the other hand, one should also not blindly rely on supposed CIA "documents" declassified through the efforts of the National Security Archive, an organization that may be a front for the CIA.[10]

Even more important is the fact that, unlike historians, intelligence analysts are guided in their work by a cardinal principle of intelligence and espionage: things are rarely what they appear to be.

Introduction

Most books and articles that have been written about the U.S. Central Intelligence Agency mention the first two CIA covert warfare operations: the overthrow of Prime Minister Mohammed Mossadegh in Iran in 1953, and the overthrow of President Jacobo Arbenz in Guatemala in 1954. A few of these articles and books mention the CIA's intervention in the Italian elections in 1947-1948 to prevent Italians from freely electing members of the Communist Party.

Some of these books and articles also mention what they consider the CIA's first mistake: its failure to predict the riots in Colombia that later became known as the Bogotazo. But there is much more to the Bogotazo than what the CIA, Fidel Castro, and their Council on Foreign Relations (CFR) promoters do not wish to be disclosed.

For their part, Colombians have always viewed the Bogotazo as an eruption of violence with causes rooted in Colombia's domestic politics.[1] The only ones who have tried to find any foreign influence have blamed the causes of the Bogotazo on local Communists and, secondarily, on members of international communism led by the Soviet Union. In fact, shortly after the Bogotazo, and although the connection between the Soviets and the riots was never proven, the Colombian government broke off its limited relations with the Soviet Union.

However, despite these entrenched views, I will demonstrate in this book that the Bogotazo had very little to do with Colombian internal politics or with national or international communism. On the contrary, the Bogotazo had much to do with the Wall Street bankers and the American oil magnates in their effort to implant in the gullible minds of the American people the supposed danger of communism - what at the time came to be called the Cold War. Consequently, the Bogotazo is a key event in understanding later similar operations carried out by the CIA on the orders of the Council on Foreign Relations conspirators.

So, before studying the Bogotazo, I will analyze in detail the CIA and the organizations that preceded it and, especially, who created them and why. In fact, to say that the CIA assassinated Gaitán is as irrelevant or uninformative as saying that the Communists did it. Without a detailed study of the CIA and the organizations that preceded it, as well as who created them and why, it is impossible to understand the true causes of the Bogotazo.

Therefore, although the chapter on the Bogotazo is the highlight of this book, I beg readers, and in particular Latin American readers, not to give in to the temptation to jump straight to it and read carefully the chapters that precede it.

On April 9, 1948, Bogotá, the capital of Colombia, was the scene of violent riots that later became known as the Bogotazo. The event that apparently triggered the riots was the assassination of Colombian leader Jorge Eliécer Gaitán. Participants in the riot destroyed most of the city center. Several thousand people were killed.

The riots coincided with the celebration in the city of the Ninth Pan American Conference of Foreign Ministers, which had opened its sessions a few days earlier, on March 30. The Conference was presided over by General George Marshall, U.S. Secretary of State. Marshall, like John Foster Dulles, who succeeded him, was a lawyer in a Wall Street firm and a senior executive of the Council on Foreign Relations.

In reality, the Bogotazo was not a spontaneous explosion of popular violence, but a false flag operation [2] that initiated in the Western Hemisphere a large-scale psychological warfare operation later known as the Cold War. As such, the Bogotazo is a key event in understanding many similar false flag operations carried out by the CIA on the orders of the Council on Foreign Relations conspirators - including the September 11, 2001 operation.

Almost all authors who have studied the Bogotazo mention Fidel Castro's participation in the events anecdotally, without giving it much importance, as a curious chapter in the youthful years of a man who later became a world-class political leader. Interestingly, the only article on the Bogotazo to appear in Studies in Intelligence, the CIA's in-house academic publication, is an obvious effort to downplay Castro's involvement in the events.[3] The times he has spoken on the subject, Castro himself has also tried to downplay his participation in the events. But, as we will see below, Fidel Castro played an important role in the events of the Bogotazo, let alone in the Cold War that began in the Western Hemisphere with the Bogotazo.

The Bogotazo is extremely important because in that operation the CFR conspirators used the newly created CIA to test the effectiveness of new brainwashing techniques (Manchurian candidate), use of scapegoats, false flag operations and psychological warfare operations based on the Hegelian dialectic principle of thesis-antithesis-synthesis, which were later successfully repeated in similar operations, such as the assassinations of U.S. President John F. Kennedy and his brother Robert, as well as the assassinations of U.S. President John F. Kennedy and his brother Robert, as well as the assassinations of U.S. President John F. Kennedy and his brother Robert, as well as the assassinations of U.S. President John F. Kennedy and his brother Robert. Kennedy and his brother Robert, as well as in the operation that caused the tragic events of September 11, 2001. These psychological warfare operations have resulted in the extraordinary advancement of the conspirators' plans to establish a Communo-Fascist New World Order under their total control.

Therefore, in this book I will make the first analysis of the Bogotazo from the point of view of intelligence and espionage, as a successful covert operation of psychological warfare against the peoples of the United States and Latin America. Unfortunately, very few researchers have even mentioned this possibility. However, as authors John Loftus and Mark Aarons have rightly pointed out, "Historical omission is the fundamental clue that a covert operation has been successful."[4]

Servando Gonzalez

Part One: The CIA

If the CIA's successes were made known, our enemies would
know about them, and then they would become failures.
—William Colby, CIA Director.

Most studies of the U.S. Central Intelligence Agency reinforce the belief that the CIA is a continuation of the Office of Special Services (OSS), the civilian intelligence agency created during World War II, led by General William Donovan. However, as we will see below, the CIA's true roots go much deeper.

1. The Inquiry

In the fall of 1917, Colonel Edward Mandell House, confidential advisor to President Woodrow Wilson, managed to recruit a group of about one hundred prominent intellectuals in order to discuss the post-war world —I mean World War I— that was coming. This group of academics-turned-spies and intelligence analysts, soon after called The Inquiry, drafted the plans for the peace agreements that eventually became the famous "Fourteen Points" of American foreign policy —attributed to Wilson, but actually the work of Mandell House.

Those plans first expressed the idea of what would later come to be called globalization, and included a call for the elimination of "all economic barriers" between nations (what is now known as "free trade") and the creation of a "general society of nations" —which later materialized briefly in the failed League of Nations and years later in the United Nations Organization, entirely under the control of the conspirators at the Council on Foreign Relations.

Mandell House, who was actually a secret agent of the conspirators, used psychological manipulation techniques to implant in Wilson's mind the idea of creating a private intelligence agency - which was nothing more than the lucubration of a small group of oil tycoons and Wall Street bankers. Without intending to, House had created the modus operandi, later used by the conspirators through the National Security Council, to manipulate and control American presidents.

The initial group, which grew to 126 members and was composed of a majority of socialist (Fascist-Communist) minded academics, began working secretly from the offices of the American Geographical Society, conducting historical research and writing reports on plans for a peace settlement in Paris. Although it never worked for the American people, but rather for the international bankers and oil tycoons who created it, The Inquiry was de facto the first central American intelligence agency.

From its inception, The Inquiry was organized and worked as an intelligence agency. First, it was divided into several study groups. Some of these groups analyzed the different geopolitical areas of the planet, including Latin America. Others studied diplomatic history, economics, international law, and cartography,[1] a division very similar to what the CIA later adopted with its so-called "bureaus."

Second, the activities of The Inquiry were conducted under the utmost secrecy.[2] Even the name "The Inquiry" had been selected because it meant nothing and helped to misinform about the organization's true purpose.

As later happened with the CIA, The Inquiry was an autonomous organization, theoretically reporting directly to the President and subsidized by secret funds that Wilson controlled. Congress and the State Department were totally unaware of its existence.[3] Nor were the activities of The Inquiry known to the American people, because the press never reported its existence. Armed guards patrolled its offices day and night.[4]

Third, the activities of The Investigation were divided into four general categories: planning, collection [of information], analysis, and processing [of information] into intelligence.[5] This division is very similar to what the CIA calls "the intelligence cycle": direction and planning, collection, processing and analysis [of information], and dissemination [of intelligence].

Finally, although in theory the activities of The Inquiry were only to investigate and report to President Wilson in order for him to prepare the U.S. for the possibility of a peace settlement after the end of the war in Europe, the fact that it conducted studies on Latin America indicates that its real secret objectives were much broader. In fact, The Investigation was, among other things, the first step in the systematic study of Latin America's natural resources for future exploitation by oil tycoons and Wall Street bankers, a role later assumed by the Council on Foreign Relations.

In November 1928, shortly before the armistice ending World War I was signed, Colonel House traveled to Paris accompanied by bankers Paul Warburg and Bernard Baruch, as well as a select group of members of The Inquiry and 20 military intelligence officers. A month later, Wilson himself traveled to Paris accompanied by 20 scholar-spies from The Inquiry.

As soon as they settled into the Crillon Hotel, the scholars began their espionage activities. The information they obtained served for the creation of Wilson's 14 points, the adoption of which Wilson himself proposed at the Versailles Conference.

The newly created intelligence agency had served the oil tycoons and international bankers so well that they decided to make it permanent. A few days after the end of the Conference, a group of American and British conspirators met at the Majestic Hotel, where the British delegation to the Conference was staying, to discuss the continuation of their successful experiment in espionage. Finally, they agreed to create a permanent intelligence agency, at the service of the international bankers, with branches in London and New York. As usual, in order to conceal their real intelligence and espionage activities, they gave it the innocuous name of the Anglo-American Institute of International Affairs.

However, a few months later, the American branch decided to become independent and took the name Council on Foreign Relations (CFR) and the British branch adopted the name Royal Institute of International Affairs (RIIA), later known as Chatham House. With few exceptions, most of the members of The Inquiry became members of the CFR. Prominent among these were Colonel House himself, Elihu Root, Herbert H. Lehman, W. Averell Harriman, and John Foster Dulles.

2. The CFR: The Invisible Government of the U.S.

Over the years, the average American citizen has had a fuzzy suspicion that there must be a hidden reason why most of the time his government ends up aiding his country's enemies and betraying his friends. Only a small group of scholars have seriously analyzed the cause of this phenomenon. Those who have done so have come to the conclusion that the government of the United States of America has been penetrated and has fallen under the control of a group of millionaire, powerful and unscrupulous individuals, who have been using it to promote and preserve their particular interests. This group has been referred to by various names: the Power Elite, the Invisible Government, the Great Conspiracy, the Secret Group, etc. I call them the Conspirators.

Like ninja warriors, the most powerful weapon employed by these conspirators who control the invisible government of the United States has been precisely their invisibility. Until relatively recently, this elite group, which has achieved near total control of all three branches of the U.S. government —including the CIA and the other intelligence services— the mass media, the educational system, and now extends its tentacles to penetrate the armed forces, has been almost unknown to the American people. But we should not blame the people. The main organization in which these conspirators are grouped is seldom mentioned in the mass media, and is virtually absent from textbooks.

The Council on Foreign Relations (CFR) is the visible head of what some authors call the "invisible government" of the U.S.

The CFR describes itself as a non-partisan organization - in the jargon of the conspirators "non-partisan" actually means "controlled by the CFR" - whose sole purpose is to promote international exchanges to achieve better understanding between countries. But this description is no more than what in intelligence and espionage is called a "cover story."[6] In reality, the CFR is an intelligence and espionage agency, and functions as such.

In his laudatory study of The Inquiry, CFR agent Peter Grose accidentally exposed the true character and objectives of the CFR. Like The Inquiry, the Council on Foreign Relations is an intelligence agency in the service of the American plutocracy of Wall Street bankers, oil tycoons, and top executives of transnational corporations.[7]

Like all intelligence agencies, the Council on Foreign Relations is a semi-secret society: although it is no secret where it is headquartered and who its directors are, no one really knows what its secret activities are, much less its real objectives. Like all intelligence agencies, the CFR has both recognized members and secret members.[8] Like all intelligence agencies, the CFR has a specialized area for gathering information and analyzing and evaluating it into intelligence. But unlike conventional intelligence agencies, intelligence analysts in this department do not work directly at CFR headquarters, but live a parasitic life scattered among government and other private institutions such as the National Security Council, the State and Defense Departments, the Pentagon, the press, universities, and in so-called non-profit foundations.

Like all intelligence agencies, the CFR has a branch specializing in psychological warfare, subversion, insurgency and paramilitary operations - functions that, until very recently, had been mostly carried out by the CIA's covert operations branch. Today, however, after the conspirators have taken more control over most key areas of the U.S. government, including a large segment of the senior military brass, they no longer need the CIA, and have transferred many of these functions directly to the U.S. military.

Like all intelligence agencies, the primary job of some CFR members is to recruit spies and agents of influence, as a means of infiltrating other organizations they want to control, in the U.S. and abroad. In the case of ambitious and intelligent but morally and ethically deficient young people, once they are spotted by the CFR's talent scouts[9] and, after initial screening, it is decided to go ahead with their recruitment, the first step is usually to award them a Rhodes Scholarship. If they successfully pass this first test, they are offered a scholarship to study at the London School of Economics.

As required, the CFR intelligence analysts are charged with producing their own National Intelligence Estimates (NIE), but that is exactly what they are not, for the fact that they are produced from the point of view of the interests of the conspirators, which differ greatly from the National Intelligence Estimates produced officially by the CIA, which are produced from the point of view of the interests of the U.S. This explains why the NIEs are not the same as the National Intelligence Estimates produced officially by the CIA, which are produced from the point of view of the interests of the U.S. This explains why the NIEs are not the same as the NIEs. This explains why NIEs and other types of intelligence alerts produced by the CIA are either ignored (as we shall see below this is what happened during the Bogotazo) or are forced to be changed according to the political and propaganda needs of the CFR conspirators.

Typical of this type of intelligence estimate produced by secret CFR agents is George Kennan's article published in 1947 in Foreign Affairs, the official organ of the CFR, under the pseudonym "X", in which he expounded his theory of "containment" —actually a theory created by the CFR conspirators. According to Kennan, the U.S. role in the coming Cold War should be limited to containing the spread of Soviet communism, not fighting to eliminate it. Soon after, President Truman made containment the central part of "his" Truman Doctrine.

Of course, many senior officers in the U.S. armed forces who considered their mission not to contain the enemy, but to defeat him, disagreed with the doctrine of containment. Some of them, such as Generals Curtis LeMay and Douglas MacArthur were vilified and their careers destroyed. Others, like General George Patton, were preemptively assassinated.

Another example of a secret document created by the CFR conspirators is the infamous NSC 200 (National Security Study Memorandum 200), attributed to Henry Kissinger. Kept secret for many
years, NSC 200 outlined a genocidal policy of population elimination on the African continent to make it easier for transnational corporations to plunder its natural resources and prevent Africans from
exploiting and enjoying them. Nothing exemplifies the implementation of NSC 200 better than Castro's invasion of Angola in the fall of
1975.

In theory, Castro ordered the invasion of Angola to help nationalist leader Agostinho Neto and prevent imperialist-backed forces
from taking over the country. But what was the result of Castro's
victory in Angola?

Within months after Castro's troops took control of the country,
Angola became one of the United States' largest trading partners in
Africa. Wall Street banks such as Chase Manhattan Bank, Bankers
Trust, Citibank and Morgan Guaranty lent heavily to Angola. Businesses of General Motors, General Tire, Caterpillar, Boeing, IBM,
NCR, Pfizer, Xerox and other U.S. companies flourished in the country. Ninety-five percent of Angola's oil was exported to Western countries. Castro's soldiers protected the refineries in Cabinda from possible attacks by "saboteurs" and Castro was paid in dollars for his
services. Half of Angola's Gulf oil production ended up in U.S. refineries. The De Beers consortium controlled the diamond mines.
This was a direct result of Castro's "anti-imperialist" and "anti-
colonialist" policy in Angola.

More recently, the CFR produced another interesting intelligence
estimate on Iran. The study appeared in the January-February 2012
issue of Foreign Affairs, in the form of an article by Matthew Kroenig
with the title "It's Time to Attack Iran. Why an Attack Is the Least
Bad Option." Of course, Kroenig does not explain that attacking
Iran might be the best option for the CFR conspirators, but possibly
the worst option for the American people.

The Council on Foreign Relations has become in practice in the
U.S. the closest thing to a Communo-Fascist party in power. Like
the Communist Party in the Soviet Union, the Nazi Party in Germany, or the "Communist" Party in Castro's Cuba, CFR members
hold secret meetings where they discuss the country's policy, and
then their members infiltrated into the government lobby officials to
ensure that these policies are carried out. Like members of a Communist or Fascist party in power, CFR members maintain strict party
discipline: once a policy has been approved in their secret councils,
it becomes the Party line and they support it with all their might.

Like members of a Communist or Fascist party, CFR members act as a bloc, and internal dissent on key issues is not permitted.

Although the CFR appears to be just another club composed of wealthy East Coast members, especially Wall Street bankers, the CFR is in fact a very secretive organization. Since its inception, its activities have been private and confidential.[10] It is the CFR's policy not to publish the minutes of its meetings.[11]

So, if you don't know what the Council on Foreign Relations is, who its members are, what role the CFR has played in the foreign and domestic policy of the U.S. and much of the world, or what its secret purpose is, you are no exception, because most Americans themselves are ignorant of it. And this ignorance is not by mistake, but by design, which explains why the CFR is not mentioned in U.S. history books and is barely mentioned in the press, even though many editors of major U.S. newspapers, magazines and television stations are CFR members.

These CFR members exercise almost total control over the U.S. mainstream media —in fact they own most of it[12]— and use their power to prevent the CFR from becoming the center of attention of the masses.

Proof of this is that in Baden-Baden, Germany, in 1991, during one of the secret conclaves of the Bilderbergs, an international globalist organization closely linked to the CFR, David Rockefeller, Director of the CFR from 1970 to 1985, effusively thanked members of the press for keeping the existence of his organization secret,

> We thank the *Washington Post, New York Times, Time Magazine* and other fine publications whose editors have attended our meetings and respected our discretion for nearly forty years. It would have been impossible for us to have carried out our plans for the world during those years if the light of publicity had exposed them.
>
> But now the world is much more sophisticated and is poised to march toward world government. The supranational sovereignty of an intellectual elite of world bankers is far preferable to the national self-determination of the last few centuries.

But today, primarily thanks to the Internet which has acted as an ultraviolet light to reveal harmful bacteria, this organization is losing its powers of invisibility, and more and more people have discovered who they are, how they operate, what their secret plans and objectives are, and what other organizations they control directly or indirectly. I am referring to the Council on Foreign Relations (CFR), as well as its parasitic organizations, such as the Bilderberg Group, the Trilateral Commission, the World Economic Forum, the United Nations, the World Bank, the International Monetary Fund and the like. And there is every reason to be concerned, because the conspirators' plans are to eliminate no less than 85 percent of the planet's current population and reduce the survivors to pre-industrial levels of consumption, in a global government under their total control: what the CFR conspirators euphemistically call the New World Order.

Usuaally, when their apologists mention the so-called "New World Order", they sugarcoat it with the adjectives, "more just", "more humane", "more equitable", and the like. However, as we will see later in this book, if anything really characterizes the new world order the conspirators plan to implement, it is that it is more unjust, more inhumane, and less equitable for the masses —a sort of global sweatshop.

The CFR publishes the influential journal *Foreign Affairs*. If most of the predictions that appear in its pages shortly thereafter come true, it is not because they have hired the most qualified political analysts or the best seers with their crystal balls, but because, due to their control of the U.S. government and public opinion, they force the government and the American people to accept their treasonous plans.

The CFR completely controls both the Democratic and Republican parties and, with few exceptions, they are the ones who have put most of the presidents in the White House. As noted by Georgetown University professor and Bill Clinton mentor Carroll Quigley, probably the researcher who has studied the CFR in most detail,

The belief that the two parties represent different, opposing ideas on policy is a foolish idea. Both parties are identical, and no electoral change will lead to real change in policy, because in reality both parties pursue the same ends.[13]

Like a malignant cancer, the CFR has not only expanded its influence by creating affiliates in major U.S. cities, but has also metastasized into several major organizations, all of them created and funded primarily with Rockefeller money, including the Trilateral Commission, the Foreign Policy Association, the World Affairs Councils, the Brookings Institution, and the Carnegie Endowment for International Peace, just to mention a few of the most important.

It also has close ties with international organizations such as the Bilderberg Group, the United Nations, the World Economic Forum and the Club of Rome. The ultimate goal of these organizations, openly expressed by their leaders, is none other than the creation of a Communo-Fascist New World Order controlled by transnational corporations in the hands of the Rockefellers and their Wall Street cronies. Unfortunately, in recent years the conspirators have succeeded in establishing CFR branches in several Latin American countries.[14]

Some political analysts have pointed out that in recent times the CFR has become a department of the U.S. government. In reality it is the U.S. government that has become a dependency of the CFR. The way CFR agents have managed to gain virtual control over the U.S. government has been by infiltrating it —a strategy used by the British Fabians[15] and by intelligence services around the world. Today most of the top officials in the State Department, the CIA and the military, as well as many of the top managers, advisors and members of the presidential cabinet, Supreme Court justices and members of the U.S. Congress, are members of the CFR.

CFR conspirators have also successfully infiltrated most American universities. The main tool for control used by the conspirators is money, which they generously distribute through the large number of non-profit foundations they control. Chief among these are the Carnegie, Ford, MacArthur, Mellon and Rockefeller foundations, as well as a constellation of smaller foundations that receive most of their funding through the aforementioned foundations. These smaller foundations are used as intermediaries to hide the real source of the money.

Since the end of World War II, CFR agents infiltrating the U.S. government have maintained total control over the U.S. State Department. Most of the Secretaries of State, during both Democratic and Republican administrations, have been CFR members. They also control the Federal Reserve Bank which, contrary to common belief, is not an agency of the U.S. government, but a private corporation. In the case of the Central Intelligence Agency, they never had to infiltrate it, since, as I will explain in detail later, since its creation, the CIA has always been totally under their control.

Proof of this is that, when President Truman disbanded the OSS at the end of World War II and refused to create a Central Intelligence Agency, CFR member Allen Dulles independently created in secret a private espionage and intelligence organization. This agency operated for some time from a secret office in the Harold Pratt mansion in Manhattan, headquarters of the CFR.[16]

Eventually President Truman yielded to pressure from the conspirators and created the CIA. A few years later, who was appointed CIA Director? None other than Allen Dulles. After Dulles, all but the most recent CIA directors have been members of the CFR.

Initially, the fortunes of most of the major conspirators —appropriately called the "robber barons" (Rockefeller, Carnegie, Morgan, Vanderbilt, et al.)— came from the steel, railroad and oil industries. But oil is a difficult commodity to find and expensive to exploit, and railroad construction and steel production are also difficult and time-consuming. So, in the late 19th century, the robber barons discovered a new, much better and more lucrative product to further increase their fortunes: the sale of air in the form of fiat money not backed by precious metals. This explains why, without abandoning their traditional businesses, they began to move their fortunes into banking.

Banks are basically criminal organizations that steal their customers' money using a form of swindling called "fractional banking", which essentially consists of using other people's money to increase their own money without running the risk of losing it.

To that end, the conspirators created the Federal Reserve Bank[17] and the Internal Revenue Service (IRS) to rob the American people of the money they needed for their banks. They then bought venal politicians to pass laws authorizing the creation of so-called non-profit charitable foundations, which are really a way to hide their money from the thieving IRS officials. This explains why in the U.S. the wealthiest pay proportionately much lower taxes than the poor.

At present, finance capital is the main source of wealth for the conspirators who control the CFR. And the business of lending money, especially to governments, has proven to be very lucrative. But, in order to do so, they soon realized that, like traditional loan sharks, they needed to have a strong arm to punish the few who dared to default on the interest on their loans.

Initially, the conspirators used for this purpose the armed forces of the U.S. This was, for example, the very purpose for which Teddy Roosevelt created the "Great White Fleet", which he sent out to sail around the world displaying the U.S. flag (instead of the skull and crossbones flag of the Wall Street pirates) in order to frighten potential defaulters by reminding them of the military might of the bankers. This is what was appropriately called "gunboat diplomacy."

For a long time the U.S. Marines were the military arm of the Wall Street conspirators. Paradoxically, one of the conspirators' staunchest critics was a highly decorated and worthy U.S. Marine officer, Brigadier General Smedley D. Butler.[18]

As General Butler bluntly put it in his book *War is a Racket*,

> In 1914 I helped make Mexico, especially Tampico, safe ground for American oil interests. I helped make Haiti and Cuba safe ground for the National City Bank boys to swell their profits. I helped Wall Street bankers plunder half a dozen Central American republics. The list of plunder is long. In 1909-1912, I helped pacify Nicaragua for the benefit of the Brown Brothers bankers. I did the same in the Dominican Republic in 1916 for the benefit of U.S. sugar interests.[19]

Unfortunately, due to the fact that the conspirators have always hidden their criminal activities under a cloak of legality provided by the U.S. government, Marxists, leftists and revolutionaries around the world began to blame the United States and its people for the criminal actions of the Wall Street Mafia. This was the true origin of the so-called "American imperialism" or "Yankee imperialism", which in reality is the imperialism of the oil tycoons and Wall Street bankers. It is therefore no coincidence that most of the leading American critics who point to "American imperialism" as the main source of world evil have been directly or indirectly funded by the Wall Street mafia itself through its "charitable" foundations.

Most intelligence officers of the Office of Special Services (OSS), the U.S. intelligence agency during World War II, were Wall Street lawyers and bankers or their children. However, there is abundant evidence to prove that Wall Street bankers played a cardinal role in helping Hitler seize power in Germany, and later did business with Nazi Germany before and during the war. Therefore, it makes sense to think that many of those who joined the OSS did so not out of patriotism or altruism, to fight the Nazis, rescue the Jews, or protect the interests of the American people, but to protect their own narrow interests.

In fact, one of the main objectives of the secret mission of the

OSS during World War II was to help major Nazi war criminals, especially SS officers, escape justice and hide the gold they had stolen. Another important objective was to protect German companies such as I.G. Farben, which had been collaborating closely with the Nazis while being associated with several Wall Street banks.

Just as the OSS was, the CIA has for many years been the hidden strong arm of the Wall Street Mafia. The bankers have used it to impose their wishes on victims who have refused to accept the illegal rules imposed by criminal organizations such as the International Monetary Fund, the World Bank and others they have created. To carry out their criminal activities, the Wall Street Mafia commonly uses extortion, threats, assassinations, economic aggression and direct physical aggression of all kinds, including conventional warfare and psychological warfare through covert operations.

Acting on behalf of the conspirators, some CFR members have committed genocide and mass murder,[20] carried out unprovoked wars, conducted psychological warfare operations against the peoples of Latin America and other parts of the world, and overthrown legitimate leaders of many countries through coups and assassinations, including some U.S. Presidents.

Since the end of World War II, the number of Council on Foreign Relations members in key positions in the U.S. government has been increasing. The Council has succeeded in infiltrating its agents into the government until it has virtually become its dependency. In the last 50 years, almost all Presidents, as well as Secretaries of State, Supreme Court Justices and Directors of the CIA, have been members of the CFR. The number of senior officers in the Armed Forces who are members of the CFR is increasing. The most influential people in the mass media are CFR members. CFR-controlled foundations fund almost all leftist, pro-Castro, and anti-American groups in the U.S., and many abroad.[21]

3. The Destruction of Russia and the Creation of the Soviet Union

The Soviet Union was the artificial creation of a group of oil tycoons and international bankers. Their purpose was to put Russia in an economic and political deep freeze —which they succeeded in doing it for almost 60 years— and to prevent Tsar Nicholas II from realizing his intentions of turning the country into a major oil producer competing on world markets. But apparently the Czar did not know that oil monopolists detest competition.[22]

After the assassination of Alexander II in 1881, his son, Alexander III, was crowned Tsar of Russia and his grandson Nicholas became the main heir to the throne. A few years later, Alexander III began an ambitious program of industrialization of the country, which included the construction of a modern railroad network that would unify the country. The result of this effort was the creation of the Trans-Siberian Railway, which would transform Russia's economy and turn the country into a modern industrial society.

After the unexpected death of Alexander III, his grandson Nicholas was crowned and set out to continue his father's economic policy. Alexander entrusted Count Sergius Witte, Russia's finance minister, with the continuation of the railway project.[23] A few years later, thanks to Witte's efforts, Russia had gone from being only the largest supplier of wheat to British trading houses to a thriving industrial power. Predictably, the British government strenuously opposed these changes in Russia.[24] But Witte's efforts came to a sudden end in 1905 when Czar Nicholas II was deposed as a result of the Russian "revolution."

The major problem the conspirators faced with Russia was not the efforts of the tsars to turn it into an industrialized nation, but the large oil fields that had recently been discovered in Baku, Azerbaijan, near the Caspian Sea. At the time, the reserves in the Baku oil fields were considered to be among the largest in the world. By the early 1880s, Russian crude oil production had reached 10.8 million barrels per year, almost one-third the output of the United States,[25] and was continuing to rise.

Predictably, John D. Rockefeller and his criminal associates were greatly alarmed at the possibility that Russia attempted to control the world's oil supply. Consequently, they began to actively conspire to create a plan to sabotage the Russians' efforts.[26] Eventually, they came to the conclusion that the only thing that would enable them to achieve their goal was to depose Czar Nicholas II, and that the only way to depose him was by means of a "revolution."

Most history books, many of them written by unscrupulous disinformers in the service of the CFR, describe the Russian Revolution as the result of a spontaneous uprising of the Russian working masses against an oppressive government. According to this version, Russia's disastrous participation in World War I, which cost the lives of four million men, caused widespread discontent. A growing economic crisis and food shortages contributed to the problems. Street demonstrations of people asking the government to give them food broke out in several cities. This chaotic situation created the conditions for the popular revolt that eventually led to the overthrow of the Tsarist government and transformed Russia into the Soviet Union, a new egalitarian society based on the anti-capitalist principles of Marxism.[27]

But this view is far from true.

Thanks to the efforts of scholars such as Antony Sutton,[28] G. Edward Griffin,[29] and others, we now know that the Russian "revolution" was in fact a covert operation planned and carried out by international bankers and oil tycoons, not unlike the recent "spontaneous revolutions" of the so-called Arab Spring in Egypt, Libya, Sudan, Syria and other Middle Eastern countries. Without the considerable infusion of money from some of the most notable billionaires of the time, the Russian "revolution" would never have succeeded.

Although initially Czar Nicholas II was a supporter of his father's autocratic ideas, over time he had changed his mind, and initiated a series of reforms aimed at transforming Russia from a feudal kingdom into a modern industrialized society. These measures included the emancipation of the serfs, the creation of a Duma, or National Assembly, and rural communes. These reforms would have encouraged the Russian people to think about the possibility of a shift to a benign government in which the people would participate democratically.

But some powerful oil tycoons and influential Wall Street bankers were not pleased with the changes in Russia, and conceived other plans for the country. To carry them out, John D. Rockefeller, in collusion with bankers Andrew Mellon, J.P. Morgan and steel magnate Andrew Carnegie, as well as other so-called "robber barons", pooled their resources, collected some $50 million (at that time a huge sum of money) and, under the pretext of stimulating world trade, created the American International Corporation (AIC), a powerful monopolistic cartel. The truth is, however, that the main purpose of the AIC was to provide the necessary funds for a small group of professional revolutionaries, the Bolsheviks, to overthrow the government of Tsar Nicholas II.[30]

Between 1907 and 1910, the conspiratorial bankers met on several occasions with Leon Trotsky, a Russian extremist exiled in New York, and Vladimir Ilich Lenin, another extremist living in exile in Zurich. Eventually, the arch-capitalists struck a deal with the arch-capitalists in exchange for the bankers providing them with the necessary funds to carry out their "revolution." As payment, the Wall Street arch-capitalists reserved the right to design the economic system of the country that would later become the Soviet Union - in theory the most anti-capitalist country in the world.

With the help of the bankers, Lenin returned to Russia in a special train with a large amount of gold. Shortly thereafter Trotsky, under the protection of President Wilson and his puppet master "Colonel" House, left New York for Russia on a ship with more gold. It was this gold from the bankers that made it possible for the two "revolutionaries" to carry out their "revolution."

But, from the beginning, some well-informed people knew perfectly well that the Russian "revolution" was nothing but another ploy of the oil tycoons and international bankers. In a speech he delivered in the House of Commons on November 5, 1919, English statesman Winston Churchill laid out the conspiracy in a few, but accurate words:

> Lenin was sent to Russia . . . as if a flask containing a culture of typhus or cholera had been sent to empty into the water supply of a large city, and he acted with incredible efficiency. Soon after Lenin arrived, he began to contact influential people in his mansions in New York, Glasgow, Berne, and other countries, and thus gathered these influential spirits into a formidable sect; the most formidable in the world ... . With these spirits around him, [Lenin] set to work with demonic skill to destroy every institution on which the Russian State depended to.

As we shall see later in this book, history repeated itself to the letter when the conspirators gave their secret support to Fidel Castro to seize power in Cuba and destroy the country with his "revolution" and, more recently, in the so-called democratic "revolutions" in Egypt, Libya and Sudan, and those plotting to seize power in Syria and Iran.

What Churchill failed to mention in his speech, however, was that those who had spread the Communist plague in Russia were a group of English, European and American bankers, including the Rothschilds, Sir George Buchanan and Lord Alfred Milner (members of the initial group of conspirators who created the CFR), the Warburgs, the Rockefellers, Andrew Mellon and J.P. Morgan. With this small monetary investment, the conspirators had created a pseudo-enemy largely under their control. Soon thereafter the Soviet Union, with the secret support of the conspirators, became the main enemy of the United States and other Western countries. The rest is history.

But apparently the conspirators did not foresee that communism and the Marxist economy are so inefficient that, from the very beginning, the monster they had created could not even provide for its own subsistence. So, while ostensibly fighting to eradicate it, behind the scenes they did everything they could to keep it alive and threatening.

In his massive academic study *Western Technology and Soviet Economic Development*, then in his *National Suicide: Military Aid to the Soviet Union*, and finally in *The Best Enemy Money Can Buy*,[31] Professor Antony Sutton documented in detail how the Soviet Union was kept artificially active, particularly in the military field, thanks to massive economic and technological aid, mostly from the U.S.. And this technological transfer was not the result of the good work of Soviet spies, as people have tried to make believe, but of the treacherous activities of CFR members at the highest levels of the U.S. government. In particular, the two most resounding successes of the conspirators were to provide the Soviets with the technology necessary to produce, first nuclear weapons, and then the intercontinental missiles to deliver them.

According to the official story, it was Soviet spies Ethel and Julius Rosenberg who in 1950 stole the nuclear secrets needed to produce an atomic bomb and provided them to the Soviets. But this is nothing more than a fairy tale.[32] In reality the Soviets did not have to steal the nuclear secrets because secret CFR agents infiltrated the U.S. government and provided them to them in 1943 through the so-called Lend Lease program.[33]

Professor Sutton documented in detail the second case, the transfer of American technology required to increase the accuracy of Soviet intercontinental missiles.[34] According to Sutton, without this technology Soviet intercontinental nuclear missiles would never have achieved the accuracy needed to hit the targets.

4. The Creation of Nazi Germany

There is overwhelming evidence to prove that some Wall Street bankers played an important role in helping Hitler seize power in Germany, and then traded with the Nazis before and during the war.[35] Although the fact is not mentioned in many of the official histories, Adolf Hitler was able to seize power in Germany because of the financial support provided to him by certain industrial monopolies, primarily the chemical cartel I.G. Farben.[36] But I.G. Farben achieved its economic power because of a little known source: Wall Street bankers. According to Antony Sutton, one of the authors who has most researched this relationship, "Without the capital supplied by Wall Street, there would have been no I.G. Farben, no Adolf Hitler and no World War II."[37]

G.I. Farben was created in 1924 when the American banker Charles Dawes coordinated large capital loans, totaling $800 million, to consolidate the German chemical and steel companies into giant commercial monopolies under what became known as the Dawes Plan. But the Dawes Plan was actually the brainchild of the J.P. Morgan bankers.[38] Other Wall Street bankers who collaborated with Nazi Germany were the firm of Dillon, Read & Co, Forbes & Co, and the National City Bank, which provided three-quarters of the loans used to create these commercial cartels.[39]

Because Germany did not have sufficient natural sources of oil to manufacture gasoline for the coming war, in 1927 the Rockefellers' Standard Oil provided I.G. Farben with the technology to produce synthetic gasoline from coal, a product abundant in Germany. [40]

From the beginning of the war, Rockefeller's Standard Oil had been one of the main suppliers, via North Africa, of the gasoline that the Nazi war machine so badly needed. But, after the Allied invasion of North Africa, Standard Oil was no longer in a position to supply its Nazi friends with gasoline through that route. So Standard Oil began to send oil to the Nazis through Spain and Switzerland, two neutral countries.

The American press, totally under the control of the CFR conspirators, kept these transactions hidden from the American people, who at that time stood in long lines at gas stations without complaint, because they knew that the American military was in need of gasoline. They did not know, however, that more gasoline was going to the Nazis via Spain and Switzerland than to U.S. troops.[41]

A State Department memorandum dated August 1943 shows that the trade had been authorized between a subsidiary of Standard Oil of Venezuela, the Creole Petroleum Co. and a company in Aruba. From there, the oil was shipped to Spain and ended up in Germany.[42]

The CFR conspirators not only played a key role in bringing the Nazis to power, but continued to aid the Nazi war machine even after the U.S. had declared war against Germany. This has been documented in detail in books such as Charles Higham's Trading with the Enemy,[43] Antony Sutton's Wall Street and the Rise of Hitler[44] and, more recently, by Jim Marrs in The Rise of the Fourth Reich.[45]

Moreover, the CFR conspirators, mostly with the help of their secret agents William Donovan and Allen Dulles, were not only instrumental in facilitating the escape of many Nazi war criminals, including senior SS officers, to South America, mostly to Perón's Argentina, but also in the assassination of General George Patton.

At the head of his Third Army, Patton had launched a withering attack aimed at taking Berlin long before the Russians did so. But at the Yalta Conference the plotters had reached an agreement with Stalin to cede control of Eastern Europe to him. They also needed more time for their Nazi friends to escape to South America. Consequently, CFR agents Franklin Roosevelt, George Marshall and Dwight Eisenhower cut off the supply of fuel and ammunition to the Third Army. As a result, more than three-quarters of the casualties of the Allied forces in World War II occurred after this betrayal. At the end of the war Patton commented that he was going to pull his influence to have an investigation conducted, and this led to the CFR conspirators ordering his assassination.[46] The assassin was an OSS officer.

But assassinating General Patton, helping Nazi leaders escape justice, and helping Stalin take control of Eastern Europe were not the only criminal actions carried out by Donovan and his OSS henchmen. Through special secret operations, such as Operation Paperclip, the conspirators brought Nazi scientists to work in the United States, as well as recruited Wehrmacht General Reinhard Gehlen and many of his SS thugs to work for the newly created CIA.

The OSS was also the tool the conspirators used to test the psychological warfare techniques they had developed and would later use to carry out psychological warfare operations against the American people and other peoples of the world.

5. The Office of Strategic Services (OSS)

Most books dealing with the history of U.S. intelligence services repeat over and over again that the Office of Strategic Services (OSS) was the first central intelligence agency of that country. This is the case, for example, in the book Documents by Christy Macy and Susan Kaplan, which is advertised on the cover as "an impressive collection of memos, letters and telexes from the secret archives of the U.S. intelligence community."[47] According to these authors," The CIA is the direct descendant of the Office of Strategic Services."[48]

Another author, Jeffrey T. Richelson, repeats the same piece of disinformation in his A Century of Spies: Intelligence in the Twentieth Century.[49] According to Richelson,

In 1941 President Franklin Roosevelt established America's first central intelligence agency, the Office of Information Coordination. The man chosen to head the new office, which became the Office of Strategic Services (OSS) in June 1942, was William J. Donovan.[50]

Despite its intentionally misleading name, however, the Office of Coordination of Information (IOC), was not an intelligence agency in the strict sense of the word. Its real function was not the collection and analysis of information to produce intelligence, but the execution of covert military operations. This was the first foray of the CFR conspirators into the realm of espionage, sabotage, black propaganda,[51] guerrilla warfare, and other subversive activities that had hitherto been considered contrary to American idiosyncrasies.[52]

An important part of IOC activities was devoted to psychological warfare. By late 1946, the IOC had already created detailed directives for postwar psychological warfare activities. In mid-1947, a subcommittee consisting of members of the U.S. State Department, Navy and Army was created to plan for the continued use of psychological warfare against the newly artificially created enemy: the Soviet Union.[53]

Once he created the CIA in July 1947, President Truman approved NSC-4/A, which gave the Office of Information Coordination, which was now part of the CIA, the responsibility for planning and executing covert psychological warfare tasks.[54]

The creation of the Office of Information Coordination, a veritable military arm directly in the service of the CFR conspirators, had enormous political significance. First, because the U.S. had never before had a civilian-controlled intelligence agency in peacetime, totally dedicated to covert military operations. Second, because, being under the control of the executive branch, the IOC constituted a dangerous extra-constitutional expansion of presidential power. Given the fact that since the early 20th century U.S. presidents had become puppets of the CFR, in reality this amounted to a real seizure of power in the U.S. by the CFR conspirators.

Most authors who credit President Roosevelt with the creation of the OSS miss a very important point: like most U.S. presidents, Franklin D. Roosevelt was a puppet placed in the White House and manipulated by a group of advisors, who were in reality the strings with which the CFR puppeteers controlled their puppet.[55]   Promi-

nent in this group of close advisors, which Roosevelt euphemistically called his "brain trust", were Harry Dexter White, Harry
Hopkins, George Marshall, and Henry Morgenthau, Jr. all of whom
were secret CFR agents. These individuals were a sort of early version of the National Security Council advisors who since 1947 have
surrounded U.S. presidents with a disinformation belt created at the
CFR.

Therefore, it makes sense to conclude that, like all major decisions made by U.S. presidents since Wilson, the creation of the OSS
was also an idea developed in the CFR and implanted in Roosevelt's
brain by its controllers. Moreover, given the fact that the conspirators already had their own intelligence agency, the CFR itself, it is
obvious that they had no need for another. Therefore, despite claims
to the contrary, the OSS was never a real intelligence agency, but
only the covert military arm of the CFR.

The real purpose of the OSS was never to defend the interests of the
American people, but the interests of the Wall Street bankers, the oil
tycoons and the owners of the big corporations, who had been doing
good business arming the Nazi war machine. Contrary to what is
written in most history books, the real goal of the CFR conspirators
was not to defeat their Nazi partners, but to help them save their
skins after the catastrophic collapse of Germany. This secret task
was largely accomplished by the OSS. This explains why the conspirators orchestrated the attack on Pearl Harbor as a pretext to manipulate American public opinion into willingly accepting the sending of their sons to fight in a war to which Roosevelt had shortly
before promised them they would never be sent.[56]

As I mentioned earlier, the OSS was never an intelligence agency
in the literal sense of the word, for the simple fact that the conspirators already had one: the CFR. The facts show that the OSS never
did any appreciable work in the areas of information collection, much
less in its analysis and evaluation to turn this information into intelligence. On the contrary, its main activity consisted in carrying out
covert military operations, particularly in the area of sabotage and
psychological warfare.

General William Donovan, the man the oil tycoons and Wall
Street bankers chose to command the OSS, was a millionaire lawyer
in the service of Wall Street bankers and an active member of the
Council on Foreign Relations (CFR). In 1929 he had set up his own
law firm, the law firm of Donovan, Leisure, Newton and Lumbard.[57]

His right-hand man, Allen Dulles, was also a Wall Street lawyer and a member of the CFR. From his OSS office in Bern, Switzerland, Dulles' job was not to protect the interests of the American people, but those of Wall Street bankers and other CFR members. Sullivan & Cromwell, the Wall Street law firm for which Dulles had worked since 1926,[58] maintained close business ties with I.G. Farben, the firm that produced Ziklon B, the lethal gas used to murder Jews and other minorities in the gas chambers.

Sullivan & Cromwell also represented United Fruit and other Rockefeller interests. One of the senior partners in this firm was John Foster Dulles, Allen's brother and, like him, a member of the CFR. Other lawyers in the firm were George Kennan, Paul Nitze and James Forrestal, all key members of the CFR.

Most of the OSS officers had been members of The Inquiry. Many of them later held key positions for many years in the creation of the CIA, the National Security Council and U.S. international policy.

Therefore, it must be concluded that most of those who joined the OSS were not motivated by patriotism, to fight the Nazis and protect the interests of the American people, but to protect their personal interests. In fact, the secret primary mission of the OSS during World War II was to help high-ranking Nazi officials escape with the gold they had stolen, as well as to protect German corporations associated with Wall Street banks. This explains why, when Wall Street conspirators infiltrating the American government realized that Hitler had become a kind of Frankenstein's monster, they provoked and incited the Japanese to attack Pearl Harbor and then used the incident as a pretext to take part in the war.

Nor is it a coincidence that CFR undercover agent William Donovan recruited most of the OSS officers from among members of the wealthy families whose businesses were supplying the Nazis. Among the most notorious was Andrew Mellon, son of millionaire Paul Mellon. In addition, the head of the OSS in London, David Bruce, was the son of a millionaire U.S. senator, and was married to Paul Mellon's sister, Aisla. The Mellons' links to the Nazis were well known. As a Wall Street lawyer, Donovan himself had ties to I.G. Farben, one of the major German companies that collaborated with the Nazis.

Two of J.P. Morgan's sons, Junius and Henry, also joined the OSS and held important positions in the organization. The Vanderbilts and the Duponts also allowed some of their descendants to join the OSS to keep a protective eye on their family's Nazi-linked businesses. Author Harris Smith mentions that only the Rockefellers were absent from the OSS, but Nelson was already quite busy in his espionage activities in Latin America as Coordinator of Inter-American Affairs.[59]

The Wall Street firm Goldman Sachs, allowed many of its top executives to join the OSS. And some of the Standard Oil Company's trusted men, now transformed into OSS intelligence officers, saw to it that gasoline shipments to Nazi Germany through Spain and Switzerland continued unmolested. For his part, Allen Dulles always kept hidden the close relationship, and even the shared ownership, between some American corporations and those of the Nazis.[60]

Much less well known, however, is the role these individuals played before, during, and after World War II in the development of international fascism. For example, after the Versailles Conference, John Foster Dulles, acting in his capacity as Special Advisor to the Dawes Committee, contributed greatly to the creation of so-called Dawes Plan loans, which were given to Germany after World War I to recapitalize and remilitarize.

Sullivan & Cromwell, the firm for which John Foster and Allen Dulles worked, benefited enormously from these loans. Many of the German firms that capitalized on the Dawes Plan were clients of Sullivan & Cromwell, and were instrumental in promoting Adolf Hitler's seizure of power and the creation of the German military machine.

Other Fascist European countries that benefited from Wall Street bankers' handouts were Mussolini's Italy, Franco's Spain, and Pilsudski's Poland. It should be made clear that the money the Wall Street bankers provided to the European Fascists did not come out of their pockets, but had been stolen from the American people through the Internal Revenue Service (IRS), the federal tax agency illegally created by President Wilson on the orders of "Colonel" House, the secret agent of the Wall Street bankers themselves.

Frank Wisner, a senior OSS officer who later became head of CIA covert operations, was a lawyer who had been a member of the powerful Wall Street firm of Carter, Ledyard, Milburn. William Colby, another OSS officer who went on to join the CIA and became one of its directors, had been associated with Donovan's Wall Street law firm. Other OSS members who had been Wall Street lawyers were William Jackson, Gordon Gray, and Tracy Barnes.[61] They all became CIA officers shortly after its creation in 1947.

Gray became one of the CIA's experts in psychological warfare and Wisner played a pivotal role in facilitating the escape from justice of many important Nazi war criminals. One of them, Nazi General Reinhard Gehlen, became the CIA's chief of counterintelligence in the fight against Soviet communism. Both Dulles and Wisner worked in close coordination with the Gehlen Organization.

During World War II, Allen Dulles had been in charge of the OSS office in Bern, Switzerland. Under the cover of his position at the OSS, Dulles maintained close relations with key members of the Nazi industrial and financial elite. Many of them were already known to him from the days when he worked for Sullivan & Cromwell.

Nevertheless, it must be acknowledged that, all things considered, the OSS did an excellent job. The problem is that it did it not for the benefit of the American people, but for their real masters, the oil tycoons and Wall Street bankers. Unfortunately, that was a vice that the CIA inherited.

Contrary to the established myth, the OSS was never an intelligence agency that fought to protect the interests of the American people. On the contrary, the OSS was a fifth column that the CFR conspirators infiltrated into the U.S. military. One of its secret tasks was to sabotage the efforts of true patriots like General George Patton, who were trying to destroy the Nazi military machine in order to win the war as quickly as possible and thus save the lives of American soldiers.

But the CFR conspirators had other plans. When they were forced to fight the Nazi military machine because the monster they had created turned against them, their secret plan was to replace it with another, more docile monster they had already created: Soviet Russia.

The primary mission of the OSS during World War II was to prevent the Allied troops from winning the war too quickly and to capture the Nazi war criminals before the OSS had created the necessary means to facilitate their escape.[62] The secondary mission was to create favorable conditions for the Soviets to occupy much of Eastern Europe. This explains why a large majority of the OSS officers were leftists or Communist militants.

However, the plan ran into several obstacles. Although the CFR conspirators controlled some senior Army officers, such as Dwight Eisenhower, George Marshall and Mathew Ridgway, most were true patriots who firmly believed that their primary mission was to defeat the Nazis. Unfortunately, they were wrong. These honest officers were unaware that the real purpose of the war was to protect the investments of the oil tycoons and Wall Street bankers in Germany and to make it easier for top Nazi leaders to escape justice.

At the time, not all senior military officers in the U.S. armed forces were under the control of the CFR conspirators, so Donovan and his cronies in the OSS immediately made several enemies, among them General George V. Strong, head of the Army's G-2 (intelligence) section. General Strong openly expressed his lack of confidence in Donovan's new organization and proceeded to establish his own clandestine intelligence service to compete with the OSS.[63]

Another enemy, probably more powerful than General Strong, was J. Edgar Hoover, the director of the Federal Bureau of Investigation (FBI). The FBI was the government agency responsible for counterintelligence, and Hoover, who had been doing a good job, especially in Latin America, was merely protecting his turf.

While most American military men were risking their lives fighting what they considered a just war, whose only noble purpose was to free Europe from the Nazi scourge, the secret army of the CFR conspirators, the OSS, was working in the shadows to protect the conspirators' interests in Germany and to help the Nazi leaders escape to South America with the help of the Vatican and Peron. And Donovan and his OSS men were there not only to protect the Nazis, but also to keep loyal officers in check and ensure that they did not achieve too soon what they considered their primary mission in the war: to defeat the Nazis.

It is true that some members of the OSS were also true American patriots who firmly believed that their primary role was to fight the Nazis. But all of them had been recruited under a false flag and, consciously or unconsciously, were helping the pro-Nazi conspirators of the CFR to prevent the Nazi war criminals from paying for their crimes.

6. Nelson Rockefeller and the PsyWar Against Latin America

From its inception, John D. Rockefeller's Standard Oil Company - which other oil producers called "a gang of thieves" [66] —always operated as an intelligence and espionage organization. As in the spy agencies, John D. created in his Standard Oil a cult of silence and deception, under a policy of total secrecy. It is known that some of the people who did business with John D. were obliged to sign an oath of secrecy, with the promise to keep any kind of agreement with Rockefeller strictly private.[65]

John D. Rockefeller was a pioneer in the use of industrial espionage to advance his business interests. According to author Gary Allen, "Rockefeller's system of industrial espionage was at the time the most elaborate, the most sophisticated, and the most successful ever created." [66]

Rockefeller hired agents everywhere: among his competitors, among politicians, and in the media. In his continuing effort to monopolize the oil industry by eliminating all competition, Standard Oil spies compiled information on foreign and U.S. markets,[67] and analysts evaluated the raw information and produced useful information - a process known today as the evaluation of information into intelligence.[68]

John D. Rockefeller was the inventor of a new form of economic power, the trust, on which modern corporations are based.[69] Corporations are basically criminal organizations devoid of principles, ethics, morals, morality, honesty, or human feelings. The main objective of a corporation is the elimination of competition and the creation of a total monopoly, as well as maximizing, by whatever means, the profits of its investors and executives.

The creation of corporations was the preliminary step that paved the way for the creation of the two most common types of totalitarian states in modern times: communism and fascism. Basically, communism is a type of socialist government in which the state controls corporations, while fascism is a type of socialist government in which corporations control the state. It makes sense, therefore, that the New World Order that the Rockefellers and their criminal associates plan to implement in the world will be a mixture of both types of totalitarian regimes.

The Council on Foreign Relations, basically an intelligence and espionage organization, reflects the psychology, mentality and interests of its creators, the Rockefeller brothers, especially David and Nelson. Like their grandfather John D., Nelson and David Rockefeller always felt a special fascination for intelligence and espionage activities, and proudly continued the tradition that began with their grandfather John D. Rockefeller.

Because of the scandal unleashed when the press discovered it, many people have heard of Project Camelot, a psychological warfare operation conceived by the conspirators who control the U.S. government, which was carried out in Chile as a testing ground for later implementation in other Latin American countries. Executed in part by the CIA, and financed by the Ford Foundation and the Rand Cor-

poration —evidencing that it was in fact a secret CFR operation —
Project Camelot began in 1964 as a sociological study of Chilean
society. Shortly thereafter, in his Report on Latin America, Nelson
Rockefeller would recommend to the U.S. government the seizure
of power in Latin America through coups carried out by the puppet
militaries they controlled.

But Project Camelot was neither the first nor the last psychological
warfare operation instigated by the Rockefellers against countries
south of the U.S. border.

In the late 1930s, Nelson Rockefeller was appointed to oversee a
secret U.S. government project, which soon became a covert offen-
sive of ideological and economic warfare against countries south of
the border. American Propaganda Abroad, a book written by a former
U.S. Information Agency official, describes in considerable detail
how the United States began its first psychological warfare campaign against Latin America in 1938, with the creation of the Office
of Inter-American Affairs (OIAA) in the State Department, under
the direction of Nelson Rockefeller.[70]

That innocuous name actually masked the real work of the OIAA:
waging psychological warfare against the peoples of Latin America.
Shortly after its creation, a secret psychological warfare team was
created within the OIAA.

The creation of the Office of Inter-American Affairs had strong support among politicians of both Rockefeller-controlled parties. Both
Nelson and David had been clamoring for the creation of an agency
to coordinate U.S. defense activities in Latin America and foster attitudes favorable to the conspirators' secret objectives.

Two years later, in August 1940, Nelson Rockefeller was appointed
Coordinator of Commercial and Cultural Relations with the Latin
American Republics. By this time, Nelson already had strong economic, financial and commercial ties in Latin America, and the main
secret function of his Office of Inter-American Affairs was the implementation of an extensive psychological warfare operation. This psychological warfare had been carefully planned to mold public opinion in Latin America to accept without protest the economic and
ideological subjugation plans of the CFR conspirators in the implementation of the early stages of the New World Order.

Nelson held various positions in the Roosevelt administration. But
Truman, who was not a member of the CFR, did not consider Nelson's

help necessary in his administration, and simply dismissed him from office. However, during Dwight Eisenhower's administration, Nelson's star shone again when Eisenhower appointed him as Special Assistant to the President for Foreign Policy (1954-55) and as head of the secretive "Committee of Forty" in charge of overseeing CIA covert operations.

Nelson Rockefeller always advocated the use of private organizations and foundations as government surrogates in U.S. psychological warfare. Nelson Rockefeller's criminal activities around the world became so scandalous that in 1947, when the U.S. had just won the war against Nazi Germany, widespread suspicions arose about his treasonous activities in Latin America. The reason for these suspicions was that Nelson was in charge of the U.S. intelligence services, which had turned a blind eye to Standard Oil's shipments of oil from South America to the Nazis before and after the U.S. declared war against Nazi Germany.

On the other hand, it must be recognized that Rockefeller was not the only important person in the U.S. government suspected of having participated in treasonous acts during the war. Other traitors were Prescott Bush and his lawyer Allen Dulles, then head of the OSS office in Bern, Switzerland and later director of the CIA. But it is no coincidence that both were associated with the Standard Oil Co.[71]

In his book Trading with the Enemy, Charles Higham offered abundant evidence of the treasonous activities of the Rockefellers during World War II.[72] Despite the fact that Germany lacked the oil needed to wage war, Nazi bombers continued to rain bombs on London and other European cities. This was made possible by gasoline provided by the Rockefellers' Standard Oil.[73]

After the U.S. became involved in World War II, President Roosevelt appointed Nelson Rockefeller Coordinator of Inter-American Affairs. But all indications are that his main task was actually to coordinate the secret resupply of German ships and submarines in South America with Standard Oil tanks. Nelson also used this position to obtain important concessions in South America for his private company, the International Basic Economy Corporation (IBEC), which included an important participation in the Colombian coffee market.

As soon as Nelson gained control of the coffee market, the first thing he did was to raise prices, a decision that allowed him to buy several billion dollars worth of real estate in South America. This once again affirmed the stereotype of "Yankee imperialism" that the

CFR conspirators and their secret agents like Fidel Castro have always used as a smokescreen to hide the real imperialists.

The Rockefellers have always used espionage as their main tool to promote their personal interests. For example, Stephen Schlesinger, a specialist with expertise in the field of cryptography, wrote an article in which he revealed some of the unethical espionage activities carried out by the CFR conspirators.

Before and during the 1945 San Francisco Conference, which culminated in the creation of the United Nations, OSS officials working for their CFR masters spied on delegates and intercepted their secret communications with their respective countries to learn in advance the positions of each country in the negotiations. Knowledge of this private information allowed the CFR conspirators to have total control of the Conference, to the point that the Charter of the United Nations adopted by the delegates was the one the conspirators had previously drafted at the Harold Pratt House in New York, the CFR headquarters.[74]

7. The National Security Council and the CIA

At the end of the war, many members of the defunct OSS became part of the War Department's Strategic Services Unit (SSU). Shortly thereafter, the SSU split into two separate organizations, the Office of Special Operations (OSO), and the Office of Policy Coordination (OPC). Richard Helms and James Jesus Angleton joined OSO, while Frank Wisner, Richard Bissell, Edward Lansdale, Desmond Fitzgerald and Tracy Barnes joined OPC. Needless to say, almost all of them were members of the Council on Foreign Relations.

Shortly thereafter, the OSO disappeared and the OPC took the intentionally misleading name of the Office of Coordination of Information (COI). But, like its predecessor the OSS, the COI was never properly an intelligence agency. The COI never conducted intelligence gathering and analysis, but rather covert military operations. This was the second direct foray by the CFR conspirators into the field of "espionage, sabotage, 'black' propaganda,[75] guerrilla warfare, and other subversive practices."[76]

Author John Loftus found that the Office of Information Coordination was actually a secret covert action department controlled by the CFR through Secretary of Defense James Forrestal, a CFR agent, and what Loftus calls "the Dulles [John Foster Dulles] faction in the State Department."[77]

A major part of IOC activities was devoted to psychological warfare. By late 1946, the IOC had already created detailed directives for postwar psychological warfare activities and, in mid-1947, created a subcommittee consisting of members of the State Department, the Navy, and the Army to plan the continued use of psychological warfare against the newly artificially created enemy: the Soviet Union.[78]

The creation of the Office of Information Coordination, a covert military arm in the direct service of the CFR conspirators, had enormous political significance in U.S. history. First, because the country had never before had a civilian-controlled intelligence agency in peacetime, let alone one dedicated to conducting covert military operations. Second, because, being under the direct control of the president, the IOC constituted a major unconstitutional extension of executive power. This expansion of the president's power, which granted him quasi-dictatorial powers, allowed the CFR conspirators to control the U.S. government simply by controlling the president.

Once the CIA was created, President Truman approved NSC-4/A, which gave the Office of Information Coordination, now a part of the CIA, the responsibility for planning and executing covert psychological warfare operations.[79]

On July 26, 1947, President Harry S. Truman signed the National Security Act creating the National Security Council (NSC). This act also created the Central Intelligence Agency (CIA), as well as the positions of Secretary of Defense and Joint Chiefs of Staff. It also created the Air Force as an independent branch of the U.S. armed forces. This marked the official beginning of the Cold War, an artificial creation of the conspirators at the Council on Foreign Relations.[80]

In theory, the National Security Council was created in order to better control the departments conducting foreign policy and the military and intelligence activities of the U.S. government. However, the National Security Act, like the most important documents of the U.S. government, had been written neither in the White House nor in Congress, but in the Harold Pratt House in Manhattan, headquarters of the CFR.

One must take into account the fact that at that time some U.S. presidents were not yet fully under the control of the conspirators. Therefore, the real purpose of the conspirators was to create a shadow organization, whose members would surround the presidents and manipulate them by selectively controlling the information reaching them. It is no coincidence that, since its inception, most of the members of the National Security Council have been also secret CFR agents.

The National Security Act only gave the National Security Council advisory duties, not executive powers. More importantly, the Act did not give the newly created CIA the authority to conduct covert operations abroad. Yet just a few months later, in December 1947, CFR operatives on the National Security Council secretly issued NSC Directive 4-A, which made the CIA director responsible for psychological warfare.

Then, less than a year after its creation, CFR agents on the National Security Council went a step further and illegally assumed executive powers. On June 18, 1948, the National Security Council produced NSC 10/2, a secret directive that replaced NSC 4-A and was kept hidden from the American people and government for many years. NSC 10/2 authorized the CIA to conduct not only psychological warfare but also all types of covert military operations.

Finally the CFR conspirators had achieved what they had set out to do: the creation of an invisible army to carry out their plans for world domination, hidden under the cloak of legality of a legitimate U.S. government organization.

The NSC 10/2 directive is perhaps the most important document if we are to understand the true essence of the CIA. Written in June 1948, just two months after the successful Operation Bogotazo, NSC 10/2 actually divided the CIA into two basically operationally distinct organizations: one to carry out basically passive tasks of espionage and intelligence analysis, and the other to execute active tasks of psychological warfare and covert military operations.

As in Italo Calvino's well-known novel The Viscount's Two Halves, NSC 10/2 split the CIA into two, one good and one bad. The intelligence and espionage branch was staffed by true patriots who believed they were doing important work to ensure the security of their country. On the contrary, the covert operations branch was totally controlled by secret agents of the CFR, who were not fighting to look after and defend the interests of the country but the interests of the oil tycoons, Wall Street bankers and top executives of transnational corporations.

This explains why all the alleged failures that have been blamed on the CIA have always been in the area of information analysis and intelligence. According to the official story, most of the time the CIA has been unable to alert the government in time to the possibility of enemy action. This seems to be exactly what happened at the time of the Bogotazo.

However, as we will see below, both in the case of the Bogotazo and the other "failures" that followed, the CIA did inform in advance, but nobody paid attention to it. And nobody paid attention to it for the simple reason that those who planned to carry out the action were precisely CFR agents in the covert operations branch of the CIA.

If this dichotomy is ignored, it is impossible to understand why, in most cases, after an alleged failure of the CIA to predict an event, it is later discovered that in fact the CIA (i.e., the intelligence and espionage branch of the CIA) had previously warned about the possibility of something happening, but was ignored.

CFR conspirators infiltrating the U.S. government have always explained these "failures" as the inability of the CIA and other intelligence agencies to "connect the dots." What the conspirators conveniently fail to say is that, if the dots were connected, the lines would point directly to traitors in important positions in the U.S. government and military, all of whom are secret CFR agents.

From time to time, some amateur conspiracy theorist expresses his suspicions that the CIA has fallen under the control of an internal conspiracy of rogues and ill-intentioned crooks, who are using it to further their own monetary interests. This idea, however, is not new. It has been mentioned before, and reinforced by Senator Frank Church, when, during the congressional inquiry he presided over in 1975 to investigate CIA misconduct, he called it "a mischievous elephant." [81]

However, unlike most conspiracy theories about September 11, 2001, this one is totally false. There is no private criminal group that has taken over the CIA. In fact, since its inception, the CIA has always been a criminal organization that has nothing to do with the U.S. government and has never worked for the people who pay the bills with the money the government takes from them in taxes: U.S. citizens.

The National Security Council was the first step in the creation of a Fascistic aberration later known as the National Security State. Soon after its creation, this state within the state, totally under the control of the oil tycoons, Wall Street bankers and top executives of transnational corporations, was transformed into an unaccountable and out-of-control state, which soon became the greatest source of insecurity for the American people.

The National Security Council is a key element in understanding how the CFR conspirators indirectly control the U.S. government. The National Security Council is the visible head of the fifth column of CFR conspirators infiltrated within the U.S. government. This was confirmed a few years ago by one of them.

On February 8, 2009, at the 45th Munich Conference on Security Policy at the Bayerischer Hof Hotel, Barack Hussein Obama's[83] National Security Advisor, General James L. Jones,83 stated:

> Thank you for your wonderful tribute yesterday to Henry Kissinger [CFR]. Congratulations. As America's newest National Security Advisor, I take my daily orders from Dr. Kissinger, filtered through General Brent Scowcroft [CFR] and Sandy Berger [CFR], who is also here. We've always had a chain of command in the National Security Council and it exists today.[84]

A few months later, U.S. Secretary of State Hillary Clinton also confirmed this. In a July 15, 2009 speech at the opening of the new CFR affiliate in Washington, D.C., Hillary stated:

> I am delighted to be here at this new affiliate. I often visit the mother ship in New York City, but it's nice to have a Council affiliate right across the street from the State Department. We always get a lot of advice from the Council, so it means I don't have to go far to be told what we should do and what we should think about the future.[85]

So, in their own words, General James Jones and Hillary Clinton destroyed the myth that the National Security Council (and the CIA) are tools in the hands of the President. By their own admission, the chain of command of America's national security advisors and secretaries of state has nothing to do with the White House, but comes directly from the Harold Pratt House in Manhattan, where the oil tycoons, Wall Street bankers, and top executives of transnational corporations maintain the real seat of power in the U.S..

This chain of command was officially established in 1947, when CFR secret agents infiltrating the U.S. government forced the creation of the National Security Act. However, shortly after its creation, CFR agents infiltrating the National Security Council turned it into a tool to control and filter information reaching the eyes and ears of presidents, thus creating a smokescreen of disinformation around them.

Since the end of World War II, the CFR conspirators, through their secret agents in the National Security Council, have been pouring disinformation into the eyes and ears of American presidents and "suggesting" to them what decisions to make. This has ensured that the most important policy decisions made by American presidents have actually been conceived in the Harold Pratt House.

Some wayward presidents, who tried to act independently, soon suffered the consequences: Kennedy was assassinated, Nixon was deposed by a palace coup, and Reagan nearly lost his life, but was miraculously saved.

After what I have stated above, one might ask: Why did the conspirators need a new intelligence agency, the CIA, when they already had an excellent one, the CFR?

The answer is relatively simple: they had no need for another intelligence agency, and in fact they did not create a new one, because, as I have explained above, the CIA has never been an intelligence agency in the true sense of the word, at least, not for the CFR conspirators who created it. So the proper question might be, why did they create the CIA if not to capitalize on its ability to obtain information and, through a process of evaluation and analysis, turn it into useful intelligence for the president to make appropriate decisions?

According to a certain anecdote, when Soviet leader Joseph Stalin was informed that the Vatican had declared war on Nazi Germany after receiving news that the Red Army had surrounded Berlin with an iron fist, the Soviet dictator laughed good-naturedly and asked, "How many divisions does the Pope have?"

Like the Vatican, the Wall Street bankers and oil tycoons had succeeded in gaining enormous economic power to buy off corrupt politicians and critics in the countries they wished to control. But they also needed to resort from time to time to brute force to intimidate cowards and punish rebels. So, from the end of the 19th century, they began to use the U.S. armed forces as their military arm to impose their imperialist policies. The long list of military interventions around the world, starting with the Spanish-Cuban-American war, marked the beginning of the misnamed "American imperialism", which is really "Wall Street imperialism." These military interventions for the benefit of the Wall Street Mafia, but carried out on behalf of the American people, resulted in many honest people around the world blaming the American people for these imperialist aggressions.

CFR agent Donald Rumsfeld often quoted a phrase from Al Capone: "You get more with a kind word and a gun than with a kind word alone." All indications are that the philosophy of the Chicago Mafia closely resembles the guiding philosophy of the Wall Street Mafia: "You accomplish more with a lie and an army than you do with a lie alone."

A simple cursory analysis of U.S. military interventions around the world since the mid-1800s shows how Wall Street bankers and oil tycoons have used the U.S. military, particularly the Marines, to carry out their criminal actions against other peoples of the world.[86] Latin America is undoubtedly one of the areas of the planet that has suffered most from these criminal activities. A list of U.S. military interventions since 1890 would show that very few countries have not experienced firsthand the presence of U.S. troops acting to protect the interests of Wall Street bankers and oil tycoons.

But eventually the world changed, and it became increasingly risky and problematic for the CFR conspirators to openly use the U.S. military, particularly in Latin America, as the main tool to impose their will on other peoples. The fact was recognized by Franklin D. Roosevelt himself, a secret CFR agent, when in one of his meetings with Winston Churchill during World War II he pointed out to him that naked colonialism, such as had been used in the past, was no longer a suitable option in the Caribbean.[87] And this was not only because the Marines had become a worldwide symbol of American aggression and oppression, but also because of growing discontent among senior officers in the U.S. armed forces. The opposition of some of these, who were not entirely under the control of the conspirators, made it more difficult for them to continue openly using the U.S. military to achieve their nefarious purposes.

Nevertheless, the CFR conspirators needed a short-term option to continue to use direct U.S. military action when coercion and intimidation alone failed to do so. Therefore, perhaps after remembering that Sun Tzu had said that all warfare is based on deception,[88] the conspirators decided to create their own illegal private army. And the best way to create this army without alarming the American people and the world was to create an invisible army. They therefore created it surreptitiously, keeping it hidden from public scrutiny under the cover of a legitimate U.S. government organization.

To that end, using their secret agents infiltrated into the U.S. government, in 1947 the conspirators forced the naive, or corrupt,

American politicians to pass the National Security Act, which created the organization they planned to use to exercise full CFR puppet control over American puppet presidents: the National Security Council. And an important component of the National Security Act was the creation of a Central Intelligence Agency, which they never planned to use as a real intelligence agency, but as a cover to hide their military arm, now in the form of covert operations.

In a short time the CIA proved to be exactly the kind of organization the conspirators needed to help them achieve their illicit ends of carrying out their pillaging and plundering around the world. First, it was free, because American taxpayers paid for it. Second, because, thanks to the CIA's operating principles of secrecy, compartmentalization and need-to-know inherent in all intelligence services, it was relatively easy to conceal its real activities, both from the American public at large and from CIA employees themselves who were not under the control of the CFR.

Allen Dulles himself, a secret CFR agent who was Director of the CIA for several years, acknowledged the fact when he wrote:

> An intelligence service is the ideal vehicle for a conspiracy. Its members can travel in and out of the country carrying out secret orders and asking no questions. Every scrap of paper in the files, its membership, the use of funds, its contacts, even contacts with the enemy, are secret.[89]

Although Dulles was referring specifically to the German intelligence services, everything he said could very well apply to the CIA or any other intelligence service. The fact that the CIA is essentially a conspiracy was also noted by political analyst Michael Parenti. According to him,

> In most of its operations, the CIA is, by definition, a conspiracy, relying on covert operations and secret plans, many of which are of the worst kind. What is a covert operation if not a conspiracy? At the same time, the CIA is an institution, a structural part of the national security state. In short, the CIA is an institutionalized conspiracy.[90]

Like many other important documents in recent U.S. history, NSC Directive 10/2, which authorized the CIA to conduct covert military operations, was written at the Harold Pratt, House in Manhattan by George Kennan, a secret agent of the conspirators.[91] The document cites as a proven fact "the virulent covert activities of the USSR, its satellite countries and Communist groups to discredit and derail the objectives and activities of the United States and other Western powers." These alleged "virulent covert activities" of the Soviet Union were the justification given by the CFR conspirators to the American people, whose country was supposed to be the antithesis of the Soviet Union, for allowing the CIA to engage in virulent covert activities around the world.

Some years later, former OSS officer and CFR agent Arthur Schlesinger, Jr. expressed exactly the same idea as Kennan in an article he wrote in 1967 for Foreign Affairs magazine, the CFR's disinformation organ. According to Schlesinger, Western countries were forced to confront the Soviet Union because Stalin was paranoid.

However, without falling into the leftist error of believing that the Soviet leaders were saints guided by lofty moral principles, there is ample evidence to indicate that the Cold War, like the Soviet Union itself, were artificial creations of the CFR conspirators, conceived and maintained as a credible threat to keep the American people in a constant state of terror. This threat justified the arms race resulting from confrontation with the enemy they had created out of thin air. It is also a known fact that the CFR conspirators served Stalin Eastern Europe on a silver platter as a sure way to increase the fear of communism in the world.

Stanford University revisionist historian Barton J. Bernstein found abundant evidence to prove that, "by refusing to accept Soviet interests, American leaders in charge of formulating foreign policy contributed to the Cold War."[92] A similar view was expressed by political analyst H.W. Brands. According to him, "The Cold War was largely the result of U.S. efforts to export capitalism to the whole world." [93] It should be added that what they exported was monopoly capitalism, the greatest enemy of true capitalism.

These views are not very different from the thesis formulated by Frank Kofsky in one of the best documented books on the causes of the Cold War, which he attributes to a conspiracy carried out by the CFR power elite. According to Kofsky,

> Regardless of whether some "conspiracy theories" are fanciful or nonsensical, it is an established fact that in the 1940s members of the American ruling class and power elite resorted to conspiratorial machinations whenever they felt it necessary.[94]

The process by which the CFR conspirators brandished the specter of communism for half a century to stoke fear in the American people was repeated in exactly the same way in 2001 with the fear of terrorism, after the unexpected implosion of the Soviet Union had deprived them of the necessary enemy. I have always suspected that the real reason for the first war in Iraq - a trap into which Saddam Hussein foolishly fell - was to provoke the Soviets into the conflict. But by that time the Soviet bear was already dead, and even that direct provocation failed to revive it. Unfortunately for the American people, the failure to resurrect Soviet communism brought them the events of September 11, 2001, which justified the War on Terror as the interim substitute for the Cold War.

However, it appears that the War on Terror has not proved to be entirely convincing, so the CFR conspirators are doing their best to start a new Cold War with China and Russia. Unfortunately, as always, it is the people, not the conspirators, who pay the highest price in these unjustified and unnecessary wars.

Part Two: Fidel Castro

> *A common characteristic of all intelligence officers is that they have an open mind. For them nothing is impossible just because it is improbable.*
> —Thomas Powers, *The Man Who Kept the Secrets.*

> *When we eliminate the impossible, whatever remains, however improbable it may seem, must be the truth.*
> —Sherlock Holmes, *The Sign of the Four.*

At noon on April 9, 1948, the lawyer and popular political leader Jorge Eliécer Gaitán, who many predicted would be the next president of Colombia, was assassinated as he was leaving the building where his office was located. Fidel Castro and three other students from the University of Havana, Rafael del Pino,[1] Enrique Ovares and Alfredo Guevara (no relation to Che Guevara), were in Bogota at the time. They had arrived a few days before the inauguration of the Ninth Pan American Conference to be held in that city. The reason given to justify the Cubans' presence in the country was their participation in an anti-imperialist student congress that had been planned to coincide with the Conference.

Only a few days earlier, Castro and del Pino had contacted Gaitán on the pretext of inviting him to speak at the inaugural session of the student congress, and Gaitán had agreed to meet with them that day to discuss the matter. But, just under two hours before the meeting, someone fired several shots at him, and he perished a few hours later. When Gaitán was assassinated, Castro and del Pino were very close to the place where the events took place.

Gaitán's assassination unleashed a frenzied orgy of death, destruction and looting that destroyed most of the center of the populous city of Bogotá and virtually cut off communications with the rest of the country for several days. The riots resulted in the deaths of more than a thousand people. 150 important buildings were totally burned or partially destroyed.

The riots marked the beginning of a bloody period in Colombia's history known as *La Violencia*, (The Violence) which has cost the lives of more than 200,000 people and has continued almost to the present. *La Violencia* was the main cause of a massive emigration of Colombians from the countryside to the cities. It also created the necessary conditions for the emergence of guerrilla groups that still exist today.

Some of the books that have been written about the CIA briefly mention the events of the Bogotazo as the first failure of the CIA. According to these authors, the newly created CIA did not alert the U.S. government to the possibility of such an incident occurring. However, what none of the books that have been written about the CIA mention is that the Bogotazo was actually the first successful large-scale psychological warfare (psyop) operation carried out by the newly created Central Intelligence Agency on the orders of its real masters: a group of Wall Street bankers, oil tycoons, and transnational corporate executives grouped together in the Council on Foreign Relations.[2] In this operation the CIA tested new covert warfare, propaganda and mind control techniques that it later used in similar operations ranging from the assassination of President John F. Kennedy to the psyop of September 11, 2001.

Moreover, the Bogotazo was the operation in which the CFR conspirators first used their new agent they had recruited shortly before: a young student at the University of Havana named Fidel Castro.

Some years ago, a Washington D.C. psychiatrist whose patients included members and former members of the CIA learned so much from them that she decided to create a typical spy personality profile. According to her, spies fit perfectly into the classic description of individuals with antisocial personalities, also known as psychopaths.[3] Psychopaths are people incapable of professing loyalty to individuals or groups. They are immensely narcissistic and selfish. They are also insensitive, manipulative, and contemptuous of other people. They are incapable of guilt, remorse or regret for their actions and do not learn as a result of experience or punishment. Most psychopaths are impulsive, show very little tolerance for their frustrations, and tend to blame others for their mistakes. Although superficially charming, they are actually distrustful, liars, and insincere.

Most psychopaths are incapable of feeling love or friendship of any kind, and never feel anxiety or inner conflict, as they are usually people of action, not feelings. They are dramatic, exhibitionist, and impostors. It is common for them to commit criminal acts.[4] As we will see below, this description of a psychopath fits Fidel Castro's personality perfectly.

The CIA talent scouts[5] at the U.S. Embassy in Havana were already aware of Fidel Castro's activities and decided to recruit him and send him to Bogotá as an agent provocateur on an important mission. Apparently, Fidel Castro's already impressive record as a gangster, murderer and psychopath totally lacking in ethics, morals and principles, convinced them that he was the right person to carry out this delicate and important mission. There is no doubt that they were not wrong.

1. Fidel Castro the Gangster

On December 8, 1946, when he was still a student at the University of Havana, Fidel Castro was arrested and accused of making an attempt on the life of Leonel Gómez, his opponent for the candidacy in the next elections for the presidency of the University Federation of the Law School. But the judge decided that there was not enough evidence. Therefore, he decided to suspend the indictment and ordered Castro released.

In mid 1947, Fidel Castro joined a group of Cubans and Dominicans who were undergoing military training on a small island off the northern coast of Oriente province. The objective was to overthrow Rafael L. Trujillo, the president-dictator of the Dominican Republic. The expedition ended in total failure when the participants were captured by the Cuban Navy. Castro was able to escape without being arrested and, a few months later, participated in a failed attempt on the life of Rolando Masferrer, one of the leaders of the unsuccessful expedition.[6]

A few months later, on February 22, 1948, Manolo Castro, former president of the University Student Federation, was assassinated as he was leaving a movie theater in downtown Havana, in a Chicago gangster-style shootout. Two days later, Castro was arrested and charged with the murder. But, as in the previous case, he was later released when the judge claimed there was insufficient evidence that he had committed the crime.

The criminal activities of young Fidel Castro's were extensively reported in the Cuban press, and were public knowledge, and CIA intelligence officers at the U.S. Embassy took note of it. A confidential message dated April 26, 1948, sent to the State Department and signed by the Embassy Counselor, proves that Castro's activities were known,

> He [Castro] is a student leader at the University of Havana Law School who came to the attention of the Embassy in connection with the shooting and murder of Manolo Castro (no relation to Fidel), former president of the University Student Federation. Fidel Castro is believed to be a member of the Revolutionary Insurrectionary Union (UIR), a gang of "student" thugs and assassins who

are suspected to be the killers of Manolo Castro as the culmination of a long-running feud between the police and the students.[7]

A confidential document for the record, written by J.L. Topping, CIA Station Chief at the U.S. Embassy in Havana, indicates that the CIA's interest in Castro's criminal activities had not been a passing thing. According to this document, declassified in 2002,

On December 20, 1957, Manuel Márquez Sterling y Domínguez, youngest son of Dr. Carlos Márquez Sterling, stated that, according to his personal knowledge, he knew that Fidel Castro had had an active participation in the conspiracy to assassinate Manolo Castro, when Fidel was a student at the University of Havana.

Manuel explained that, although Fidel was not in the same class as him, he was a classmate of his older brother. Manuel did not explain how he obtained the information, but added that Fidel Castro had acted as a watcher or finger-man for the assassins. Fidel had disguised himself as a lottery ticket seller, and had positioned himself in front of the movie theater, from where he kept watch waiting for Manolo to come out of the theater.[8]

It seems that the CIA agents at the American embassy were not the only ones who shared the suspicion that Fidel Castro had been the assassin of Manolo Castro. It is rumored that Ernest Hemingway, who was a personal friend of Manolo Castro, took Fidel Castro as a model to create the main character in his short story *The Shot*.[9]

But Hemingway was not the only writer motivated by Fidel Castro's gangster activities. Venezuelan writer Rómulo Gallegos, then in exile in Cuba, said that he had been inspired by Fidel Castro to create the fictional character Justo Rigores, "El Caudillo", one of the main gangsters in his novel *La brizna de paja en el viento* (The blade of straw in the wind).[10]

Many people in Cuba knew that, as a student at the University of Havana, Castro always carried a .45 caliber pistol. As soon as he began attending law school at the University of Havana, Castro created his own Nazi SA-style gang, which he called "the Manicatos." He later joined one of the gangs that swarmed the University, the Movimiento Social Revolucionario (MSR) and, after a dispute with Rolando Masferrer, the leader of the MSR, Castro switched to the rival faction, the Unión Insurreccional Revolucionaria (UIR). The two organizations combined politics with the purest gangsterism.

Luis Conte Agüero, at the time one of Castro's best friends, stated that Fidel Castro had "the mentality of a gangster."[11] UIR members engaged in gun fights with the police, with other students, and with almost everyone else, over issues that were purely personal rather than political in nature. Fidel Castro found in the UIR his natural habitat.[12]

It was in the UIR in 1945 that Castro began his real career as a professional gangster. UIR assassins had a habit of leaving a note next to their victims that read, "Justice takes time, but it comes", and Castro made the phrase his own.[13] Ernst Halperin, one of the scholars who has analyzed Castro's life, noted the high frequency with which the word "justice" appears in his speeches. It is possible, Halperin speculated, that Castro's fixation with the word "justice" could have arisen while he was preparing the "macabre notes."[14]

What is most striking about Castro's passion for gangsterism is that it did not begin at the University of Havana when he joined the gangster groups, but several years earlier, in his adolescence, when he was still a high school student. As soon as Fidel started attending the Colegio de Belen in Havana, he organized a gang with four or five of his cronies and used it to harass his classmates. The Jesuit fathers were terrified. Never before had they had a student like Fidel Castro.

One day one of his teachers expelled him from class for fighting with another classmate. Fidel threatened the teacher, shouting, "I'm going to bring my gun and I'm going to kill you", and ran out of the classroom. No one believed him, but a few minutes later he returned wielding a .45 pistol.

Another day he started a fist fight with Ramon Mestre, a classmate. Mestre won the fight, however, and the enraged Fidel returned with the .45 pistol. Only the intervention of Father Larracea, one of the teachers, who convinced Fidel to give him the pistol, saved Mestre's life. But now comes the most incredible part. When Father Larracea convinced him of the impropriety of his behavior, Fidel, in an act of repentance, went to his room and returned with another .45 pistol, which he gave to the astonished Father Larracea.[15]

2. CFR Conspirators Recruit Fidel Castro

Many people have tried to find a rational explanation for the fact that, despite his incessantly proclaimed American hatred, Fidel Castro has actually never been bothered by the U.S.[16] Nevertheless, only a few, including this author, have come to the conclusion that the only ratiional explanation for this anomaly is that Castro was actually secretly working for those he claimed to hate.

In my case, I managed to find abundant circumstantial evidence tconfirming my suspicions.[17]

However, it was not until 1995 that someone provided me with the first direct evidence that Fidel Castro had been recruited by the U.S. intelligence services.

In a 1995 self-published book,[18] Ramón B. Conte, a Cuban who collaborated with the CIA in minor activities where brute force might be necessary, mentions in some detail how Castro's recruitment took place in early 1948 during a secret meeting at the residence of Mario Lazo. Lazo was a U.S.-educated Cuban lawyer who represented many American business interests in Cuba.

In his book, Conte tells how he and another CIA operative were in a car parked on the street in front of Lazo's house. According to Conte, both were armed and ready to intervene in case Castro, known for his hot temper and passion for firearms, refused the CIA's offer and became violent.

According to Conte, Castro arrived at the meeting accompanied by his friend Rafael del Pino Siero, a CIA collaborator who had been a member of the U.S. Army during World War II. Among those who attended the meeting were Lazo himself, CIA officers Richard Salvatierra and Isabel Siero Pérez,[19] former U.S. Ambassador to Cuba Willard Beaulac,[20] and two other Americans whom Conte identifies only as Colonel Roberts and a CIA officer known only as Mr. Davies.[21]

Several years after Conte published his book, I had the opportunity to interview him by telephone from his home in Miami. In the interview, Conte added to the list of people who attended the meeting an important name that he had not mentioned in his book: William D. Pawley.[22]

At the time of the meeting, Pawley, a millionaire businessman and close friend of both President Eisenhower and Allen Dulles, was the American ambassador to Brazil. Since the days of the Office of Special Services (OSS) during World War II, Pawley had been closely linked to the U.S.. intelligence services. One of his associates, Colonel J.C. King, became Chief of the CIA's Western Hemisphere Division. Moreover, Pawley was one of the organizers of the Ninth Pan American Conference of Foreign Ministers that was to take place in April in Bogotá[23]

According to Conte, a week after the initial meeting, Castro and del Pino met again with CIA officer[24] Richard Salvatierra, who had been assigned to be the handler of the newly recruited new agent Fidel Castro, who had adopted the pseudonym "Alejandro." At this second meeting, Salvatierra briefed Castro on his first assignment in the service of the CIA (actually, in the service of the Wall Street conspirators who control the CIA).

It is likely that Salvatierra did not inform Castro in detail about the entire plan, because Salvatierra himself was probably unaware of it. Castro's mission was to travel to Bogota, Colombia and, true to his role as agent provocateur, to participate in the assassination of Gaitán, which would be the pretext for unleashing the riots that later became known as the Bogotazo. An important part of this mission was to plant false leads that would later be used to frame Colombian Communists for the events. U.S. Secretary of State George Marshall (CFR) used the riots to stoke fear of communism and to convince the delegates attending the Ninth Conference that the threat of communism was real and dangerous.[25]

3. The Soviet Union and Latin America

The evidence indicates that, despite all the CFR conspirators's efforts to implicate the Soviet Union in the Bogotazo events, the Kremlin's attitude towards Latin America in the decades before and after the Bogotazo painted an entirely different picture.[26]

Soviet strategy toward Latin America in the postwar years could be described as restrained and cautious. The cause of this change in behavior had been dictated both by the weakness of its puppet Communist parties in Latin America and by the lack of an industrial proletariat, a necessary condition —according to Marxist dogma— for the emergence of revolutionary movements.

Therefore, it is unlikely that Stalin would have tried to initiate a Communist experiment in Latin America at that time. Everything indicated that, for the time being, the Soviets preferred to maintain good relations with the United States than to incite Communist revolutions in Mexico, Argentina, Cuba, Chile or, especially, Colombia.

In those days the Union of Soviet Socialist Republics (USSR) had just emerged from a devastating war that had left it highly weakened economically. Consequently, recognition by the United States of the Soviet Union as a power in international politics, access to American high technology and industrial equipment, as well as economic aid as a result of the victorious alliance, were far more important to the Soviets than a relatively minor Communist successes in a geographical area where the U.S. had traditionally focused its interest and cemented its influence.[27]

Proof of this is that in the 1930s, when a very volatile revolutionary situation arose in Mexico, the Soviet government did not give any support to the local Communists in their struggle to seize political power in the country. In keeping with this policy, throughout these years the activities of the Latin American Communist parties were reported without much interest in the Soviet press. Also, they were aware that Americans had come to grudgingly accept the tiny Communist Party of the U.S.A. as a minor nuissance, but a Communist state in the Americas, the Soviet leaders reasoned, would have provoked a violent American reaction which the Soviets did not need at the time.

Of course, Soviet leaders were aware of the rising tide of anti-American sentiment among members of the Latin American intelligentsia, as well as the chronic economic and social problems the continent was suffering. Nevertheless, despite the early signs of the onset of the Cold War and the rapid changes in the power structure in Latin America, prudence had apparently advised them to continue their cautious policy even after the successful end of World War II.

And this was nothing new, but rather the continuation of a long-established policy. For example, on November 7, 1933, coinciding with the anniversary of the Bolshevik revolution in Russia, the Cuban Communists tried to implement a revolution of their own and established a "Soviet" of workers and peasants in the province of Oriente, in eastern Cuba. The peasants took over the land on which they worked, and a mini-Communist regime, supported by a militia of "red guards", took control.

To the revolutionaries' surprise, the Soviets expressed their displeasure, and gave no encouragement or material aid to the rebels. As a result, the Cuban "Communist" experiment lasted only a few months and ended in a resounding failure.

Paradoxically, it was Cuban President Fulgencio Batista —the same one who years later became dictator and was later overthrown after a popular rebellion involving several organizations in addition to the 26th of July Movement to which Castro belonged— who in his first term as democratically-elected president legalized the Cuban Communist Party. First, Batista authorized the Communists to publish their newspaper, Noticias de Hoy, which began publication in May 1938. Then, in September, Batista legalized the Communist Party for the first time in Cuban history.

In the years that followed, the Communists advanced in Cuba as never before. In the 1940 elections, ten Communist Party members were elected to the House of Representatives, and a Communist was elected mayor of the city of Santiago de Cuba, the second largest city in the country.

During World War II, the collaboration between the Communists and Batista became even closer and, in 1943, the President, in return for the support he received, appointed some Communists to his cabinet. More importantly, Batista allowed the Communists to infiltrate the labor movement and even control the Confederation of Cuban Workers, the most important labor union in the country, as well as to occupy certain positions in the Ministry of Labor.[28]

Thus, long before 1959, the year Fidel Castro took power in Cuba, there was already a cohesive and efficient Communist nucleus in the country. But all indications are that, despite their growing political victories, the Cuban Communists were satisfied with their meager gains and never showed any enthusiasm for taking political power in Cuba through democratic elections, much less in a revolutionary way, through armed violence. And this policy of moderation was welcomed by their masters in the Kremlin.

The overthrow of Guatemalan President Jacobo Arbenz in 1954, following a crude CIA operation to protect United Fruit interests, drew only a feeble diplomatic protest from the Soviet Union. This caution in international politics seemed to begin to fade in 1957, when Soviet successes in space technology shocked the world and Premier Nikita S. Khrushchev launched his aggressive campaign of "Sputnik diplomacy"[29] on a global scale.

But despite all these successes, it is clear that the Soviets did not consider the political climate in Latin America ripe for revolution and therefore did not see it as one of their immediate political objectives. On the contrary, the Kremlin was dedicated to expanding the Soviet presence in the area, projecting a respectable international image and portraying the Soviet Union as a country with a developed industrial base, whose advanced technology had achieved enormous triumphs in the space field; a country eager to share those achievements with other countries through traditional economic and cultural relations. This new policy, which Khrushchev called "peaceful coexistence", was aimed at "showing the world the superiority of communism over capitalism."[30]

According to Khrushchev, the struggle between communism and

capitalism was to continue, but only on the economic, political and social plane, not on the military one. Nikita Khrushchev, who had directly experienced the struggle against the Nazis and the death of 20 million Soviet citizens in World War II, knew that in a nuclear war there would be neither winners nor losers, but the annihilation of a large part of life on the planet.

But most likely Khrushchev ignored that his new doctrine soon became the casue for great concern to the American military-industrial complex.[31] Unnowingly, Khrushchev's doctrine of peaceful coexistence was a direct threat to the flourishing of its lucrative business. The U.S. military-industrial complex, which Wall Street bankers control, thrives on wars, revolutions, low-intensity conflicts and terrorism, for these are the elements that allow them to keep the people terrorized and thus ensure that Congress approves large sums of money to invest in the arms race. And Khrushchev, without intending to, with his doctrine of peaceful coexistence, wanted to spoil their business. No wonder they were so worried.

An analysis of Soviet policy towards Latin America in that period shows several interesting trends. First, although the Soviets had always been ready to take advantage of any political developments in the area, it had no priority in Soviet foreign policy. Second, despite all their efforts to make inroads in Latin America in the diplomatic and commercial fields, these efforts had not been very successful until 1960. Finally, they did not even seem to be enthusiastic about the unexpected political change in Cuba in 1959, which might allow them to extend their sphere of influence in the continent. Apparently, Soviet leaders were not convinced that it was in their interest to assume responsibilities - whether economic or political - that had unexpectedly fallen into their laps as a result of the strange and inexplicable Castro revolution.[32]

Prior to 1959, Soviet foreign policy objectives had been two-fold: on the one hand, the Kremlin's short-term goal was to increase the number of countries that diplomatically recognized the Soviet Union. On the other hand, and somewhat in conflict with the former, the long-term goal remained the same: to achieve, in the name of Marxist ideology, influence and control over the countries of Latin America.

In the previous four decades, the Soviets had had some success in achieving diplomatic recognition. In the 1920s Mexico and Uruguay were the first Latin American countries to establish diplomatic relations with the Soviet Union. Colombia did so in 1935, but, shortly thereafter, Mexico and Uruguay broke off relations, so that, at the outbreak of World War II, Colombia was the only Latin American country to maintain at least limited diplomatic relations with the USSR. However, the alliance of the Soviet Union with the United States and England in the fight against Nazi Germany persuaded several Latin American countries to extend diplomatic recognition to the USSR - Cuba in 1942; Nicaragua, Chile and Costa Rica in 1944; Bolivia, Brazil, the Dominican Republic, Ecuador, Guatemala and Venezuela in 1945; and Argentina in 1946.[33]

But the beginning of the Cold War, which the Bogotazo served as a pretext to implement, marked the beginning of a contrary trend. Based on the accusation that the Soviets were meddling in the internal affairs of the countries with which they maintained diplomatic relations —probably true to some extent, but also applicable to other powers—,[34] several Latin American countries broke off diplomatic relations with the USSR.[35] At the beginning of 1948, the Soviet Union had only embassies in Argentina, Bolivia and Mexico, as well as a trade delegation in Uruguay and a consulate general in Colombia.[36]

4. Was Castro a Communist in 1948?

Some authors such as Nathaniel Weyl[37] and Angel Aparicio Laurencio,[38] have tried to explain the Bogotazo as an operation carried out by the Communists and that from an early age Castro was an active Communist. Both authors have relied primarily on Alberto Niño's book *Antecedentes y secretos del 9 de abril*.[39] Niño was Colombia's Chief of Security at the time of the riots, and his book shows an obvious anti-Communist bias that manifests itself in the tendency to see everything as the result of Communist actions.

According to Niño, "In these same days the well-known Cuban Communists Fidel Alejandro Castro and Rafael del Pino arrived in Bogotá."[40] However, contrary to what Niño alleges, there is not a shred of evidence to indicate that, prior to the Bogotazo, Castro or del Pino were linked in any way to the Cuban Communist Party or to any international organization of Communists. On the contrary, some who knew him closely assert that Castro was never a Communist and that del Pino, a WWII vet who fought in the U.S. Army, was furiously anti-Communist.[41]

However, despite being a convinced anti-Communist, Niño shows a supreme ignorance about the ideology and tactics of the Communists. For example, as proof that Castro and del Pino were Communists, Niño provides the information that, the day before the riots, the Cubans attended a meeting of the Colombian Labor Organization, where they discussed coup d'état techniques and the organization of a general strike.[42] However, only a cursory study of Communist literature shows that Communists have always opposed coups d'état as a Fascist technique.

In an effort to convince the public that Castro was a Communist, a United Press press release dated April 19, 1948, details how, according to an employee of the Claridge Hotel, two Colombian detectives came to the hotel and, after a thorough search of the Cubans' room, found some of their personal correspondence, which they opened in his presence. According to the employee, the correspondence showed that the Cubans were members of the Cuban Communist Party.[43]

According to the press release, the detectives also found, and confiscated as evidence, identification cards with photos, which identified Castro and del Pino as first class agents of the Third Front of the Soviet Union in Latin America.[44] Other sources mentioned that in some of the Cubans' letters, the investigators found plans of the Colombian Capitol and the building where the Conference was being held.[45] Alberto Niño also mentions that among the Cubans' belongings seized by the police on April 3 was a letter from a "Mirtha" addressed to Fidel Castro —this was Mirtha Díaz-Balart, Castro's fiancée, whom he married shortly thereafter.

Although essentially a love letter, it contained a revealing sentence: "I remember that you told me that you were going to Bogotá to provoke the outbreak of a revolution."[46] Another source mentions that, upon saying goodbye to his girlfriend in Cuba, Castro told her that he was traveling to Colombia to start a revolution.[47]

The phrasing of the letter also seems to be confirmed by the fact that the day before the riots broke out, Castro and del Pino had attended the aforementioned meeting, where Castro discussed the techniques of a general strike and the seizure of power by way of arms - known as a putsch or coup d'état.[48]

After the Bogotazo, Castro maintained his preference for the Fascist tactic of the coup d'état. In 1957, when he was in the Sierra Maestra mountains engaged in his guerrilla struggle against the regime of President-dictator Fulgencio Batista, Castro called for a revolutionary strike as an initial step to provoke an uprising to overthrow President Batista.

Few heeded his call, and the strike was a total failure. The Cuban Communist Party did not support the strike, calling it "another failed putsch by Castro."[49] But most significant is the date Castro chose for the uprising: April 9, the anniversary of the Bogotazo.

5. The Cuban Communists and Fidel Castro

The Cuban Communist Party had languished for many years in the normal apathy of Latin American Communist parties, showing no interest in taking political control in Cuba. In 1958, when Castro was already in the Sierra Maestra mountains engaged in his guerrilla struggle against Batista's forces, the Communists established the first contact with Castro. Although at that time Castro's forces numbered only a few hundred men and his victory was uncertain, Batista's days seemed numbered and Castro was becoming - with the help of the U.S. media - the symbol of armed resistance against the Batista dictatorship. Under those circumstances, an alliance with the man who was leading the largest armed force against Batista seemed the most appropriate thing to do.

However, if we take into account the strict pro-Soviet discipline of the Cuban Communists, it is not unreasonable to conclude that this rapprochement had to have been authorized, and perhaps suggested, by the Kremlin. In fact, this was not at all unusual, particularly at a time of Soviet alliances with nationalist movements and leaders such as Nasser in Egypt, Sukarno in Indonesia, Nkrumah in Ghana, Sekou Toure in Guinea and the FNL in Algeria. So, whatever the motive, it is clear that the Kremlin gave them the green light and, from mid-1958, the Cuban Communists began to give Castro timid support.

Little has been written about the actual role of the Popular Socialist Party (PSP, the name adopted by the Cuban Communist Party in 1944)[50] during the struggle against Batista. But it was vox populi in Cuba that the ñángaras (the derogatory nickname by which many Cubans designated the local Communists) never showed much friendship for Fidel Castro. On the contrary, the animosity was mutual, and Castro's first clash with the Communists occurred in December 1944, when he was in his last year of high school at the Colegio de Belén in Havana.[51]

What prompted the initial quarrel was that Castro used Belen as a platform to attack a bill in Congress, popularly known as the Marinello Law,[52] because its creator was the president of the Popular Socialist Party and Senator, Juan Marinello. In his attack, which was published in the national press, Castro insinuated that the plan had been conceived according to the ideology of Soviet Russia or Nazi Germany. However, the real reason for Castro's attack was that, if passed by Congress, the law would negatively affect private education in Cuba, including the Colegio de Belen, where the Jesuits educated the privileged children of the wealthy.

Although young Fidel Castro was only a high school student at the time, the Communists were so outraged by his attack that they counterattacked with a strong article in the pages of Hoy, the Communists' official newspaper. The author of the article called Castro "*pichón de jesuita*" (Jesuit lackey) and "*come gofio*" —which in popular Cuban parlance means imbecile. That may have been the first time American intelligence officers at the U.S. Embassy in Havana heard Fidel Castro mentioned.

A few years later, in 1947, when Castro was a student at the University of Havana, he ran for vice president of the Law School. Knowing that the Communists had a strong following among the students, he immediately began to use the anti-imperialist and anti-American rhetoric of the Communists, and succeeded in attracting certain students who later voted for him. But, once elected, he began a virulent anti-Communist campaign at the University. The Communists retaliated by calling him a traitor.[53] From that early period, relations between the Cuban Communists and Castro became even more strained.

At the end of February 1948, the newspaper *Hoy*, main organ of the Cuban Communist Party, published on its front page a report on the arrest of the alleged assassins of student leader Manolo Castro. The article continued on an inside page, which included a photo of the accused, among them Fidel Castro.[54]

Nevertheless, apart from personal discrepancies and the Communists' antipathy for Fidel Castro, this attitude was the result of the Cuban Communists' blind adherence to the Soviet version of dogmatic and doctrinaire communism. For that reason, the Soviet Communists must have been the first to be surprised when, in 1961, without the guidance and support of the sacrosanct Cuban Communist party, Castro claimed to have carried out a Communist revolution right under the nose of U.S. imperialism.

It should not be forgotten that when Castro and his men attacked the Moncada Barracks in Santiago de Cuba on July 26, 1953, several leaders of the Popular Socialist Party were in the city to attend a semi-clandestine meeting. As soon as Batista learned of the attack on the Moncada Barracks, he blamed the usual suspects: the Communists. The latter defended themselves by claiming that they had had no part in the assault, and that they were in Santiago purely by chance, to attend the birthday celebration of Blas Roca, one of the founders of the Cuban Communist Party and a member of the political bureau of the Popular Socialist Party.[55] The Communists then denounced and strongly criticized the Moncada assault. One of the leaders of the PSP, Joaquín Ordoqui, distinguished himself from the rest by his vituperation of Fidel Castro.

On the othar hand, the Cuban Communists had every reason to be indignant with Castro. Although they were not involved in the action, the Moncada assault brought them serious repercussions. Batista then outlawed all Communist publications and, shortly thereafter, outlawed the PSP. As a result, the resentment of Cuban Communists towards Fidel Castro grew. A few weeks later, the Cuban Communists issued a statement which, because their local publications had been outlawed, was only published in the Communist newspaper *Daily Worker* of New York, in which they strongly criticized the attack on Moncada,

> We oppose the actions of Santiago de Cuba and Bayamo.[56] The putschist methods used are characteristic of certain bourgeois groups. This has been an adventurist attempt to capture military bases. The heroism manifested by the participants has been erroneous and unproductive, based on erroneous bourgeois ideas ...
>
> The country knows very well who organized, directed and carried out the actions against the barracks. The political line of the PSP and the mass movements has always been and is the same: to fight against Batista's tyranny and to unmask the putschists and adventurers of the bourgeois opposition who act against the interests of the people. The PSP considers it necessary to consolidate the masses in a united front against the government in order to find a democratic way out of this situation, resurrect the Cuban Constitution, guarantee civic liberties, hold general elections and form a democratic national front government.
>
> In its struggle, the PSP bases its support on the masses, and condemns putschist adventurism directed against the masses and the democratic solution sought by the people.[57]

It is highly revealing that Cuban Communists repeatedly used the word putschist —which in postwar Communist parlance meant "Fascist"— to criticize Fidel Castro's revolutionary methods.[58]

The animosity felt by Cuban Communists toward Fidel Castro was more than justified. Although several of Castro's friends at the University of Havana were Communists, Castro was never a member of the PSP. Moreover, there is evidence that the animosity was mutual. In 1956 Castro was embroiled in a controversy due to an article that appeared in the prestigious weekly magazine *Bohemia* entitled "El grupo 26 de julio en la cárcel" ("The 26th of July Group in Jail"), in which its author accused Castro of being a Communist. The article was written by Luis Dam, a Spanish Republican in exile. According to Dam, the Mexican police had evidence that Castro was a member of the Communist party.[59]

Castro's angry response, written from prison in Mexico where he was being held for preparing the invasion of Cuba from Mexican territory, was not long in coming. In the following issue of Bohemia Castro published an impassioned article he titled "Enough lies!" According to Castro,

Naturally, the accusation that I am a Communist is absurd in the eyes of all those who know my public conduct in Cuba, without any ties to the Communist Party. I totally deny Mr. Dam's report in which he states, "Incidentally, the Federal Security Police claims that Fidel is a member of the Communist Party." Captain Gutiérrez Barros himself read me the report sent to the President of Mexico after a week of thorough investigation; among his observations it is categorically stated that we do not have [since that time Castro was already using the rhetorical plural to refer to himself] any nexus with Communist organizations. I have before me the [newspaper] Excelsior of July 26, page 8, column 6, paragraph 5, which reads: "The Federal Security Bureau emphasized that the 26th of July group has no Communist links nor does it receive help from the Communists."[60]

Castro continued his attack against Dam, accusing the Batista government of plotting against him and also recalling the past collaboration of the Communists with the Cuban dictator,

The intrigue is ridiculous and without the slightest foundation because I have only been a militant in one political party, and that is the [Orthodox Party] founded by Eduardo Chibás. Besides, what morals does Mr. Batista have to talk about communism, if he was the presidential candidate of the Communist Party in the 1940 elections, if his electoral leaflets were covered under the hammer and sickle, if there are photos of him with Blas Roca and Lázaro Peña, if half a dozen of his current ministers and close collaborators were well known members of the Communist Party.[61]

Castro's words recalling Batista's past collaboration with the Communists was the worst attack that both the dictator and the Communists could receive. Even more so was his defamatory insinuation that the Communists were still collaborating with Batista.

Theodor Draper, one of the authors who has best studied that stage of Cuban history, rightly pointed out that it is very difficult to believe that a Communist would justify himself in such a bizarre way.[62]

For their part, the Communists did not remain silent, and countered in various ways, among them insinuating that Castro was crazy and that he was a homosexual. A columnist for the newspaper Hoy, who signed under the pseudonym "Esmeril", called him in several articles "the chaste Fidel", an insulting nickname with homosexual connotations inspired by the title of a movie in vogue at the time.[63]

On the other hand, it would be unfair to blame Cuban Communists for criticizing Castro in the way they did. Despite all the theories provided accusing Castro of having been a Communist at the time, there is in fact an enormous amount of circumstantial and documentary evidence indicating that, at least at the time, Castro was not, and many confirm this. For example, Javier Felipe Pazos, who personally interviewed Castro when he was in the Sierra Maestra mountains, expressed his total lack of conviction that Castro was a Communist and that his revolution from the beginning had been a Communist conspiracy.[64]

Nevertheless, after Castro unexpectedly declared in 1961 that he had always been a Marxist, some authors, with different intentions, have tried to prove a posteriori the veracity of his words. Lionel Martin, for example, claims that the leadership of the nucleus that attacked the Moncada was studying Marxism and, on this basis, traces a circle of Marxist ideology around several leaders of the 26th of July Movement who, according to him, were related to the Cuban Communists.[65] Nathaniel Weyl, for his part, claims that Castro had been recruited by agents of international communism long before the Bogotazo, and emphasizes Castro's relations with some radical politicians.

Now, let us accept just for a moment that at the time before the Bogotazo Fidel Castro was a crypto-Communist and a secret agent of international communism. If this had been true, upon his return from Colombia, where he had "burned" his cover, since all the Colombian officialist press had accused him of being a Communist, the most logical thing would have been that the Cuban Communists would have received him as a hero and Castro would have become an official member of the PSP. In fact, if Castro had publicly declared himself a Communist, that would not have been cause for outrage. Cuban history is full of names of political figures, such as Julio Antonio Mella, Carlos Baliño and Rubén Martínez Villena, who declared their secret Communist militancy after having achieved a certain political preeminence.

But, on the contrary, upon their return to Cuba, Castro and del Pino did not become members of the PSP, but of the Partido del Pueblo Cubano (Ortodoxo), led by the nationalist and anti-Communist leader Eduardo Chibás. According to Ramón Conte,[66] both Castro and del Pino served for some time as informants for the CIA which, faithful to its work for the benefit of Wall Street bankers, viewed all nationalist leaders in Latin America, Chibás among them, as "rosados", that is, sympathizers of communism.

Moreover, far from showing any Communist leanings, after the Bogotazo Castro continued to express his Fascist ideas. For example, on July 26, 1960, in a speech he delivered at the commemoration of the failed attack on the Moncada Barracks, Castro declared his dedication to the "liberation" of the rest of Latin America.[67] What he did not make clear was that the means by which he intended to achieve his objective consisted essentially of the indiscriminate use of putschist coups d'état in the purest Fascist style, which included the assassination of some presidents democratically elected by popular vote.

In conclusion, if the historical data I have mentioned are correct, and the abundance of reliable sources confirms it, everything indicates that Fidel Castro was not a Communist before, during or after the events of the Bogotazo. Moreover, it is very likely that Castro's recruitment by the U.S.. intelligence services did indeed take place, as well as his role during the disastrous events of the Bogotazo as an agent provocateur in the service of the CFR conspirators who control the CIA.

In his typical *cantinflescque*[68] style that characterized him, Castro had tried many times to prove that during the Bogotazo, although he was not a member of the Cuban Communist Party, in reality in his mind and heart he was already a convinced militant Communist. For example, in the interview he gave to Arturo Alape in 1983, Castro makes use of his extraordinary linguistic juggling skills, in which he intermingles lies and truths in an effort to prove that, although he was not a Communist in 1948, he was in fact a Communist,

> "At that time I had already come into contact with Marxist literature, had already studied Political Economy, for example, and had knowledge of political theories. I was attracted to the fundamental ideas of Marxism, I was acquiring a socialist consciousness throughout my univer-

sity career, as I came into contact with Marxist literature. At that time there were a few Communist students at the University of Havana and I had friendly relations with them, but I was not a Communist youth, I was not a Communist Party militant. My activities had absolutely nothing to do with the Communist Party at that time. We could say that I had an anti-imperialist conscience.

"I had already had the first contacts with Marxist literature and I felt inclined to Marxist ideas, but I had no affiliation, no connection with the Communist youth, except for friendship with various young Communists, very hard-working, very stoic, with whom I sympathized and whom I admired. But neither the Communist Party of Cuba nor the Communist youth had absolutely nothing to do with the organization of this Congress in Bogotá."[69]

But the facts, which are much more credible than his words, categorically deny that at any time Castro was attracted to Marxist ideology.

6. The Myth of Fidel Castro's Communism

Fidel Castro is a unique case in the history of mankind: a political leader who is accused by his enemies of the very thing he boasts of being: a Communist. No one in his right mind would have thought of accusing Stalin of being a Communist, Mussolini of being a Fascist or Hitler a Nazi. However, despite the fact that there is not a shred of evidence to prove that Fidel Castro has been a Communist, the anti-Castro exiles, with rare exceptions, have been accusing Fidel Castro of being one for more than half a century, and still continue to do so. There is no worse blind man than the one who does not want to see.

On the other hand, this attitude perhaps explains the real cause of the continuous failures of the Cuban anti-Communists in their fight against Castro. If they had read Sun Tzu,[70] they would have understood why the oldest theorist of intelligence and espionage stated that only he who knows his enemy and knows himself will win every battle. Unfortunately, the anti-Castro Cubans have demonstrated time and again that they neither know their enemy nor know themselves.[71]

It is difficult to try to find an explanation for this irrational behavior of most anti-Castro Cubans in exile, but I believe that there are two reasons for this anomaly. One is the fact that, from the beginning, the original anti-Castro exile was almost entirely controlled by the CIA, and the CFR conspirators, who have always controlled the Agency, found the myth of Castro communism convenient for their plans. That is why the CIA instilled the myth of Castro-communism in the minds of the original anti-Castro Cubans in exile, and these, in order to ingratiate themselves with their CIA "friends", accepted it without question.

Another reason is that most Cubans in the initial exile were militant Catholics, and promoting the myth of Castro-Communism helped them to hide the hard truth that, far from being the product of the assemblies of the Popular Socialist Party [Communist], Fidel Castro is a pure Fascist product of the Jesuit classrooms of the Colegio de Belen.[72]

In their confrontation against the man who had taken the political and economic control of the country out of their hands, the Cuban oligarchs, most of them already in exile in Florida, desperately tried to find an ideological position to justify their opposition to Castro, without admitting that perhaps the main reason was only because he had stolen their property and forced them to leave the country.[73]

What they could not ignore, however, was that Fidel Castro, the son of a wealthy landowner who had amassed his fortune in the service of the interests of the United Fruit Company, was one of them. Proof of this is that, as was customary for members of the Cuban oligarchy, Angel Castro sent his son to study in Havana with the Jesuits at the exclusive Colegio de Belen. And when Fidel Castro married the daughter of a high ranking member of the oligarchy, also following tradition, he traveled to the United States to spend their honeymoon, and to spend the thousand dollars that President Batista, a good friend of Castro's father, had sent them as a wedding gift.

So the anti-Castro exiles were caught in the dilemma that if they attacked Fidel Castro for what he really was, they would find themselves in the difficult situation of having to attack themselves. So they embraced the myth of Castro's communism.

In November 2002, the Mexican cultural magazine *Letras Libres* devoted an issue to the theme "Futures of Cuba", in which appeared an interesting article by Antonio Elorza, entitled "Fidel Castro, power and its mask." In his timely and necessary article, Elorza focused his analysis on the duplicity, lies and simulation in the conduct of Fidel

Castro, whom he described not only as "an excellent trickster", but as having been perhaps "the best demagogue of the 20th century."

However, despite the existence of countless proofs, such as those provided by Elorza, that Castro is a stubborn liar, most people —and I am not only referring to his admirers, but also to his critics— still insist on believing the tyrant's assertions at face value. Unfortunately, the prevailing image of Castro, which Elorza strives to clarify, is based on what he says. But if we look at what he does, we discover a very different individual. Take, for example, Castro's oft-repeated myth of Marxism and communism.

In an effort to decipher Castro ideologically, Theodor Draper, one of the sharpest analysts of the Castro phenomenon, concluded,

> From the historical point of view, Castroism is thus a leader in search of a movement, a movement in search of power and a power in search of an ideology. From its origins until now it has had the same leader and the same path to power, but its ideology has changed.[74]

However, I believe that, contrary to Draper's assertion, Fidel Castro has never changed his ideology. Fidel Castro always was, is, and always will be, profoundly Castroist, that is, a murderous psychopathic gangster in the style of Al Capone or Lucky Luciano. This fact explains why throughout his long gangster-political career, Castro has changed ideologies as easily as a snake changes its skin, for the simple reason that he lacks political ideology. But the cornerstone of Fidel Castro's personal ideology is to assassinate anyone who opposes him or is an obstacle to carrying out his secret plans - something he may have learned from his Jesuit preceptors.[75]

On the other hand, Luis Ortega, a Cuban journalist who knew him closely, also concluded that Castro is simply a common gangster whose only ideology is violence. According to Ortega,

> In the search for the origins of Castroism, the mistake has been made of oversimplifying things by framing Castro within a simply gangster activity, which is not entirely true, because it is deliberately ignored that the gangster stage corresponds to the final moment of the action groups. Before falling into gangsterism these groups had been something else. And in that other thing, in that atmosphere of delirious violence, of expeditious justice, is where we must look for the deepest roots of Castroism.

Castro's subsequent behavior is perfectly explicable

if we refer to the center from which it emanates. Castro's great contribution to Cuba's political struggles consists, precisely, in having transplanted the dynamics of the gangs to the rural areas, which in 1956 seemed unfeasible. The discredited gangs of 1946 came to be hierarchized in the process that went from 56 to 59 with the more suggestive name of guerrillas. The delirious character is the same. The method is similar. The codes applied are the same. The terminology is in line with that of the action groups. The absence of a doctrine continues to predominate in the guerrillas.[76]

7. Fidel Castro the "Marxist"

The essential proof of Fidel Castro's supposed true ideological affiliation, which is cited again and again by almost all the "serious" authors who have studied the subject, is the self-confession offered by Castro himself on December 2, 1961 in a speech in which he proclaimed, after several hours of his typical cantinfleo in which he insisted on explaining the inexplicable, how, in spite of the fact that he had never been a member of the Popular Socialist Party, that the Communists detested him, and that he was a total ignoramus in matters of Marxist theory, he had always been a Marxist at heart, and would be so until the last moment of his life.

The unexpected revelation took not only the Cuban Communists by surprise, but also the Soviets, who received it with justified skepticism. Paradoxically, it was the anti-Castro Cubans in Florida who welcomed it.

Exile anti-Castro activists have always maintained that Castro is a compulsive liar —it was Mario Lazo who nicknamed him "the great deceiver"[77]— and most of those who knew the tyrant personally in his younger years agree. So when Castro claimed that Cuba was now the most democratic country in the world, anti-Castro exiles responded: "Liar! When Castro said that he had put an end to illiteracy, they said: Lies! When Castro claimed that there was no unemployment in Cuba, they cried out: Liar, and so on and so forth. But, when one fine day the great liar affirmed that all his life he had been a Marxist and a Communist, the anti-Castro exiles shouted all together: "Look: He is telling the truth. He is a Marxist. He is a Communist."

In their desperate urge to find an argument that would discredit the tyrant, the exile anti-Castroists unreservedly adopted a Castroist definition of Castroism. They implicitly accepted the liar's words in a key ideological area in which they should never have accepted his ideas without prior in-depth analysis. Without intending to do so, they not only helped to legitimize the tyrant, but also contributed to giving Marxist ideology a cardinal role it had never had in Latin America. An intelligence officer would have concluded that the phenomenon was a typical example of individuals who have been conquered by enemy propaganda.

Anti-Castro exiles have based their analysis of Castroism on what they want to believe, not on what the facts point to. They insist on believing that Castro is a Communist, therefore they have created a non-existent ideological infrastructure to support that belief. Without knowing it, they have fallen into one of the most common traps used by the intelligence services to deceive the enemy, which is based on this principle: if you want to be deceived, someone will deceive you.

Moreover, there is something that adds further to the ideological confusion of the anti-Castro exile: the well-documented fact that Castro's intelligence services have successfully penetrated most of the anti-Castro exile organizations.[78] An axiom of intelligence and espionage work is that things are rarely what they appear to be.

We may never be able to determine to what extent the anti-Communism of the anti-Castro exiles has been self-generated or artificially implanted in their minds by the CIA and Castro's intelligence services, although it is most likely the product of all these factors. An essential rule of intelligence and espionage work is that disinformation cannot be created in a vacuum, but must be based on already existing beliefs in the mind of the person or persons who are the target of the psychological attack.

That is why intelligence services use disinformation to finish convincing the person of something he or she is already half convinced of. In the case of the anti-Castro exiles, the target was already ripe for disinformation.

But the problem of accepting Castro's self-portrait as a Communist has more implications than simply ideological ones.

First, because it is an image createded by the great deceiver himself to create a smokescreen behind which he could hide his true face. But Cuban and Soviet Communists, true experts on communism, never believed for an instant that Castro was, or perhaps one day would become, a Communist. His partnership with the Soviets was a forced marriage, with Castro riding shotgun, consummated because the Soviets believed they would benefit from the partnership. But, like many others, the Soviets soon found that it is not easy to derive any benefit from a relationship with Fidel Castro.

Secondly, because the reduction of the Castro problem to the Communism/anti-Communism dichotomy resulted in the error of simplifying a much more complex phenomenon. The proof that this has never been a good idea is that, after more than half a century, Castro is still in power in Cuba and anti-Communist Cuban exiles are still in the U.S. and continue to invent elaborate plans to overthrow him.

Finally, because they were always more anti-Communists than anti-Castroist, the Cuban exiles never realized the deep disagreements between Castro and the Soviet Union —the Soviets tried unsuccessfully to overthrow Castro in 1962, in 1968, and were probably planning to do so again in 1998— and apparently never thought of using those differences to their advantage through an alliance with the Soviet Union. To be sure, it has not been easy for Cuban exiles to explain how, after the fall of communism in the Soviet Union and Eastern Europe, Castro, the supposed Soviet puppet, is still alive and in power in Cuba.[79]

Nevertheless, despite the overwhelming evidence that Fidel Castro was never a member of Cuba's pro-Soviet Communist party, nor that he even read much Marxist literature, some authors have endeavored to prove Fidel Castro's secret links to international communism. For example, Salvador Díaz-Versón, a Cuban journalist in exile, alleges that in February 1948 Soviet intelligence agent Frances MacKinnon Damon recruited Fidel Castro in Havana, and ordered him to travel to Bogotá to organize the World Federation of Democratic Youth, a Communist front.[80]

In May of the same year Díaz-Versón testified similarly before a U.S. Senate Internal Security Subcommittee in Washington, D.C.[81] However, Díaz-Versón was unable to present before the subcommittee the documents proving his allegation because, according to him, "his private file containing the personal files of 943 Cuban Communists" had been confiscated in January 1959 and then destroyed by Castro's troops.[82] According to Díaz-Versón, Castro's dossier contained documents and photographs of his secret meetings with members of the Soviet embassy in Havana.

This theory seems to have been confirmed by Alberto Niño, who was Colombia's Chief of Security during the Bogotazo. According to Niño, both Castro and del Pino arrived in Colombia carrying credentials from the World Federation of Democratic Youth.[83] If true, this information lends validity to the thesis that the Bogotazo was a Communist operation, carried out by the Soviet intelligence services.

But there is abundant circumstantial information that indicates that none of this is true. The most important is the irrefutable fact that Fidel Castro was never a member of the Cuban Communist Party.

In his testimony before the U.S. Senate subcommittee, Diaz-Verson mentioned his close relationship with Lieutenant Castaño Quedado, head of the Bureau of Repression of Communist Activities (BRAC) in Havana.[84] Therefore, given that Diaz-Verson did not have an organization capable of directly obtaining these documents and surveillance photos, it is not unreasonable to assume that much of the information Diaz-Verson had in his files came from BRAC.

However, there is a little known detail about BRAC, and that is that it was an organization created by the CIA. In fact, BRAC was created in January 1955 due to a proposal by Allen Dulles, a secret agent of the CFR who became director of the CIA. To that end, Dulles traveled to Havana to certify his support for the new organization.[85] Therefore, given the interest of the conspirators who controlled the CIA in validating Fidel Castro's non-existent relationship with communism, one must conclude that the famous documents and photos that Diaz-Verson claimed to have in his files were nothing more than disinformation created by the CIA.

Another author, Nathaniel Weyl, wrote that the young Fidel Castro had been recruited by an international Communist conspiracy, and emphasized Castro's student activities in Cuba's radical politics.[86] But, despite Weyl's claims, there is no evidence to prove this accusation. For his part, Hugh Thomas, one of the scholars who has analyzed Castro's life in detail, stated categorically that "Castro was not a Marxist in 1953." [87]

Yet, after Castro shocked the world when he declared in 1961 that he had been a Marxist at heart all his life, some authors have tried to prove it a posteriori, perhaps with different intentions. For example, Lionel Martin alleges that the leadership of the group that participated in the attack on the Moncada Barracks had studied Marxism, and adds that several leaders of the 26th of July Movement had been indoctrinated in Marxism and had close relations with the Cuban Communist Party.

In an effort to prove his theory that Castro was a Marxist, Martin alleges that at the University of Havana Castro was friends with Leonel Soto, Alfredo Guevara, Flavio Bravo and Luis Más Martín, all members of the Communist Youth.[88] But this friendship proves nothing, because Castro was also friends with several homosexual students, and there is no evidence that he was a homosexual.

Carlos Franqui himself, a former member of the Communist Party who knew Castro closely, expressed his doubts about Castro's Marxism at the time when Fidel was a student at the University of Havana,

> If Fidel was a Marxist since that time, how does he explain that he was a member of the UIR [Revolutionary Insurrectionary Union], a militant anti-Communist organization, which has in its history the assassination attempt on the life of the Communist union leader Aracelio Iglesias, general secretary of the Havana dock workers?[89]

Another aspect that those who accuse Fidel Castro of being a Communist strive to ignore is Castro's supreme ignorance of Marxist doctrine and theory.

In a speech he delivered shortly after the air raid that preceded the Bay of Pigs invasion, Castro proclaimed for the first time that his revolution was democratic and socialist. Even with the qualifier "democratic" before socialist, his speech most likely caused a tremendous stir in the Kremlin.

Finally, on December 2, 1961, Castro turned the screw again when, after admitting his bourgeois "prejudices", he declared that he had always been a Marxist-Leninist at heart.[90] Castro began his marathon speech at midnight on December 1 and finished it around 5 a.m. the next day. Loree Wilkerson, the researcher who has made the best study of the speech, observed that Castro's self-analysis was nothing more than a desperate attempt to alter the past to fit the present.[91]

Castro's self-confession of Marxist faith was greeted with surprise by the Kremlin leadership and with extreme suspicion by the heads of the Soviet intelligence services. Anyone with a minimum of training in this field would have noticed that what Castro had tried to create for himself was what is known in intelligence and espionage as a "legend", a false biography used by secret agents to cover his true identity. The Soviets were not the only ones surprised. Castro's unexpected conversion to communism caused an uproar in pro-Communist and leftist circles around the world.[92]

However, true to the saying that he who too much makes too misakes, in January 1962 Castro confessed to a French journalist that he had never read beyond page 370 of the first volume of Marx's *Capital*. Historian Hugh Thomas, who made some of the most detailed studies of modern Cuban history, asserted that, if Castro's claim is true, he must be the first Marxist-Leninist leader who has read almost nothing of the masters of Marxism and whose speeches do not evidence any influence of Marxist terminology and concepts.[93]

Thomas was not wrong. Many years later, Gabriel García Márquez, who undoubtedly knows Castro closely, had to admit that, "He has never been heard to repeat any of the cardboard slogans of Communist scholasticism or to use the ritual dialect of the system." [94] And the reason Castro has never been heard to repeat any of the slogans of the Communist dogma is because Castro is a total ignoramus in matters of Marxism and communism. If Castro was a Marxist, most likely he was of the Groucho type.[95] What Fidel Castro has always been, is, and was until the last moment of his life, is a full-blooded Castroist, albeit with a great admiration for fascism.

It is interesting to see how the CFR conspirators have used the press and the CIA to change the supposed Castro ideology, adjusting it to the needs of the moment. When the Bogotazo happened they made it Communist, because that was what was convenient for them if they wanted to blame the events on the Communists. Later, when Castro was in the Sierra Maestra in his fight against Batista, they turned him into an anti-Communist, so as not to frighten his naive followers and those who supported him in the United States. This façade of the anti-Communist Castro was useful to them until the beginning of 1961.

After they served Castro on a silver platter the Bay of Pigs victory that consolidated him in power, they changed the tune and transformed him overnight back into a Communist, because that was what they needed to sell him to the unsuspecting Soviets, who were desperate to win new friends. Unfortunately, no one warned the Soviets that it was unwise to accept gifts from the Americans, especially when the gift was a horse.[96]

Therefeore, the much vaunted Marxism and communism of the Caribbean Fascist tyrant is nothing more than an entelechy conceived by the great liar to hide his true ideology behind a smokescreen. Today, after the worst evils and vices of unbridled capitalism have reappeared in Cuba, corrected and augmented, and the tyrant has been transformed into a clone of Batista, Duvalier, Trujillo and Somoza united in a Frankensteinian monster, very few still dare to speak of Castro's communism and Marxism —although there are those who still speak unashamedly of "a more equitable state" in Cuba.

So why do North American and Latin American "leftists" and "progressives" still have a particular admiration for him? What is the last stronghold of the fidelistas? Well, no matter what anyone says, Fidel Castro is the only Latin American leader who has stood firm in the face of U.S. imperialism, despite more than half a century of harassment, aggression and assassination attempts - an image that Castro himself and his CFR masters have worked hard to create and maintain.

But, given Castro's long history of demonstrated duplicity, might this anti-American image not be another of his well-crafted lies? His youthful friend, Luis Conte Agüero, wrote in 1968 that Castro "has discredited Communist imperialism and favored the Americans." And he added that, "So beneficial has been his work for the cause of the "hated Yankee", that it would not be strange that at some point he would be accused of being a traitor and CIA agent."[97]

8. The Fascist Roots of Castroism

In his long political career, Castro has proven to be a great destroyer of organizations. Once he took power in Cuba in 1959, he used the Rebel Army to destroy his own 26th of July Movement (M-26-7). Then, he used the newly created militia, "controlled" by the Communists, to destroy the Rebel Army. Finally, he regained control over the army and militia, and created his own "Communist" party after destroying the real one.

Those members of the tratidional Communist Party who bent to his will and joined Castro's new "Communist" party earned political survival. Those who refused, ended up in exile, in jail, or in front of firing squads.

Like the corrupt politicians of yesteryear, Fidel Castro is an opportunist. It should be noted that his main goals in life have been survival and political power. The evidence indicates that, despite verbal tributes to Marxism and communism, Castro has never committed himself to any political movement or ideology, at least not to the point of being forced to defend ideological positions that hinder his true goals.

What, then, are Castro's true ideals, his raison d'être? It is difficult to say, but we have some clues. Castro has always been a dreamer and has never considered himself a politician. One of the reasons for his inability to succeed in any field before he became Cuba's ultimate leader was his scattered interests. Castro has always been the great dilettante, vehemently against specializing in any particular field. His talents are more of the supervisory type than those of execution. It is therefore not surprising that he has been successful in the field of politics. In fact, politics was a job tailor-made for him. Politicians usually know nothing about anything except the broad outlines of their party program, but have their own ideas as to how it should be carried out. However, in Castro's case, if one digs deep enough to find an underlying political ideology, we find that his think-ing and actions are closer to fascism than to any other ideology.

Fidel Alejandro Castro Ruz was born on August 13, 1926, in Biran, a small town founded by the United Fruit Company near Mayari, on the northern coast of Oriente province. He spent his early years on the Manacas farm, near Biran, owned by his father, Angel Castro.

When Fidel reached middle school age, his parents sent him to Santiago de Cuba, the capital of Oriente province, to study at the Catholic school of the De La Salle Brothers. After a short period of time he was transferred to the Jesuit School of Dolores. In 1942, after finishing high school, he was sent to attend the prestigious Colegio de Belén in Havana, also operated by the Jesuits.

At Belén Fidel stood out as an athlete, tireless orator and good student, perhaps not very bright, but with a prodigious photographic memory. Some of his former classmates claim that in Belen young Fidel fell under the influence of Jesuit priests Armando Llorente and Alberto de Castro (no relation to Fidel).

The Jesuit priests at Belen College, like most Spanish Catholic priests in Cuba, were strong supporters of Francisco Franco's Falange,[98] a particular type of Spanish fascism, and harbored deep anti-Ameri-can sentiments. These priests instilled their enthusiasm for their anti-American cause in the impressionable minds of some of their young disciples in Belen.

In particular, Father Alberto de Castro (not related to Fidel), who taught Latin American history, played a cardinal role in instilling these ideas. According to him, Latin American independence had been thwarted by the adoption of Anglo-Saxon materialistic values and traditions, which supplanted Spanish cultural domination. De Castro always emphasized how Franco had liberated Spain from the Anglo-Saxons and Marxist-Leninist Communist materialism. He also emphasized that those who have the truth, which is only revealed by God, have a moral duty to defend it against all. Castro's father al-ways rejected ideological compromises and clamored for the purifi-cation of society.

The young Fidel was quickly captivated by the teachings of his Jesuit professors, and in particular by the ideas of Father de Castro.[99] Some of his fellow students affirm that, from that time on, Fidel had read most of the works of José Antonio Primo de Rivera, founder of the Spanish Falange. José Pardo Llada, a radio commentator and politician who at one time was a close collaborator of Castro, noted that in his camp in the Sierra Maestra Fidel had the complete works of Primo de Rivera.[100] It seems that Fidel was so fascinated with Primo de Rivera's speeches that he knew many of them by heart. He also felt admiration for the image of Primo de Rivera, a rich man who abandoned everything and went to fight for what he believed in.

Some of his friends in Belen claim that Fidel was also a great admirer of other Fascist leaders, such as Hitler, Mussolini and Peron. Among Castro's favorite reading material was an eight-volume collection of Mussolini's speeches.[101] Moreover, Castro once told a friend that he had learned many things about propaganda by studying Hitler's My Struggle, which he also knew by heart. Some friends recall that the young Fidel had put on one of the walls of his room a large map of Europe, where he had marked the victorious advances of the Wehrmacht panzers.

Carlos Rafael Rodriguez, a former leader of Cuba's original Communist Party who later became a Castro supporter, has confirmed these stories. In an interview with one of Castro's biographers, Rodriguez told him that he remembered an article about Castro published in the conservative newspaper *Diario de la Marina*, when Castro was a student at Belen College. The article mentions that Castro always "spoke about Fascism in a favorable way."[102]

Another favorite book of Castro's was Curzio Malaparte's *La técnica del golpe de estado*.[103] This book had such a strong influence on the young Fidel Castro that when he traveled to Colombia in 1948, one of the first things he did was to give a talk on coup d'état techniques.

Father Alberto de Castro had founded at the Colegio de Belen an elitist secret society called *Convivio*, through which he attracted young students with leadership qualities. Since the Jesuit Order is in charge of intelligence and espionage for the Catholic Church, it is not unreasonable to assume that Father de Castro was actually a talent scout[104] for the Vatican intelligence services. Like their counterparts in the CIA and KGB, the Jesuits are aware of the advantages of early recruitment of agents[105] and agents of influence[106] among the student ranks. Most of the students at the Colegio de Belen came from the Cuban upper class, and the Jesuits knew that many of them would eventually end up in high positions in the Cuban economy, the press, the armed forces, and the government.

Fidel Castro soon became one of the most active members of

Convivio. In 1943, Castro's father and his Convivio disciples signed a secret pact in which they vowed to fight for a great and united Hispanic America, one that would oppose the control of the treacherous Anglo-Saxons over the New World.[107]

Dr. José Ignacio Rasco, Fidel's schoolmate at Belen, recalls that on one occasion, during an academic discussion, Fidel defended, as a thesis, the need for a good dictator instead of a democracy. Fidel believed that, in the specific case of Cuba, the problems would remain unsolved unless a strong hand took control of the island, since democracy had proven incapable of solving the problems.[108]

The Cuban Communists, and the Soviets through them, knew Fidel's ideas regarding the class struggle, which explains why they never trusted him or considered him one of their own. In one of his enlightening studies on Castroism, Theodore Draper published a letter Castro wrote to his friend Luis Conte Agüero on August 14, 1954. In it Fidel informs him of his goal to "organize the men of July 26 and unite all the combatants into an indestructible bundle (haz)."[109] *Haces* (the plural of bundle in Spanish), is the Spanish version of *fasces*, the Latin word later used to designate fascism.[110]

Fidel firmly believed that, instead of the mass struggle of the organized proletariat preached by the Communists, leadership alone could provide the catalyst that would mobilize the people in revolution. In a letter to his friend Luis Conte Agüero, Castro emphasizes the two conditions he considers most important for his M-26-7 movement to achieve. They are discipline and leadership, especially the latter. Castro's axiom "leadership is basic", which he repeated again and again in his articles, letters and speeches,[111] is more closely related to the Nazi principle of leadership (führerprinzip) than to any known Marxist principle.

The leadership principle is a basic integral part of all Fascist systems. Contrary to what we have seen in most Communist countries, the personality of the leaders has played a crucial role in all Fascist regimes. As the scholar of fascism Walter Laqueur has rightly pointed out, "leadership as an institution and symbol has been an essential part of fascism and one of its specific characteristics, in contrast to earlier forms of dictatorship, such as military rule."[112]

Although not all Fascist leaders have been charismatic, the personality of the leader has always played an important role in Fascist regimes. It is symptomatic, however, that the two best known Fascist movements in human history have been precisely those led by two charismatic leaders: Mussolini and Hitler.

On the contrary, the idea of the charismatic leader is totally absent from Marxist thought. Not even in the times of Stalin or Mao were they called "charismatic" - one of the major criticisms of Stalin after his death was his so-called "cult of personality." On the contrary, Marxists and Communists have always downplayed the role of the individual, giving more importance to the role of the masses. Moreover, Castro's visceral hatred of capitalism, one of the supposed proofs of his Communist leanings, is not evidence that he was a leftist or a Marxist, because Fascists were also characterized by attacking capitalism and foreign imperialism.[113]

During the years prior to World War II, it was fashionable among Cuban intellectuals to sympathize with the totalitarian theories of the then members of the powerful Rome-Berlin-Tokyo axis. It was only after World War II and the Nazi defeat, when Fidel Castro was a student at the University of Havana, that the ideas of communism began to gain popularity in Cuba, although fascism still attracted a large number of the Cuban intelligentsia.

From a very early age Fidel evidenced a strong totalitarian vocation. Knowing his psychopathic personality and his craving for absolute personal power, it is easy to conclude that it was just a matter of political pragmatism which of the two ideologies, fascism or communism, would better serve his purposes. Dr. Raúl Chibás, for some time Castro's political ally, stated that he believed that Fidel was "using communism as the system best suited to achieve the objectives of one-man rule." Chibás was of the opinion that Castro used totalitarian communism to implement dictatorial rule in Cuba, but, "Twenty-five years earlier it could have been Nazism or fascism."[114]

Several years after Castro took power in Cuba, it became known that some people in the U.S. State Department were convinced that Castro was going to follow a Fascist path. The reasons for such a belief were that Castro's leadership style was closer to the Spanish Falangist dictatorship than to that of the Marxists. Other reasons were the similarities between Castro's techniques and those of the Nazis and Mussolini. Those techniques emphasized nationalism and mass mobilization, exactly the same techniques that Castro was using in Cuba.[115]

Apparently they were not wrong. A detailed analysis of Castro's strategy from the early days of the revolution shows that his ideas more closely resemble fascism than Marxism[116] and, from the beginning, Cuban Communists noted the similarities. As I mentioned earlier, after Castro assaulted the Moncada barracks in 1953, Cuban Communists criticized the action and labeled its participants as "coup plotters", term in the Communist jargon of the time meant Fascist.

Moreover, the revolutionary movement led by Fidel was never defined by Cuban Communists as Marxist or Marxist-Leninist, but as "petty bourgeois" and "nationalist", a common description used by Marxists to describe fascism. Cuban Communists, who were true experts in ideological matters, always saw Castro as a Fascist. That is why they called the attack on the Moncada barracks "a putschist attempt." History has proved them absolutely right.

9. A Caribbean Führer?

A cursory study of Fidel Castro's political thought and behavior clearly indicates not only a lack of the most elementary rudiments of Marxism but also a strong influence of the classics of fascism - a fact detected many years ago by Hugh Thomas,[117] this author,[118] Georgie Anne Geyer[119] and UC Berkeley professor A. James Gregor, who described Fidel Castro as a "führer of the Caribbean." James Gregor, who described Castroism as a "tropical variant of fascism."[120] It is not Marxism, but fascism, the repeated mentions that "leadership is basic" that appear in his writings from the Sierra Maestra. It is not Marxism, but fascism, that oozes from the foquista theory of taking power through coups d'état, which Castro blew in Regis Debray's ear.

But these are not the only indications of Fidel Castro's Fascist tendency. For example, the final words of his self-defense in the trial for the assault on the Moncada barracks, "Convict me, never mind, History will absolve me", are all too similar to Hitler's final words in his own defense in the trial for the foiled putsch of 1923, "Convict me, never mind, the Goddess of History will absolve me."[121] The similarity did not go unnoticed by Cuban Communists

Certain elements of the symbols selected by Castro for his political movements also point toward fascism. For example, the colors of the 26th of July Movement's flag were red, black and white. This is unusual because, although red and white are the colors present in the Cuban flag, black does not appear in any of the Cuban national symbols.

According to Hugh Thomast, unconsciously, Castro took the idea from the colors of the anarchist flag.[122] However, red, white and black are also the colors of the Nazi flag with the swastika. The fact that Castro approved or suggested the use of the color black in the flag of M-26-7 may have been just the product of coincidence, but when one sees it in conjunction with other information it becomes clear that it had a very specific symbolism.

The first militia units, created at the University of Havana, wore dark shirts very similar to those of the Nazis.[123] Moreover, in some of the first mass rallies at the University the militias paraded carrying torches. The resemblance to Nazi storm troopers became so evident that the University militia soon changed their uniforms to more conventional ones.

But, far from being a new idea, the University militia with its torches and dark shirts was actually an old dream of Fidel Castro. On January 27, 1953, on the eve of the centenary of José Martí's birth, a group of Fidel's followers showed up at the University. They then marched down the central staircase shoulder-to-shoulder and carrying torches in an impressive Nazi-style parade.[124]

When Castro was in Mexico engaged in preparations for the invasion of Cuba, someone reported him to the Mexican secret police, who arrested some of the revolutionaries and searched the house where they lived. Among the things the Mexican police found was a copy of Hitler's My Struggle, which, according to some who knew him closely, Castro always kept on hand.[125]

An American author and journalist found that, "during his university days in Havana, Castro read Marx, and Hitler's My Struggle", and both books exerted a great influence on him.[126] For his part, Mario Llerena, a prominent member of M-26-7, stated that some had noticed in Fidel many of the characteristics of a Fascist dictator, and that he had often heard that one of Fidel's favorite books was My Struggle.[127] The evidence shows that Castro was always very familiar with the ideas of Adolf Hitler.

His closest followers called Hitler "the Führer" (the boss). Among his inner circle Fidel Castro is called "el jefe" (he boss).[128] Hitler dehumanized his enemies by calling them vermin. Castro called his opponents "gusanos" (maggots.)[129] Castro used the word "bandits" to refer to Cuban patriots fighting a guerrilla war against him in the Escambray mountains. For his part, a special instruction from the Nazi Oberkommando, dated August 23, 1942, ordered that, for psychological reasons, the term "guerrillas" was not to be used, but "bandits." It is evident that Castro, an avid reader of Nazi literature, copied the use of these terms from the Nazis.

In the early years of the revolution, it was common to hear attendees at rallies and mass assemblies rhythmically chanting in chorus, "*Fidel!, Fi-del!, Fi-del!, Fi-del!*" (pronounced Fee-del!)The monotonous chorus too closely resembles "*Zieg-Heil!, Zieg-Heil!, Zieg-Heil!*" [pronounced "Sig Hill"] of the Nazis.

A common slogan in Hitler's Germany was: "The Führer orders, we obey." The Castro motto was, "Commander-in-Chief: Order!" Evidently, there are too many similarities between Castroism and Nazism to be just a product of chance.

In a speech delivered in Santiago de Cuba in early 1959, Castro denounced the "ill-intentioned" U.S. press and launched the idea of an international Latin American news service, written in our own language. Castro immediately began recruiting journalists and, in early March 1959, created the *Prensa Latina* news agency, totally under his control.

Interestingly, Castro's idea was very similar, even in name, to a similar one that another Fascist dictator in Latin America had had many years before. That dictator was none other than Juan Domingo Perón, who created *Agencia Latina*, a news service that faithfuly carried out the propaganda work of his regime. The analogy between the names and objectives of the two news agencies becomes even more striking when one discovers that Castro appointed as director of Prensa Latina Jorge Ricardo Massetti, an Argentine journalist, a close friend of Che Guevara, who had worked for *Perón's Agencia Latina*.[130]

Not only Cuban Communists, but also Trotskyists, noticed the strange affinity between Nazism and Castroism. In April 1961, *The Militant*, a Trotskyist magazine, published an article entitled "Signs of Danger in Cuba", in which the author pointed out the similarities between Hitler and Castro.[131]

Despite Castro's more rhetorical attempts to turn the rebellion against Batista a posteriori into a revolution of the poor, the truth is that to a large extent the rebellion was a petty bourgeois phenomenon. In reality, Castro's armed rebellion was rejected by the majority of black Cubans, who swelled Batista's army, as well as by the majority of the urban and rural poor masses, who apathetically watched the bulls from the sidelines.

A cursory study of the rebellion against Batista reveals that neither "Yankee imperialism" nor economic conditions in Cuba were responsible for Fidel Castro's alleged conversion to "communism." Further adding to the mystery and complexity of the enigma is the fact that the Cuban Communist Party never opposed Batista. On the contrary, the Cuban Communists opposed all movements against Batista, including that of Fidel Castro. So how could Cuba become a Communist state, when Cuban Communists opposed the revolution that produced that state? If Castro was a Communist, why did the

Communist party initially maintain such a contemptuous attitude towards his military operations? If Castro was indeed a Communist, why did a CIA officer, testifying in 1959 before a U.S. Congressional subcommittee, state that the available evidence did not justify that conclusion?[132]

There is circumstantial evidence to indicate that the main reason Castro sought to prove his Marxist affiliation was not because he believed in Marxism, but because he knew that only communism or fascism would enable him to maintain the unlimited power he had suddenly gained. However, as I have explained above, Fidel Castro's history shows that his ideas were closer to fascism than to communism.[133] But fascism, especially after the defeat of Nazi Germany, was no longer fashionable, so he adopted the guise of communism.

As UC Berkeley professor Paul Seabury rightly observed,

> At another juncture of international conflict, Castro might well have been simply an anti-American Fascist. In fact, Castro's philosophy of revolutionary activism more closely resembles that of Mussolini than that of Lenin.[134]

The decision to declare his revolution Marxist was the ploy Castro used to deceive friend and foe alike. Since what he feared most was the loss of the power he had illegally obtained, he took the only path that would make it easier for him to maintain his leadership forever; the path of "communism."

In February 1959, Castro passed a decree called the "Fundamental Law of the Revolution." The decree not only cancelled all constitutional rights of citizens, but also shifted legislative power to the cabinet, which he controlled. This draconian and anti-democratic law was the equivalent of the Enabling Act in Germany, which gave dictatorial powers to Adolf Hitler, or the *Patriot Act* in the U.S., which gave dictatorial powers to George W. Bush. Immediately after passing the law, Castro assumed the office of Prime Minister and forbade the puppet President he had appointed to attend cabinet meetings.

Just six months after Castro seized power in Cuba in 1959, the exodus of Cubans fleeing the country had gained momentum. Day after day, hundreds of Cubans —young children, the elderly, and young and middle-aged couples— stood in long lines at the counters of airlines with flights from Havana. Their personal luggage included children's tricycles, blankets, photographs of loved ones, their silverware and virtually everything of value they owned, such as jewelry and gold watches. In dramatic scenes reminiscent of the escape of Jews in early Nazi Germany, Castro's State Security agents at the airport seized the valuable property of those who escaped.[135]

In the early months of 1962 opposition to the Castro regime spread throughout the country. Raids by government troops became common. Although Castro went on to graduate from the University of Havana Law School, he never believed in the rule of law, but in the rule of men. Within months of taking power, Cuba's judicial system was radically overturned. As in Hitler's Germany, in Cuba the power of the leader (führergewalt) became the absolute law of the land, and all of Castro's maniacal whims immediately became codes and regulations of law.

In 1962 Castro created the "mobile military tribunals", an extermination technique that made all of Batista's crimes look pale by comparison. Covered panel trucks traveled throughout the countryside, conducting summary trials in the field. These military tribunals were dispatched to areas of the countryside where someone had anonymously reported disturbances or infractions of the new law. The infractions covered a wide spectrum, from being "enemies of the state", "speaking out against the regime", to "refusing to attend school" or "refusing to do voluntary work to cut sugar cane." Trials took only minutes, and most defendants were executed on the spot. In many cases, the coffins had been brought in beforehand and the "judges" themselves served as members of the firing squad. Those fortunate enough not to be shot were sentenced to 30 years of hard labor.[136]

By early 1964, Castro had already created a large system of mass detentions, with 57 prisons and 18 concentration camps with an estimated 100,000 political prisoners in a state of total servitude to the tyrant.[137] Although many people still believe that, unlike other totalitarian tyrants, Castro never engaged in arbitrariness or personal vendettas, the reality is quite different. Although Castro has denied that prisoners in his jails are tortured or treated inhumanely, many of the political prisoners who have managed to escape have testified extensively to the contrary.[138] Unfortunately, the U.S. has now implemented in the military prison of Guantánamo, and in other secret prisons in different parts of the world, mental and physical torture techniques very similar to those applied in Castro's prisons.

By the 1980s, widespread repression in Cuba had reached intolerable levels. In April 1980, out of desperation, a group of Cuban families in search of freedom hijacked a city bus and, after crashing it into the wall of the Peruvian Embassy in Havana, tried to enter the embassy through the breach in the wall. Cuban soldiers surrounding the compound opened fire and killed several of them, including small children and women. Those who managed to penetrate the embassy grounds requested political asylum.

A few hours later, a furious Fidel appeared on television and insulted the Cubans who had taken refuge in the embassy with epithets ranging from "worms" to "CIA agents." Castro ended his speech by shouting, "We don't want them here. Anyone who wants to leave, leave!" The next day, Castro's words were reproduced in big, bold letters on the front page of the newspapers. But apparently most Cubans took his advice at face value. The gigantic tsunami of Cubans who fled the island through the port of El Mariel was later dubbed "the Mariel exodus."[139]

Concerned by the spectacle of thousands of Cubans trying to leave the island legally, Castro reversed himself. First, he began calling the desperate Cubans trying to escape the island "scum", adding that they were criminals. Soon after, he came up with the diabolical idea of "acts of repudiation", in which those who, following his own suggestion, planned to leave the country legally were physically and psychologically harassed. A detailed description of the "acts of repudiation" is beyond the scope of this book, but suffice it to say that they were a new staging of the initial persecution of the Jews in Nazi Germany.[140]

The behavior of his mobs in the "acts of repudiation" inspired Castro to create another of his Fascist abominations, the infamous *Rapid Action Brigades*; government-sponsored groups of thugs and common criminals, apparently inspired by the squadristi,[141] Mussolini's Fascist street thugs, and the Nazi SA. The main task of the Rapid Action Brigades is the brutal repression of Cuban dissidents.

Another Fascist-inspired abomination created by Fidel Castro in Cuba are the Committees for the Defense of the Revolution (CDR); groups of informants on every city block to spy on their fellow citizens. Lacking originality, Castro drew his inspiration for the CDRs from the blockwarts, a very similar institution created by Hitler in Nazi Germany.[142]

Although it took some time, it seems that more and more people in Cuba became aware of the similarities between Castroism and Nazism. In 1986, the newspaper *Granma*, the official organ of the Castro government, published on its front page a photograph of Castro at a meeting of the dreaded Ministry of the Interior (MININT),

Castro's secret police similar to the Nazi Gestapo. The photo showed Castro with his right hand raised in the typical Nazi salute and, behind him, the word "*ario*" (Aryan) on a banner on the wall. The photo had been taken by an astute photographer who had purposely framed the last four letters of the word "*revolucionario*" on the banner. Only a few copies of the newspaper reached the streets before the Castro authorities discovered the subterfuge and confiscated and destroyed the entire edition. A severe purge followed at *Granma*, and several journalists and photographers ended up in Castro's jails.

10. Was Castroism Fascism Disguised as Communism?

What most of President Batista's opponents had in mind when they fought against the Cuban dictator was just to get rid of him and return the island to normality under the guidelines of the Cuban Constitution. In other words, the struggle against Batista was in reality a popular rebellion to reestablish the constitutional order, not a revolution to change it totally and drastically.

Castro's secret plans, however, were very different. His goal was not only the political transformation of Cuba, but also the total transformation of Cuban society and the creation of a "new man" - an old Fascist idea.[143] But such profound and dramatic change was not possible with only superficial social changes, so the changes in Cuba were radical. These changes did not contemplate a return to democracy, but the total destruction of what Castro saw as an oppressive social system. So the political and social system that Fidel Castro established in Cuba and which, unfortunately, many Cubans were so eager to embrace, began with a utopian idea and ended in a system of prisons and concentration camps.

In short, what Castro implemented in Cuba was his version of the "total state." The term, from which the adjective "totalitarian" is derived, was coined by Benito Mussolini.

Castro's idea of the "total state" implied the concentration of power in the state and the concentration of state power in his own hands, at the expense of individual freedom. In short, Castro's revolution did not represent a new type of government, but rather the continuation of the political absolutism that has characterized most of human history, as evidenced by absolute monarchies, oligarchies, theocracies, dictatorships and tyrannies.

However, although some Latin American dictators often preached the unlimited power of the state, most of them proved incapable of applying it. As a general rule, even during the most iron-fisted Latin American dictatorships, the citizens of those countries, including Batista's Cuba, enjoyed a kind of partial freedom that, if not a de juri freedom, was at least a de facto freedom. Proof of this is that the case of Castro's Cuba, a country from which several million citizens have escaped at the risk of their lives for political reasons, is unique in the history of Latin America.

While it is true that the initial exile was nourished by members of the upper middle class and some of the Batista regime's collaborators, it is no less true that shortly thereafter they were followed by members of all segments of the population. Finally, as evidenced during the Mariel exodus in 1980, those fleeing the island were members of the poorest sectors of the population. The reason for this was because the only haute bourgeoisie that now exists in Cuba is the one formed by Castro, his close collaborators and their families.

It is evident that Castroism was not just another example of the dictatorial regimes that have plagued the history of Latin America, but a different and virulent form of statism that is only present in totalitarian regimes. Even the *de facto* freedom is absent in Castro's Cuba. Castroism has evidenced many of the typical characteristics of Fascist regimes, among them, an extraordinary efficiency in the domination of its subjects, the pervasiveness of coercion, the total regimentation of the masses on a scale involving millions of people, and the systematic massacre of citizens by their own government. None of these things has any parallel in recent Latin American history, including the worst crimes committed by the governments of Argentina, Chile or El Salvador. The fact that the mainstream media in the U.S. and Latin America have not informed the world about Castro's crimes does not mean that they have not been committed and are still being committed.

Castroism shares with other totalitarian regimes the idea of the infinite flexibility of human beings, which explains its emphasis on education as an efficient form of propaganda. In addition, the constant rejection of the present in expectation of a luminous future that never comes, manifested itself in grandiose plans of social reconstruction and human remodeling. This served Castro as the basis for the expansion of his totalitarian power to all segments of Cuban society.

It was Castro's total determination to bring about these radical changes that led to political terror in Cuba. All change, even for the better, always involves resistance and opposition. In a free society, total radical change simply cannot occur, since it involves great resistance from a wide variety of groups and interests. In Castro's totalitarian society this resistance was eliminated by the imposition of total terror that eventually spread to all citizens.

In democratic societies political opponents are seen as people to be convinced or defeated at the polls. Today's opponent may well be tomorrow's ruler. In contrast, both Fascists and Communists see opponents as enemies to be eliminated. This explains the appearance of concentration camps in all Fascist and Communist societies.

Concentration camps are not a distortion of totalitarian regimes, but part of their very essence. Fascist and Communist regimes cannot exist without a system of concentration camps to "re-educate" opponents and annihilate recalcitrants. The real purpose of slave labor camps is to destroy the legal and moral personhood of human beings and deprive them of the last remnants of their individuality. Since Castro assumed power in Cuba in 1959, a widespread system of prisons and concentration camps has expanded and multiplied throughout the island.[144]

Another characteristic of Castroism that has been common in Fascist regimes is its passion for unanimity. Fidel Castro is convinced that history has proven him right about everything, and he expects others to agree with him, which further justifies the certainty of his historical vision. This passion for unanimity makes Castro insist that the entire population under his control be in complete agreement with whatever measures the regime imposes on them. This agreement, which in Cuba has been expressed in periodic controlled elections and rigged plebiscites, must not be passive. On the contrary, Castro expects enthusiastic behavior on his political measures from the captive Cuban people. Cubans must always show the world that they are enthusiastic prey to a passion for self-affirmation and self-realization. When this enthusiasm and passion do not materialize, the Maximum Leader becomes very angry.

Two cardinal characteristics of the Fascist mentality are the direct result of the rejection of reason and intellect, and their replacement by will and spirit. The first is the lack of importance of theory, and the second is the idea that politics and society are only one stage of permanent revolution and war.[145] It is not theory that mobilizes Fascists, but the will of the leader.[146] Despite Castro's initial failed attempts to disguise his nationalism under a cover of Marxist theory-which he completely ignores-his main tool for mobilizing the masses was always his personal will.

The similarities between Fascist and Communist regimes have been extensively and thoroughly documented by many authors. In fact, fascism is an economic system in which corporations control the state, while communism is one in which the state controls the corporations. But unlike Communist movements, whose followers are mostly from the working class, Fascist movements, such as Castro's revolution, draw their followers primarily from the middle classes. Another fundamental difference is that Communist regimes emphasize the concept of class, whereas in Fascist regimes, as in Castro's Cuba, the emphasis is on the nation and the state.

Contrary to Marxist leaders, who try to identify themselves with the proletariat and whose supposed objective is the emancipation of the workers from bourgeois exploitation, Castro's alleged main objective has been the emancipation of the Cuban people from exploitation by the capitalist nations, especially the U.S. Shortly after he seized power in Cuba, Castro coined the slogan "The people united will never be defeated."

As in Castroism, to Fascists "socialism" is the socialism of the whole people, not just the proletariat.[147] By merging the class with the nation, Castro deftly transferred the agent of revolution from the proletariat to the nation.[148] In this way, the Cuban proletariat was removed from its position as the agent of history, as Marxist theory indicates, and replaced by the nation, in accordance with Fascist theory.

When Castro took power in Cuba in 1959 the island had one of the largest working classes in Latin America, organized in powerful unions. Some of the unions were controlled by the Communists, who used them to foment class division. One of the first things Castro did, to the surprise of most of his non-Communist supporters and to the even greater surprise of the Communists, was to unify all the unions into one and give control of it to the Communists.

However, the unexpected victory of the old-style Communists turned out to be pyrrhic. Instead of an organization fighting for the rights of Cuban workers, the new unified union became in theory an organization of the entire Cuban people, without class distinctions. A few months later, the new unified union became just another political tool in Castro's hands, with no effective power to fight either for the rights of Cuban workers or for the rights of the Cuban people.

Traditionally, Marxists see society as divided into classes in an internal struggle, but Castroism sees it as the struggle of one state, one people and one nation against other states, other peoples, and other nations. But, as happened in other Fascist states, the objective of Castroism, as has become evident in Cuba, was not the emancipation of the Cuban working class, but the total domestication of the masses.[149] And there is no doubt that it has achieved it.

Castroism has castrated the Cuban working class, and has deprived it of all the rights and privileges it had won after long years of struggle. As such, Castroism has turned out to be a useful tool in the service of the worst kind of monopoly capitalism. That explains why Castro's Cuba has lately become a haven for unscrupulous capitalists who have enthusiastically allied themselves with Castro in the most iniquitous exploitation of Cuban workers.[150]

Contrary to communism, which is a strictly atheistic ideology, Castroism shares with fascism its vaguely deistic bent. Hitler and Mussolini reached an agreement with organized religion on condition that the Church accepted their Fascist states as their supreme political leader and supported them.[151] For his part, Castro never objected to a tacit agreement with the Catholic Church, as long as the Church accepted him as its supreme leader and supported him. This explains why the top leaders of the Catholic Church have always viewed Castro as a Fascist rather than a Communist.

The main reason for the initial clashes between Castro and the Catholic Church was because Castroism is itself a secular religion with a sense of messianic mission, and could not tolerate the activities of a rival religion. Castroism's ultimate goal is to dominate all aspects of Cuban life. It therefore frowns upon Cubans spending any time in non-Castro religious activities.

Both Communist and Fascist regimes rely heavily on mass propaganda to legitimize their power. But propaganda in Communist societies is based more on ideological indoctrination than on emotional issues. In contrast, Castroism shares with Fascist regimes its quasi-religious use of symbols and rituals, as well as its appeal to emotion and belief rather than to intellect and political ideology.

There is still one more basic difference between the two systems that should be emphasized. Contrary to the Communists, Fascist leaders of all shades, including Fidel Castro, glorify war.[152] One of the main characteristics that Castroism shares with Fascist totalitarian regimes is its immanent violence, which is turned inward as well as outward, and manifests itself in a constant state of readiness for war.

The Fascist view of war contrasts with the Communist one. For Communists, war is first and foremost the struggle between social classes rather than between nations. But this class struggle, which culminates in revolution, is not an end in itself. In fact, although communism rejects the possibility of peace between communism and capitalism, it envisages, at least in theory, a peaceful order in the Communist world. The attitude of the Communist countries to prepare for war is explained by the fact that they consider capitalist man to be a class-ridden being, motivated only by economic interests. But this bellicosity will disappear, according to the Communists, when the world revolution is consummated after capitalism is abolished from the face of the earth. War is therefore a necessary means to the ends which the Communist Party strives to achieve, but, at least in theory, it is not an end in itself.

Fascists, on the other hand, have a totally different view of war. The glorification of war and the warrior, as well as the worship of military technique and the goals of destruction for their own sake, are cardinal elements of the Fascist view of man. This glorification is the direct result of the ideological importance of the collectivity in its total dedication to carrying out the orders of the leader. As Benito Mussolini so aptly put it,

> "Fascism . . . believes neither in the possibility nor in the usefulness of perpetual peace . . . Only war brings to its highest tension all human energy and imposes the seal of nobility on the peoples who have the courage to confront it. All other activities are no more than substitutes which in reality never place men in the situation where they have to make the great decision - the alternative of life or death."[153]

Che Guevara's letter to the *Tricontinental Conference* in Havana in 1966, in which he called for the creation of "two, three . . . many Vietnams", is a message of such virulent and visceral hatred that it is found only in Fascist literature, not in Communist literature. As Guevara crudely put it,

> Hatred as a factor of struggle; intransigent hatred of the enemy, which drives beyond the natural limitations of the human being and turns him into an effective, violent, selective and cold killing machine.[154]

Che Guevara's description of the perfect guerrilla could be aptly applied to Himmler's SS troops.[155]

Castro created in Cuba the largest armed forces in Latin America, second only to those of the United States. Since coming to power in 1959, the entire Cuban society and economy has remained in a constant state of readiness for war. Preparation for military service begins early in the lives of Cuban citizens, and extends into old age.

The degree of militarization of Cuban society is unknown in the rest of Latin America, even in the most reactionary authoritarian dictatorships. Not even the Soviet Union, except during periods of war, has come close to the degree of total militarization of Castro's Cuba. This type of total militarization of society has only manifested itself in Fascist regimes, and had its highest expression in Nazi Germany.[156]

The glorification of war as an end in itself and the total disregard for international law and order have characterized the Castro regime from its beginnings. This glorification of war in Cuba is only a continuation of Castro's own life and his passion for violence and constant military adventures.

Nothing is more evidence of Castro's Fascist ideology than his foreign relations activities. Only a few weeks after taking power in Cuba, Castro launched military incursions against Santo Domingo, Panama, Venezuela and other countries. Since then, he has always maintained an active role in promoting subversive activities in Latin America, Africa, North America and Europe.

It was no coincidence that Che Guevara, who in his youth had been a fanatical follower and admirer of Juan Domingo Perón, was the one who developed the Fascist project that he called the theory of the focus of the revolution, later popularized by Regis Debray in his pamphlet Revolution in Revolution.[157] According to this revolutionary theory, it is not the organized proletariat, but small bands of armed men, the elite who, with guerrilla attacks in the countryside, will act as the "detonator" of the masses to rise up in arms until the overthrow of the old regime and put the "heroic guerrilla" in power.

As Professor Irving Louis Horowitz rightly pointed out, at the ideological level, the theory of the focus of the revolution,

> It represents the transformation of the guerrillas into gorillas, into advocates of the total militarization of Latin America. This is tantamount to incorporating right-wing doctrine into a left-wing framework.[158]

The fact was also noted by Professor James A. Gregor. In a book he wrote on fascism, Gregor noted that,

> The relationship between what Debray calls "revolutionary nationalism or Fidelism" and fascism is far more intimate than contemporary radicals are willing to admit. . . . The political commitments with which Castro came to

power were almost indistinguishable in style and content from Mussolini's original programmatic commitments in 1922.[159]

The Debray-Guevarist theory of the revolutionary "*foco*", largely the expression of Castro's ideas, asserted that the construction of the new society depended on "enlightened" rulers with the interests of the masses at heart.[160] The Castro elite, considered to be among the most enlightened "saviors" of the masses of all time, apparently believed that they could impose their desires on society.

The theory of the elitist revolutionary *foco* was in reality a Fascist idea, which is why it was never accepted by most of the traditional Communist parties in Latin America. However, it was favorably received by many like-minded revolutionaries, particularly those of the petty bourgeoisie and the Latin American left intelligentsia, who share with Castro and the CFR conspirators a deep hatred and contempt for the lower classes, and whose fondest dream, even if they do not admit it, is a techno-Fascist world dominated by the United States.

In reality, the Debray-Guevarist theory of the revolutionary "*foco*" was nothing more than a disguised form of the Fascist technique of the coup d'état that Castro has always admired. Focoism was diametrically opposed to the Communist theory of revolution, which is based on the conscious and organized struggle of the working masses under the leadership of a Communist party controlled by Moscow. That was the reason why the Soviet Communists and their puppets in Latin America always viewed Che Guevara's activities with extreme distrust. This also explains why the Bolivian Communist Party did not help Guevara, and played a key role in his capture and death.[161]

Like most Fascist leaders, Fidel Castro has a great passion for action itself, as well as a total contempt for intellectuals. In a speech he delivered in the 1960s, during one of the meetings with some Cuban writers and artists at the National Library in Havana, Castro insisted on his ignorance of the things that concerned the audience, in particular the problems of aesthetic form and attitude of intellectuals towards the revolution, and made it clear that he had attended the discussion as a ruler and as a revolutionary, not as an intellectual.[162] And all indications are that Castro was proud of it.

In an interview with French journalist Jacques Arnault, Castro confessed to him that, "I am not an intellectual. I am a man of revolutionary action."[163] Likewise, in Oliver Stone's documentary *Looking for Fidel*, Castro categorically told the American film director,

"I am not a theoretician of the revolution; I am an activist."[164]

The code of conduct of Fascist regimes emphasizes violence and lies in all aspects of human relations, both within the Fascist nation and between nations. Contrary to the democratic view, in which politics is seen as a mechanism by which social conflicts and different interests are resolved peacefully through compromise, the Fascist view sees politics as a friend-enemy relationship.

In the democratic way of thinking, the antithesis of the friend is the adversary, who is potentially tomorrow's ruler. In the Fascist view there are no adversaries, only enemies. Because the Fascist sees all opponents as enemies, and enemies represent the embodiment of evil, the only solution is their total annihilation. An example of this way of thinking was Castro's treatment of the friendly countries that voted at the 59th Session of the Commission on Human Rights at the United Nations. Session of the Commission on Human Rights in Geneva in 2003 condemning human rights violations in Cuba. Even countries like Mexico, which abstained from voting, did not escape the wrath of the Cuban Fascist tyrant.

It was not difficult for Castro to fool amateur anti-Communist Cubans[165] exiled in the U.S., because they were ripe for disinformation —people generally believe what they want to believe. But, despite his repeated claims about his alleged Marxist ideology, Castro never fooled the world's three leading experts on communism: the Communists themselves, the CIA, and the Catholic Church. None of them, perhaps for different reasons, believed the theory that Castro was a Marxist or a Communist, although both the CIA and the Vatican have used it to their advantage.

Some observers have interpreted the rapprochement between Castro and the Catholic Church as proof that Castro has succeeded in deceiving the Church's top hierarchy. But the rapprochement can also be interpreted as proof that Castro never managed to fool them.

Until recentlym the history of the Catholic Church showed a visceral hatred for communism. This hatred was formalized in 1937 by Pope Pius XI in his anti-Communist encyclical Divini Redemptoris, in which he described communism as "intrinsically perverse", and added that "it cannot be admitted that those who wish to save Christian civilization from ruin collaborate with communism on any ground whatsoever." Furthermore, he called communism a "satanic scourge."

In contrast, although fascism has also proven to be an intrinsically evil satanic scourge, the Vatican has shown a deep love for anything that smacks of fascism. Although the Vatican has always maintained cordial relations with Fascist leaders —Hitler, Franco, Peron — it has never had them with Communist leaders, and Castro was no exception. Therefore, if the Catholic Church has agreed to collaborate with Castro, as evidenced by the visits of John Paul II and Benedict XVI to the island, this is one more element that confirms my theory that the Vatican considered Castro a Fascist leader.[166]

Many people find it difficult to accept the fact that a leader whose methods, symbolism and ideology resemble fascism is not right-wing. However, although most people believe that fascism is, by definition, a political manifestation of the right, this is not entirely true. The Nazis, for example, considered themselves to be socialists, defenders of the German working classes and enemies of capitalism.[167]

The similarity between Castroism and fascism explains why Georgie Anne Geyer noted that Fidel Castro has created, "the first left-wing Fascist regime in history."[168] But Geyer was wrong. In reality what Castro created is the first Fascist regime disguised as Communist in the history of mankind.

However, the idea that Castroism is not communism, but fascism, is not new. As early as 1978, Hugh Thomas wrote:

> Fascist techniques were used so much during the early days of the Cuban revolution in 1959 and 1960 that, in fact, that useful term "Fascist left" could have been coined to apply to it. Castro's cult of heroic leadership, endless struggle and exalted nationalism was a feature of all Fascist movements in Europe. The emotional oratory, the carefully orchestrated mass rallies, the deliberate creation of tension before the "leader" speaks, the banners and the intimidating mobs, are Castroist techniques reminiscent of the days of Nazism.[169]

In an earlier book, Thomas had already expressed the similarities between Castroism and fascism so clearly that it deserves to be quoted in detail:

> "It is tempting to analyze the characteristic coloration of fascism that Castro has given to his Cuban-style communism. It is evident that Castro, like Chibas, and also like Mosley or Hitler, believes that political power lies in "the reaction of a large audience to a stirring speech." Large sectors of the Cuban population, including intelligent and humane people, have expressed their desire to submit their

individuality to Castro, just as many submitted to Fascist leaders. Present in the propaganda of the [Castro] regime is the continual elevation of the principle of violence and calls for martiality, as well as the cult of leadership, the emphasis on physical fitness in the educational system, and the continual criticism of bourgeois democracies.

"Guevara's own statement in *Socialism and Man in Cuba*, which defines Cuban socialism, shares with fascism such expressions as, "the need to recover the 'total man,' who has been atomized and alienated by society", a man who cannot find himself in "bourgeois democracy." The "New Man", whose prototype is Guevara himself, is a hero and man of action, will and character, who would have been admired by the French Fascists, such as Brasillach, or Drieu, or the D'Annunzio of the demagogic era of the Republic of Fiume, who seems to have been an intellectual precursor of Castro. Castro's moralizing desire and his interest in breaking with all material incentives is a reflection of Fascist regenerationism, and the presentation of himself as an attentive and benevolent father is reminiscent of Mussolini."[170]

Hugh Thomas was one of the first scholars to note the similarities between Castroism and fascism. However, a well-known ideologue of the Castro revolution, he perceived the true nature of Castroism long before Thomas and Geyer. In January 1960, only a year after Castro seized power in Cuba, Che Guevara gave a concise definition of the ideology of the Castro revolution when he stated that "it could be schematized by calling it leftist nationalism."[171] As a faithful follower of Perón, Che was never fooled by Castro's "Communism."

However, probably the first mention of Castro's true ideology was made by his brother-in-law Rafael Díaz-Balart. During a visionary speech he delivered before the Cuban Congress in May 1955, House Representative Diaz-Balart expressed his opposition to the Congressional bill that approved amnesty for Fidel Castro and his followers imprisoned for their participation in the attack on the Moncada Barracks. According to Diaz-Balart,

Fidel Castro and his group only want one thing: power, but total power, which will allow them to definitively destroy every vestige of Constitution and law in Cuba, to establish the most cruel, the most barbaric tyranny, a tyranny that would teach the people the true meaning of tyranny, a totalitarian, unscrupulous, thieving and murderous regime that would be very difficult to overthrow in at least twenty years. Because Fidel Castro is nothing more than a Fascist psychopath, who could only make a pact from power with the forces of International Communism, because fascism was already defeated in the Second World War, and only communism would give Fidel the pseudo-ideological garb to murder, steal, violate with impunity all rights and to definitively destroy the entire spiritual, historical, moral and legal heritage of our Republic. [Emphasis added.][172]

Unfortunately, the only thing that Diaz-Balart was wrong about was how long Castro's tyranny would last.

Eventually, more and more people came to a similar conclusion. José Fernández González, a Spanish businessman who lived in Cuba for nearly fifteen years doing business with the Castro government, finally discovered that Castro's "socialism" is really fascism by another name, and he laid it out in great detail in a book he wrote in 1996 entitled *Del socialismo al* fascismo (From Socialism to Fascism).[173] For his part, Rogelio Saunders, a Cuban poet and writer living in Havana, wrote an interesting article in which, although he apparently refers to fascism in general, he actually provides a fairly accurate description of the Castro regime.[174]

Another person Castro failed to fool was U.S. President Ronald Reagan. In a speech he gave in Miami on May 20, 1983, Reagan asserted that Castro was basically a Fascist.[175]

Even some of Castro's intelligence officers in charge of disinformation activities have not been able to avoid reaching a similar conclusion. Jesús Arboleya, a professor at the University of Havana and a member of Castro's intelligence services, stated: "The Cuban revolution is a project of social justice that finds its viability in anti-imperialist nationalism."[176] And Arboleya's conclusion is apparently not the product of an error, because a few pages further down he again mentions "the nationalist and anti-imperialist orientation adopted by the revolution."[177] Arboleya's definition of the Castro revolution makes no mention of communism or Marxism.

It is good to remember that, although Mussolini's fascism and Franco's Falange were definitely right-wing regimes, the position of the Nazis in the political spectrum was not entirely clear, and some of their policies were to some extent left-wing oriented. It should be kept in mind that, before it took power in Germany, the National Socialist German Workers' Party (Nazi) was a left-wing party; a revolutionary movement that had sprouted in the underworld of Munich.[178]

On the other hand, some authors consider the popular Fascist movements of Juan Domingo Perón in Argentina and Getulio Vargas in Brazil, as a type of fascism essentially progressive and a precursor of Castroism, whose regimes leaned to the left more than the respective caudillos had envisioned.[179]

As I explained above, the idea that Castro created the first left-wing Fascist regime in the history of mankind is debatable. What no one can deny is that it was the first Fascist regime disguised as communism.[180] In conclusion, it seems that, contrary to his claims of Marxist and Communist militancy, the Maximum Leader is nothing more than a Fascist of the Nazi type, and will remain so until the last day of his life.

Or maybe not.

11. Castroism or Jesuitism?

Those who have seen Fidel Castro simply as a nationalist, anti-American political leader have missed the true essence of Castroism. Although Castro has benefited from the use of organizational and political techniques copied from other political and religious organizations, especially Communist and Fascist ones, Castroism's emphasis on the creation of a new man with a new consciousness indicates that, basically, Castroism is not a political movement but a pagan cult very similar to that which originated in Sparta, then was reborn in Germany with Nazism,[181] and eveything indicates it is being reborn in the U.S.[181]

As we have seen above, Fidel Castro's true ideology is an enigma that has confounded not only most of the scholars who have tried to decipher it, but also his closest collaborators and his enemies. The fact that Castro has been able to hide his true beliefs and ideological affiliations is due to his extraordinary ability to create false clues to disorient enemies and friends. This is undoubtedly one of the reasons why he has been so successful in deceiving almost everyone.

However, there is a great deal of evidence to indicate that, contrary to what he himself claims and what most people believe, Fidel Castro never was, never has been and never will be a Marxist or Communist. Moreover, it seems that he is not even a true Fascist. The relationship that Fidel Castro managed to establish with the Cuban people and with his close collaborators has always been with his person, not with his ideas or with any particular ideology.[182] This is why Castro has changed his ideas many times without danger of damaging this relationship. As Herbert Matthews observed,

> "Early in the revolution I suggested that Castro wore movements and ideologies like articles of clothing; putting them on, taking them off, throwing them in the trash, hanging them in the closet, but always the one who wore them was Fidel Castro himself."[183]

Also, taking into account the peculiar characteristics of his way of thinking, it is very difficult to believe that, throughout his life, Fidel Castro was anything other than a fanatical Castroist. However, as I have mentioned in this book, a cardinal axiom of intelligence and espionage is that things are seldom what they appear to be. To what extent, one might ask, is the ideology that has inspired Castro not Marxism, as he claims, nor fascism, as some believe, but Jesuitism? To what extent was the failed attack on the Moncada barracks, which the Cuban Communists called a "putschist attempt" —a code phrase that in Communist language means Fascist— not Marxist but Jesuit-inspired? To what extent was the failed Nicaraguan operation not a Castro-Soviet operation, as some claim, but a joint Castro-Jesuit operation?

A critical analysis of the Castro doctrine of proletarian internationalism, which is alleged to have been inspired by Marxism, uncovers extraordinary points of contact with the Jesuit doctrine of ultramontanism, the Jesuit practical affirmation of universalism.[184] On July 21, 1773, Pope Clement XIV abolished the Jesuit Order. However, in 1776 the renegade Jesuit Adam Weishaupt created the Order of the Illuminati, a secret society whose aim was to destroy all the religions and governments of the world and merge them into a new world order, through a process he called "internationalism." Is Castro's internationalism really a version of Weishaupt's Jesuit internationalism? Apparently it is.

Castro's totalitarian control over the Cubans is not unlike the ideas of Ignatius of Loyola, who thought that the unity of the Church was not possible without total submission to the Pope.[185] But the Jesuits did not limit their totalitarian designs to the Church; they also wished to extend this monastic absolutism to civil society.

In their eyes, sovereigns were only temporal representatives of the Pope, the true head of Christendom. As long as the monarchs remained subservient to the Pope, the Jesuits were their most faithful servants, but if any of these monarchs rebelled, the Jesuits became their sworn enemies. This view is very similar to the attitude that Fidel Castro has always maintained in his relations with Latin American governments.

The word *compañero*, initially used by Castro and later adopted by his followers, has been erroneously interpreted as a synonym for comrade, a term with obvious Communist connotations. But, far from being a Communist usage, compañero is actually the term chosen by Ignatius of Loyola for the members of the Society of Jesus to address each other, as a means of emphasizing their collective struggle to achieve their religious goal.

Few seem to have noticed the many similarities between Castroism and Jesuitism. However, the facts indicate that the "socialist" state Castro created in Cuba is not much different from the one the Jesuits created in Paraguay in the early 17th century, where the Guarani Indians were indoctrinated and forced to live a regimented life under strict communal discipline. As in Cuba today, the Jesuit state did not allow freedoms of any kind. The natives could not dispose of their time and persons freely, and all property belonged to the state. However, according to the Jesuit ideologues of the time, the natives were happy, because they enjoyed free education and public health and the state guaranteed them a permanent job.

The Jesuits ruled the Indians with an iron fist, and punished even the slightest violations of the code of conduct they had imposed on them. Fasting, penance, public floggings, and imprisonment were used indiscriminately to keep the "happy" Indians under control.[186] The Indians were kept isolated from the outside world and traders could not approach the Jesuit socialist commune. The picture described above looks very much like the society Castro has imposed on Cuba, including the so-called economic "embargo. Is it possible, one might ask, that just as the Jesuits did in Paraguay, Castro has all these years been trying to create a Jesuit theocratic state in Cuba?

As in Castro's Cuba, the Jesuit socialist experiment ended in total failure. Lacking material incentives, the Indians lost all interest in work. Just as Castro has blamed the Cubans for his failure, the Jesuits blamed the Indians for theirs. According to the Jesuits, the Indians were lazy, greedy and narrow-minded. According to Castro, Cubans are lazy, greedy and lack "revolutionary consciousness."

In the Jesuit paradise, fruits spoiled in the fields without anyone harvesting them, farm implements deteriorated without being used and livestock died abandoned. A few years after the beginning of the socialist experiment, hunger was such that it was common for the

Indians to unharness an ox, kill it on the spot, light a fire, cook it, and eat it.[187]

Hardly a better description can be given of Cuba today after more than half a century of Castroism. The illegal slaughter of cattle has become so common that the National Assembly had to pass a law modifying the existing penal code to create harsher penalties for this type of activity. According to Granma, in 1986 about 17,000 head of cattle were illegally stolen and slaughtered. In 1998 this number rose to 48,656.[188]

In 1750, Spain and Portugal signed a treaty delimiting the borders in America. Through this treaty, Spain ceded to Portugal the rights to a vast territory located east of the Uruguay River, precisely in the area where the Jesuits had established their socialist state. As a result, the Jesuits were ordered to withdraw with their Indians to the Spanish side of the border. Far from obeying the order, the Jesuits armed their Guarani subjects and began a long guerrilla war against Portugal. Finally, after many years of struggle, they remained owners of the land, which finally had to be returned to Spain. Is it possible that the guerrilla war first against Batista and then against most Latin American governments was not inspired by Mao, as Castro claimed, but by the Jesuits?

The totalitarian socialist organization on which the Society of Jesus is based has always been so attractive to totalitarian-minded leaders that some have successfully copied it. For example, Heinrich Himmler took it as a model for his Schutzstaffel organization (the infamous SS), which he created according to Jesuit principles. The service statutes and the spiritual exercises prescribed by Ignatius of Loyola were from the beginning an integral part of the SS. As in the Jesuit Order, absolute obedience to the leader was the cardinal principle. Each and every order of a superior was to be accepted by his subordinates without question or mental reservation, perinde ac cadaver (as a corpse).[189]

In an effort to counter criticism of the lack of democracy and freedom in Cuba, Castro has responded on several occasions by asserting that, on the contrary, the regime he has imposed on the people of Cuba is an example of true democracy. One might wonder whether the "democracy" that Castro has implemented in Cuba may have been inspired by the Jesuit idea of democracy within the Order. Within the Order the Jesuits are free to discuss how best to serve the system, but the system itself is sacrosanct.[190]

Castro amassed an immense fortune, but he nrever seemed to care much about money or the enjoyment of earthly goods. He made no secret of the fact that he has great admiration for the Jesuits because, he says, "The Jesuits have never been motivated by profit." Castro once told his biographer Carlos Franqui how the Jesuits formed people of character, and that he admired their Spartan lifestyle.

Nevertheless, it would be unfair to blame the Jesuits entirely for the creation of the monster that turned out to be Fidel Castro, rather than the monster himself.[191] However, it is no less true that the Jesuit fathers of the Colegio de Belen committed a grave violation of their religious duties when, instead of trying to neutralize the evil creature they had on their hands, they encouraged and cultivated the dark side of Fidel Castro.[192]

On the other hand, it seems that the role of the Jesuits in cultivating the monster of Biran was not the product of mistakes, but of a conscious effort. Argentinian journalist Alfredo Muñoz Unsaín, who for many years was a correspondent in Havana for the *France Press* agency, has told a revealing anecdote.

When Father Pedro Arrupe was visiting Cuba in the early 1980s, Muñoz Unsaín spoke with him. Muñoz recalled that, during the conversation, the black pope told him of the excellent educational work of the Jesuits, and ended by telling him that he was very pleased with the work of the Jesuits in Latin America, especially how many of their disciples had risen to important positions in all kinds of professions. To which Unsaín replied: "Good, but I don't think you are proud of everyone. Don't forget that Fidel Castro was one of his disciples." To which Arrupe, in typical Jesuit style, replied in turn with a question, "And what makes you think we are not proud of Fidel Castro?"[193]

Contrary to what Castro and his enemies claim, it is difficult to believe that, during his long life, Fidel Castro was anything other than a fanatical fidelista. The similarity between Castroism and Nazism is due to the fact that both Nazism and Castroism are not political movements but religious cults. Nevertheless, if I were forced to define Fidel Castro's ideology, which is not easy, I would say that he is a kind of renegade Jesuit[194] who came to power and has maintained it using Fascist tactics.[195] His passion for lying is but one more evidence of his crypto-Jesuitism —what the Society euphemistically calls "mental reservations."

Part Three: The Bogotazo

The Communists did it.
—Gen. George C. Marshall.

Most Colombians who have studied the Bogotazo consider that the tragic events were merely an explosion of violence resulting from national politics. But, as I will show below, that view does not agree with the facts.

On the contrary, everything indicates that the Bogotazo was a false flag psychological warfare operation[1] that had nothing to do with Colombia's internal politics. Proof of this is that a secret report on the riots, made by the Attaché of the U.S. Office of Naval Intelligence, Colonel W.F. Hausman, mentions that initially the riots had been planned to break out during the Pan-American Conference that had taken place in Rio de Janeiro in 1947. But the Brazilian police did a good job and efficiently dispersed the rioters before the disturbances became generalized.[2]

In reality, the Bogotazo was the event that initiated a psychological warfare operation of enormous proportions in the Western Hemisphere: the so-called Cold War.

1. Use of Agent Provocateurs

As I explained in the previous chapter, Fidel Castro was recruited by the CIA in early 1948 and sent to Colombia as an agent provocateur to participate in the Bogotazo and the assassination of Gaitán. His objective was to plant false leads that would incriminate the Communists for both events.

On their way to Colombia, Castro and his friend Rafael del Pino Siero made a brief stopover in Panama, where they were introduced to President Enrique Pérez Jiménez. True to his role as agent provocateur, del Pino took advantage of the occasion to deliver a virulently anti-American speech.[3] But those who heard his passionate anti-American harangue were unaware that, a few months earlier, del Pino had been honorably discharged from the U.S. armed forces. Moreover, his presence at Mario Lazo's house when Castro was recruited indicates that del Pino still maintained relations with members of the U.S. intelligence services.

A few days later, the newly recruited agents provocateurs moved from Panama to Venezuela, where they repeated their performance when they met with a group of university students. They then met with former President Rómulo Betancourt, who had been appointed to head the Venezuelan delegation to the Bogotá Conference.[4] Because of his nationalist and anti-imperialist stance,[5] and the fact that as a young man he had been a leader of the Venezuelan Communist Party, the CFR conspirators considered Betancourt problematic and therefore accused him of being a Communist.

It is evident that the real purpose of Castro and del Pino's activities in Panama and Venezuela had been planned in advance by the CFR conspirators to solidify the false cover of the agents provocateurs as agents of international communism. From Venezuela, both agents provocateurs went to Colombia.

From the moment Castro and del Pino arrived at the Medellin airport, the Colombian National Security Office kept them under close surveillance. Alberto Niño, at the time Colombia's head of security, later wrote that he had been informed that the Cubans had replaced two Soviet intelligence agents stationed in Cuba.[6] But, as we shall see below, Niño was apparently one of those who believed that being anti-Communist earned him points with the overlords to the north.

Continuing their mission as agents provocateurs, in the days leading up to the Bogotazo, Castro and del Pino openly distributed Communist propaganda in various parts of the city. They also conveniently placed Communist literature in plain view in their Claridge's hotel room to be later found by the authorities.

The day before the riots broke out, Castro and del Pino attended a meeting with representatives of the Colombian Workers Union where, among other things, Castro lectured on coup d'etat techniques. However, even Claudia Furiati, a pro-Castro Brazilian author, has had to admit that the strongly leftist tone used by Castro in his dissertation "resembled that used by the provocateurs.[7]

According to yewitnesses, at about 4:00 p.m., a few hours after Gaitán had been assassinated, they saw a street mob, with Fidel Castro at the head, shouting "To the Palace" [referring to the Presidential Palace]. According to these witnesses, Castro wielded a rifle, and boasted of having killed two priests.[8]

In an effort to add credibility to the accusation that Castro was a Soviet agent, William D. Pawley, U.S. Ambassador to Brazil and delegate to the Conference, later testified before a U.S. Senate investigation that, as he was driving to the U.S. Embassy in an official car on the day the riots began, he heard on the radio someone say:

> "This is Fidel Castro from Cuba speaking, This is a Communist revolution. The President is dead. All the military establishments are in our hands. The Navy has capitulated and the revolution has triumphed."[9]

Some authors have interpreted Pawley's statement as definitive proof that already at that time Castro was an active Communist serving the interests of the Kremlin. But the evidence points to the contrary. In the first place, because, according to Ramon Conte's statement, Pawley attended the secret meeting at Mario Lazo's residence where Castro was recruited by the CIA. Secondly, because years later Pawley played an important role in 1958 as President Eisenhower's personal envoy in an attempt to convince Batista to leave the country voluntarily and leave the way open for Castro to take power in Cuba. Therefore, the veracity of Pawley's statement is questionable.

The use of agents provocateurs to incite rebellious and immature people to commit terrorist actions, or even simulate them, is not foreign to the techniques of the CFR conspirators who control the U.S. government. In a book published in 2001, James Bamford mentions Operation Northwoods, the code name for a false flag operation that would include sabotage, provocations and assassinations of American citizens.[10]

The plan, attributed to CFR agent Major Lyman Lemnitzer, is described in great detail in a secret Joint Chiefs of Staff document, later declassified, dated 1961. The document details a plan by the U.S. military to covertly create various pretexts to justify an invasion of Cuba. The plan included the assassination of several anti-Castro Cubans in the U.S., a fake attack by Cuban troops on the Guantanamo base, and the sinking of a U.S. ship in waters near Cuba to create a "remember the Maine" type incident." [11]

Bamford considers Operation Northwoods to be perhaps the most corrupt scheme ever conceived by the U.S. government, but it should not be forgotten that he wrote his book before the disastrous false flag operation of September 11, 2001. Nevertheless, there is no doubt that the military men who conceived that document[12] consciously disgraced their uniforms, their military branch, and their country.

However, the activities of CFR agents in creating false flag operations still continue. Some years ago, Secretary of Defense Donald Rumsfeld (CFR), mentioned a plan by the conspirators for the creation of an organization called the Proactive, Preemptive Operations

Group (P2OG). The main purpose of P2OG is to give a final push to fearful or hesitant terrorists to commit acts of terrorism that would justify a government reaction, even if these terrorist actions cost the lives of American citizens.[13]

2. The Creation of False Leads

Since their arrival in Bogotá, Castro and del Pino devoted much of their time to planting false leads in an effort to implicate the Soviet Union and Colombian Communists in the Gaitán assassination and the Bogotazo riots.

Proof of this is a confidential report by Colombian police detective number 6, reproduced in El Grafico de Caracas on September 22, 1949. The report, originally published in the newspaper El Siglo of Bogotá, refers to the results of the surveillance kept on Castro and del Pino in the days before and during the Bogotazo.

According to the report of detective number 6,

"I was commissioned by Dr. Iván Arévalo, Chief of Detectives of the National Police, to guard the President of the Republic, Dr. Mariano Ospina Pérez and his wife during the function that both were going to attend at the Colón Theater on the night of April 3.

"Around 10:00 p.m., shortly after the beginning of the third act of the play they were witnessing, a shower of loose leaves fell from the gallery. The loose sheets had been printed in Havana [speculated Detective No. 6]; they lacked the municipal tax stamp of Bogotá; the text was definitely revolutionary in phraseology and contrary to the democratic principles of our country, England and the United States.

"Together with two other detectives, [Detective No. 6] went to the gallery, where he captured two Cubans in the act of raining loose sheets of revolutionary propaganda on the boxes and orchestra pit of the Colón Theater."

"Detective no. 6 arrested Fidel Castro and del Pino and led them to their lodging - room no. 33 of the Claridge Hotel. Once there, the two Cubans voluntarily [emphasis added] showed the detectives several documents, some of them important. Among them was a letter from Rómulo Betancourt recommending the two, as well as several

Communist or leftist books [emphasis added], including one by Betancourt, "with whom they [Castro and del Pino] claimed to have relations of friendship and political affinity."[14]

According to the report, the detectives requested written authorization from their superiors to take Castro's and del Pino's passports and take the detainees to the National Police Detective Bureau for further questioning about their Communist activities. But, strangely, the authorization was denied.[15] Apparently, some important people in Colombia needed Castro and del Pino to continue their work as agents provocateurs without being interrupted.

The same day Gaitán was assassinated at 1:30 p.m., Castro and del Pino were in a café in front of the building where Gaitán's office was located. According to them, they were waiting to go to an interview with Gaitán that was to take place at 3:00 p.m. Castro and Gaitán had already met a few days earlier.[16] The date and time of the interview is recorded in Gaitán's diary. According to journalist Jules Dubois, the interview was to take place at the offices of the newspaper *El Tiempo*.[17]

3. The Trip to Colombia According to Castro

On several occasions, Fidel Castro has offered different versions of his participation in the Bogotazo. Although some of these differ considerably, I have decided to analyze the one he told Colombian journalist Arturo Alape,[18] not because it is the most coherent -as we shall see, Fidel Castro's thinking is characterized by its incoherence- but because it is the longest. This does not mean that it is the most complete or the one that most conforms to the historical truth, because, despite his extraordinary photographic memory,[19] Castro conveniently forgot to mention some important aspects of his participation in the events and his version of them is quite distorted.

In the introduction to the interview, Alape states his conviction that his interest in interviewing Fidel Castro about his participation in the events of the Bogotazo was due to his conviction that "the version, the definitive and true one, could only come from the main actor's mouth."[20] This statement, incredible in the mouth of a self-respecting journalist, indicates that Alape apparently ignores the most elementary principles of his profession.

The journalist's job is not reduced to regurgitating whatever politicians blow in his ear, but to publish it as one more version of the facts and, if possible, accompanied by a personal analysis based on information from other sources, preferably antagonistic ones. Besides, it should not be forgotten that, to the list of questions that every aspiring journalist learns on the first day of school: what, who, when, where and how, a true journalist has to add the most important one, why, and make his own analysis of the case in order to try to unravel something that the interviewee will possibly not mention or about which he will give a biased version. And that is conspicuously absent from Alape's interview.

Moreover, his idea that the definitive version of events can only come from the protagonist's mouth indicates that Alape ignores not only that, by definition, all politicians are liars, but that from an early age Fidel Castro has always been a professional liar.

Despite his constant allusions to his truthfulness, the evidence indicates that Fidel Castro was a convincing and accomplished liar. Over the years, Castro has proven to be a true master at saying one thing while having in mind something diametrically different.

Just a cursory analysis of Castro's speeches shows dozens of times in which he has admitted after the fact that he lied. One author who made this analysis of his speeches noted that "the Cuban dictator is a liar who later confesses the truth - retroactively. "[21] This fact explains why Mario Lazo —who, as we shall see below, knew Castro quite well— called him "the great dissembler."[22]

I will now go on to analyze in detail the "definitive and true" version of the Bogotazo as it came out of the mouth of one of the protagonists, whose role in the events was much more important than he himself and his admirers would have us believe.

At the beginning of the interview, seeing how his interviewee begins "to dismantle history as if it had happened the day before", Alape is amazed at "the marvelous machine that is Fidel's memory."[23] But Alape ignores that this prodigious memory is prone to selectively forget key facts that Castro prefers not to remember.

In example, in other interviews, Castro has stated that he went to Bogotá acting as President of the Federation of University Students (Federeación de Estudiantes Univeristarios, FEU), to represent his organization at the University Youth Conference that was to take place in that city. But, as we will see below, this version is at odds with the truth.

According to Castro himself, "I was president of the Law School, I was an official student of the university." And, as if for the avoidance of doubt, in that same paragraph he repeats it again: "I was president of the Law School.[24]

However, in the following paragraph, Castro offers a somewhat different version of the previous one. According to him, at the Law School,

> There was a dispute, since those who controlled the majority of the University, associated with the government of [Cuban President] Grau, had an interest in control. In my School, which was the Law School, the majority of the delegates had ousted the president, who was closely associated with the government, and they had elected me. So I was vice-president of the School and I was also elected at that time president of the School.[25]

However, on the next page Castro adds some information that belies his earlier categorical assertion that he was the President of the FEU at the Law School. According to his own confession, because of his involvement in a military expedition that planned to overthrow the President of the Dominican Republic, Rafael Trujillo,

> I missed my exam time. I found myself in a situation where I had to give up my official political rights at the University or enroll again in the third year, if I wanted to be an official leader.[26]

Castro goes on to explain why, because of that situation, "at that time I was a free student and had no political rights, but I had great ascendancy among university students."

In typical Castrroliar style —Castro has always held the firm conviction that words (especially his own) have more value than facts— Castro, just as he explained that although he was not a Communist, he was in fact a Communist, now tries to convince his credulous interlocutor that, although by law he could not be, and therefore was not, president of the FEU at the Law School, he actually was de facto because "he had a great ascendancy among university students.[27]

But the fact that Castro had great ascendancy among his classmates, which we have no way of corroborating beyond his words, does not disprove the fact that, as he himself confesses, because he was not an official student at the time he could not have been legally elected President of the student association.

So it must be concluded that what Castro has always alleged, that the reason for his visit to Colombia in 1948 was to represent the FEU as President of the Law School at the Student Conference that was to take place in Bogotá, is simply a lie. The facts indicate that Castro traveled to Colombia as an impostor, posing as someone he was not.

In fact, to cover up his true mission, Castro illegally appointed himself President of the Law School and traveled to Colombia without the authorization of the FEU.

Castro himself confesses this later in the interview:

> "I *arrogated to myself* [emphasis added] the representation of the Cuban students, although I had conflicts with the leadership of the FEU, ... That is to say, I did not carry the official representation of the great majority of [the] students, who continued to consider me as a leader, even though I had not officially enrolled and could not be an official cadre of the FEU."[28]

Upon learning that crazy Fidel[29] had illegally self-titled himself President of the Law School in order to attend an event in Colombia, the reaction of the official FEU leaders to the impostor was not long in coming. According to Castro himself, he confessed to Alape,

> "A situation occurred: I was the organizer of the Congress and everywhere accepted the role I was playing,[30] but then the leaders of the FEU in Cuba, when they saw that the Congress was a reality, wanted to participate officially and sent a representation in which they included the former secretary of the organization, Alfredo Guevara, and the President of the FEU."[31]

According to his own words, it seems that the meeting was quite heated, and Castro ends by saying that "practically unanimously the students supported me" and that is why he continued in the role he had assigned himself in the student conference.[32] But, once again, there is no way to corroborate his words, and one has to rely on his selective photographic memory.

In another part of his interview with Alape, Castro explains whose idea it was to hold a student meeting in Bogotá to coincide with the Ninth Conference. According to Castro,

> "In those days, I conceived the idea, in the face of the OAS meeting in 1948,[33] a meeting promoted by the United

States to consolidate its system of domination here in Latin America, that simultaneously with the OAS meeting and in the same place, we should have a meeting of Latin American students, behind those anti-imperialist principles, ... The idea of organizing the Congress was mine.

"... So I conceived the trip in this way: first to visit Venezuela, where a revolution had just taken place and there was a very revolutionary attitude among the students; then to visit Panama and then Colombia."[34]

However, after learning that several weeks earlier Fidel Castro had been recruited by the CIA, and that the CIA is nothing but an instrument at the service of the interests of the oil tycoons, the Wall Street bankers and the top executives of the transnational corporations, it is not far-fetched to suppose that the idea for the student meeting came from the same people who planned the Bogotazo: the conspirators of the Council on Foreign Relations.

The young student Manuel Galich had traveled to Colombia as a representative of the Guatemalan university students to attend the conference organized by the Cubans. But, upon his arrival in Colombia, "we found that only the promoters of the meeting had come, which were the Cubans of the University Student Federation, FEU."[35] And he added that, "The meeting was held in the premises of the CTC, which was a tiny, poor little room, all run down."[36] In other words, the meeting was attended by only four cats.

The above is further proof that the meeting of Latin American students was nothing more than a farce; a pretext to justify Castro's presence in Colombia and to cover up his real role as agent provocateur at the service of the CFR conspirators.

4. Perón's Role

In his interview with Alape, Castro tries to explain something very difficult: the reason why the pro-Fascist, anti-Communist president-dictator of Argentina, Juan Domingo Perón, provided him with the funds to travel to Colombia and other countries.[37] According to Castro's version, there were already contradictions between the two countries,

"At that time there were already strong contradictions between Perón and the United States. We [Castro uses the rhetorical plural of kings when referring to himself]

are therefore in this movement that is circumscribed to the following points: democracy in Santo Domingo, the struggle against Trujillo, the independence of Puerto Rico, the return of the Panama Canal, the disappearance of the remaining colonies in Latin America.

"These were the four fundamental points, and this led us [me] to establish certain contacts, let's say tactical, with the Peronists, who were also interested in their struggle for some of these issues, because they were also claiming the Malvinas Islands, which were a British colony.

"At that time the Peronists were carrying out activities, sending delegations to different countries, meeting with students, distributing their material; from that coincidence between the Peronists and us [Castro always used the plural to mean "I"] came a tactical rapprochement with them."[38]

Some authors have tried to explain the initial contact between Castro and the Peronists by alleging that, by one of those coincidences of life (coincidence is not a scientific term), in mid-March 1948 several Argentine delegates to the United Nations Meeting on Employment and Trade, which was to be held in Havana, were visiting Cuba. They were the ones who provided Castro with the necessary funds for the trip to Colombia.

But the contradictions between Perón and the conspirators controlling the U.S. government were no more than a figment of Fidel Castro's imagination or of those who sent him to Bogotá. On the contrary, at that time Perón was one of the most valuable allies of the same interests that recruited Castro for his secret mission in Colombia.

Although Perón at the time had assumed an apparent anti-American stance, there is circumstantial evidence to indicate that he was in fact a secret ally of Wall Street bankers and a personal friend of Allen Dulles.

As a Wall Street lawyer, Dulles represented the business of many corporate and political interests in Argentina, particularly the Rockefellers, before and after the war.[39]

At the end of the war, the brothers Nelson and David Rockefeller (CFR), with the help of their agent Allen Dulles (CFR) and the collaboration of the Vatican and their faithful friend Perón, facilitated the escape of many Nazi officers to various Latin American countries and the U.S. via Argentina. Among these Nazi war criminals were Adolf Eichmann, Josef Mengele, Gestapo officer Klaus Barbie (the Butcher of Lyon), and other lesser known Nazi war criminals such as Alfons Sassen, Friedrich Schwend, Wimm Sassen and Walter Rauff.[40] Dulles and OSS chief General William Donovan (CFR) played a major role in recruiting former Nazi officers to work with the CIA —most notoriously Reinhard Gehlen— and, through Operation Paperclip, repatriated many Nazi scientists, including Werner Von Braun, to the U.S..

The secret operation to help high-ranking Nazi officials escape justice and take refuge in South America was efficiently coordinated by Allen Dulles from his OSS office in Bern, Switzerland. This operation began before the end of the war and continued for many months afterwards.

Among the notorious pro-Nazi war criminals who took refuge in Argentina was Ante Pavelic, head of the Croatian Fascist movement during World War II. After the end of the war, Pavelic re-emerged in Argentina, and shortly thereafter Perón appointed him his "security advisor."[41]

Another important ex-Nazi who found refuge in Argentina was SS Colonel Otto Skorzeny, Hitler's favorite commando. Skorzeny gained international fame with the successful operation he led to rescue Mussolini. It is known that at the end of 1948 Skorzeny moved permanently to Argentina, where he began to work directly for Perón.

An important figure in the Peron-Vatican cooperation to repatriate Nazi war criminals to America was Licio Gelli, an Italian Fascist financier who from very early on maintained close relations with the CIA. This is the same Gelli who in the 1970s, following CIA orders, organized and provided the funds for the creation of the Red Brigades. This was the same terrorist group that later, following orders from CFR agent Henry Kissinger, assassinated Italian Prime Minister Aldo Moro.[42] In 1947 Gelli had to flee Italy to escape justice. Predictably, he traveled to Argentina, where his friend Perón welcomed him with open arms.

But this is not the only proof that Perón's anti-Americanism is a myth.

In 1945, the American delegation to the San Francisco Conference, where the creation of the United Nations (UN) was being discussed, included 47 CFR members, among them Adlai Stevenson, John Foster Dulles, Nelson Rockefeller, Edward Stettinius, Cordell Hull and Alger Hiss. The charter for the creation of the UN that the delegates approved had been written in its entirety at the Harold Pratt House.

One of the problematic aspects during the sessions of the Conference was the pressure exerted by the American delegation to include Argentina among the member countries of the future United Nations Organization. In the end, due to strong opposition from the Soviet Union and some Latin American countries, which mentioned the Perón government's collaboration with Nazi Germany, Argentina was not part of the initial group of member nations.

However, the next year, John D. Rockefeller, Jr. (CFR), donated a plot of land in Manhattan, valued at $8.5 million, for the construction of the United Nations building. Shortly thereafter, Argentina was accepted as a member of the UN.

In his biography of Fidel Castro, Tad Szulc mentions the seemingly inexplicable fact that the Peronists chose precisely a group of Cuban students for the mission of organizing and holding the congress in Bogotá.[43] In fact, it is extremely difficult to explain why the Fascist Perón chose precisely a "Communist" student to organize a congress of anti-American students in Latin America. It is also difficult to explain why, despite the existence of a legitimate representation of Cuban university students, the Federación Estudiantil Universitaria (FEU), the Argentines ignored it and went directly to contact Castro, who was not part of this organization.

But there is an explanation that deserves consideration. According to Castro himself, the idea of organizing the student congress occurred to him a few days before the Ninth Conference was supposed to begin. That is, it was after he had attended the secret meeting at Lazo's house and his first contact with his handler, CIA agent Salvatierra. Therefore, it is not difficult to conclude that the idea of a student congress parallel to the Ninth Conference was not Castro's, but that of his masters the Rockefellers and other members of the CFR. This would be the perfect pretext to justify the presence of agent provocateur Fidel Castro in Bogotá.

Most likely, the funds for the trip were provided by the Rockefellers. But, obviously, they could not have done it directly through the CIA, as this would have been difficult for Castro to explain. Therefore, the conspirators enlisted the help of their good friend Perón to serve as an intermediary, which is a common procedure used by intelligence agencies when they want to hide the origin of the funds they supply to their secret agents.

If Perón was anti-American, he was so only in the sense that David and Nelson Rockefeller, Allen Dulles and Fidel Castro were: always acting against the interests of the American people, but in favor of the interests of the Wall Street bankers, the oil tycoons, and the executives of the international corporations that control U.S. policy. The rest is nothing more than a fairy tale created to hide Perón's close relations with the real anti-American imperialists.

5. The Bogotazo Riots

In the interview he gave to Alape, Castro stated categorically that the Bogotazo was a spontaneous explosion of mass violence as a result of the assassination of Gaitán:

> "I can assure you that April 9 was a complete spontane-ous explosion, that no one organized it, nor could anyone have organized it. ... No one can claim to have organized April 9, because precisely what April 9 lacked was orga-nization. That is the key, it absolutely lacked organiza-tion."[44]

It is highly significant that Castro's version of events coincides ex-actly with that offered by the then Director of the CIA, Admiral Hillenkoetter. However, contrary to Castro's and the CIA's opinion, most authors who have studied the Bogotazo agree that, far from being a spontaneous uprising, it was evident that there had been prior preparation to create the disturbances. Moreover, in contradiction to what he assured Alape, Fidel Castro himself has lent credibility to these suspicions.

In an interview he gave to Indian journalist Kurt Singer in late 1960, Castro mentioned how, when he was only twenty years old, "I participated in the execution *of a plan* [emphasis added] whose ob-jective was the liberation of Colombia."[45] The fact that Castro was following a previously established plan is confirmed in a letter he received from his girlfriend Mirtha,[46] in which she mentioned she was worried because, before the trip, Fidel had told her that "he was going to start a revolution in Bogotá."[47]

Now, given that at the time Fidel Castro was only 21 years old and lacked the experience, resources, and political stature necessary to carry out such a plan, one must conclude that the plan was not his, but that of someone he does not mention. However, after learning that Castro had previously been recruited by the CIA, as well as that the CIA is nothing more than an instrument of the Wall Street bank-ers in the Council on Foreign Relations, it is not unreasonable to think that the plan he mentions was not his, but was conceived by the CFR conspirators in the Harold Pratt House, and carried out by agents of the newly created CIA and the defunct OSS.

Clearly, there is much to indicate that the Bogotazo riots had been planned well in advance. Possibly the clearest indication was that, a few hours before Gaitán was assassinated, the newspaper *El Popular*, of Barquisimeto, Venezuela, published in its April 9, 1948 edition (which, logically, had been prepared the night before it was printed) the news of the assassination and the riots that followed.

Other publications took notice of the unbelievable event. A few days later, on April 14, the Venezuelan publication *El Gráfico* of Caracas, reproduced a facsimile of the page of *El Popular* in which the information had appeared. The newspaper *El Siglo* of Bogotá followed suit, and on April 29 reproduced the extraordinary information that appeared in *El Popular*.[48]

If we rule out the possibility of extrasensory perception, the only thing that explains the publication of the news about Gaitán's assassination and the Bogotazo riots before they happened is that the CIA's Mighty Wurlitzer[49] made a temporal miscalculation.

But that is not the only difficult thing to explain about the Bogotazo.

Although the rioters relied mostly on improvised explosives to cause the destruction, some eyewitnesses later recalled that they did their destructive work with great speed and efficiency. According to a study of the Bogotazo published in 1969 in a CIA academic journal, for internal circulation only, some of the rioters wore a red ribbon on their arm (the traditional symbol of the Colombian Liberal Party), but some of the red ribbons showed the hammer and sickle (the traditional symbol of Soviet communism).[50]

An eyewitness who closely observed the work of a group of about 25 rioters, and apparently joined them for some time, stated that they were disciplined and well organized. The leader of the group wore a red ribbon on his arm. Shortly thereafter, this group was joined by three other similar groups, but the leader of these groups wore a white ribbon. This new leader held in his hands a typewritten sheet with a list of the buildings they intended to loot and destroy. The witness added that, during the time he joined the groups, he did not hear any comments critical of General Marshall or the United States.[51]

The evidence offered by several eyewitnesses shows that, despite the apparent chaos, the participants in the riot acted according to a well-coordinated plan. Some witnesses observed that the destruction was very well organized, to the point that, even before the revolt broke out, tanks of gasoline had already been stored in certain strategic locations in the city, which was then used to burn the buildings.[52]

A G2 report of April 17, 1948 asserts that "the revolt has been organized to the point of carefully distributing jars of gasoline that could be used for burning" However, the famous Colon Theater, the Jockey Club, the Shooting Club, and other maximum symbols of the Colombian aristocracy, were left untouched. Moreover, although the looters stole as much private property as they could carry, they did not touch the archives of the notaries public where the contracts of property transactions were kept.[53]

Much more difficult to explain is the fact that, despite the chaotic and bloodthirsty appearance of the mass of rioters, some of them seemed to act with some coordination. For example, while some of them prepared Molotov cocktails to burn a particular building, others entered the building and, while destroying the furniture, forced those still in the building to evacuate it in an effort to avoid unnecessary deaths.[54] Moreover, despite the fact that radio stations incessantly accused General Marshall of being implicated in the assassination of Gaitán, the rioters never attempted to make an attempt on Marshall's life or to disrupt the Conference. The balance of the riots showed that no important Colombian or foreign politician lost his life in the revolt.[55]

A few minutes before 2 p.m., the mob arrived at the National Capitol and began to ransack the building. The Conference had just finished one of its morning sessions and many of the delegates were preparing to leave. Inexplicably, however, none of the more than a hundred delegates present were disturbed. The mob kept them surrounded, but without assaulting them, until a few hours later when they were rescued by military forces who took them to their respective embassies.

The next day, Carlos Atilio Bramuglia, Argentina's Foreign Minister, suggested to General Marshall that he postpone the continuation of the Conference until the riots had ceased. But Marshall, perhaps on the basis of privileged information, flatly refused to accept the suggestion. Shortly thereafter, the Conference venue was moved to a school on the outskirts of the city, where it continued its deliberations, culminating in the Bogotá Declaration, unmolested.[56]

The use during the Bogotazo of certain propagandistic elements typical of psychological warfare operations is evidence of careful preparation prior to the events. For example, only a few minutes after Gaitán was shot and wounded by the assassin (or assassins), some well-organized people distributed a leaflet in the streets of downtown Bogotá. Specialists who later analyzed it noticed several things that were difficult to explain. First, the print showed the use of six different fonts. Second, the ink with which it had been printed was completely dry. Third, the margins of the printed text were completely crisp, with no smudges or smears to indicate tampering while the ink was still wet.

The text, in theory written by Colombian Communists, accused President Ospina of being guilty of the assassination of Gaitán:[57] The fact that this loose leaf mentioning the assassination of Gaitán had evidently been printed before the crime had been committed indicates that the assassination was not the work of an isolated individual but of a well-organized conspiracy.

Within minutes after the news of Gaitán's assassination spread, the railroad stations, post and telegraph offices, as well as most of the radio stations, had fallen under the control of the rioters. These were the radio stations that immediately began to play an important role in coordinating the riots. Many of the authors who have studied the Bogotazo agree that the radio stations played a key role in instigating the riots.[58]

Less than 20 minutes after Gaitán was assassinated, some radio stations began broadcasting messages inciting the riot and giving instructions to the rioters on how to obtain weapons by looting hardware stores, how to prepare Molotov cocktails, and which key points to attack.[59] Some legitimate broadcasters realized the irreparable damage that Gaitán's assassination could cause, and advised their listeners to stay at home or at work[60] and not join the riots, but others did the opposite, and incited the rioters to loot, kill and destroy.

However, the improvised announcers who broadcast their messages from the radio stations occupied by the rioters demonstrated a high degree of professionalism that runs counter to the widespread opinion that it all happened in the heat of the moment. A secret report of the event, written by Colonel W. F. Hausman, Attaché of the American Office of Naval Intelligence, mentions "secret radio transmissions" in which the people were incited to participate in the revolt.[61] According to another report, no fewer than three clandestine stations, one of them mobile, began transmitting messages only a few minutes after Gaitán's assassination.[62] Most of the stations used in the operation used the same technique: they would transmit for a few minutes, stop, change frequency and go back on the air. This prevented the place where the transmission originated from being located by triangulation.[63]

One message that was constantly repeated in the radio transmissions consisted of a call to assassinate President Ospina, whom they accused of being sold out to U.S. imperialism. According to these messages, Ospina, in collusion with General Marshall, had ordered the assassination of Gaitán.[64] However, the radio announcers never incited the mob to interfere with the Conference or to physically attack General Marshall or any other Americans attending the Conference.

Several witnesses later reported sniper activity during the riot.[65] In fact, much of the casualties that occurred during the riot were the result of sniper fire. Because some of the snipers were firing from church steeples, unfounded rumors circulated that priests were shooting at people.

After the riots, it was widely spread that some of the rioters had stormed police stations, where they had seized weapons and ammunition. According to these accounts, it was there that the snipers found the weapons they later used in their deadly work. However, as anyone who has undergone military training can attest, sniper technique is not easy to learn.

Although it is not difficult to fire a rifle, hitting a target at a distance of more than half a block (about 50 meters) is something quite different. The difficulties increase if the shooter has had no previous experience in handling firearms, the rifle sight has not been professionally sharpened by a gunsmith,[66] and the shot is not fired when the rifle is in a horizontal line with the target, as shooting from the rooftops of buildings or church steeples requires.

Therefore, the doubt persists: Who were the snipers? Who supplied them with perfectly sharp rifles? Who trained them and placed them in their firing positions?

6. The Ninth Pan-American Conference

It was no a coincidence that the Bogotazo riots broke out during the Ninth Pan American Conference. In 1945, after the end of World War II, the U.S. military-industrial complex and its partners, the oil tycoons and Wall Street bankers, were desperately seeking a way to continue producing armaments, and they saw Latin America as an extraordinary potential market for their products. To this end, they kept active the military bases that, under the pretext of war, they had acquired in several Central and South American countries, in an effort to influence these countries to standardize their military equipment with U.S.-purchased weaponry.

The purpose was not only to increase the profits of the military-industrial complex, but also to create technological and economic dependence on the U.S. To that end, they created shortly thereafter the Inter-American Defense Board to standardize, following the U.S. model, the armaments, organization, and training of the armed forces of the Latin American countries.

The CFR conspirators infiltrating the U.S. government knew the importance of the countries south of the border as a secure source of raw materials from a geographic area where other foreign powers could not interfere. The plan was to use the Latin American military to protect the natural resources of Latin America which, the conspirators reasoned, belonged to them in their own right.

In 1945, the foreign ministers of most Latin American countries and the U.S. signed the Act of Chapultepec. An essential point of the Act was a call to take collective action in the event of an attack by an extra-continental power against a signatory state. Of course, the Act did not mention the possibility of an attack against a Latin American country by a continental power: the USA.

Another step in the consolidation of the CFR conspirators' control over the hemisphere was the signing of a military alliance between the United States and the Latin American countries (except Uruguay, which refused to sign): the Rio Pact of 1947. According to the pact, the signatory countries undertook to provide assistance to other countries in the event of an armed attack. But, contrary to the Latin Americans, the U.S. always saw the Pact as an anti-Communist alliance that gave it the right to intervene directly or indirectly in the internal affairs of the signatory countries.

However, despite pressure from the U.S., the fight against communism was not a priority among the signatory countries. Latin Americans were more concerned about the lack of economic development and endemic poverty in their countries than communism. In fact, by this time most Latin American countries had outlawed Communist parties and Soviet influence in the area was minimal.[67]

Most Latin American governments that had signed the Pact expected the U.S. to give them much-needed economic aid (most of which corrupt politicians hoped to appropriate) in exchange for their political and military collaboration. But, a year after it was signed, the U.S. economic aid had not materialized, and the politicians were not happy. Nevertheless, the U.S. was now again trying to convince them in Bogotá to sign new treaties based on new promises that they might not intend to keep.

Of cardinal importance among these new alliances was the creation of a new tool conceived by the conspirators to increase their economic and political domination over Latin American countries, the Organization of American States (OAS), as well as a declaration committing Latin American countries to fight the new threat: Soviet communism. A secret memorandum dated March 22, 1948, signed by George Kennan (CFR), Director of Policy Planning of the U.S. State Department, mentions that the problem of communism was to be discussed at the Ninth Conference, as well as the implementation of anti-Communist measures to be created and implemented in the inter-American system.[68]

But, given previous experience, most political leaders in Latin American countries were unwilling to cooperate with the U.S. in implementing such measures. This was evidenced during the first days of the Conference by the reluctance of most delegates to bow to Marshall's veiled pressures and threats. In particular, many delegates expressed concern about the inclusion of a dangerous measure added at the last minute to the proposed Charter creating the OAS, Article 15 of which originally stated that, "No state or group of states has the right to intervene, directly or indirectly, for any reason whatsoever, in the internal or external affairs of any state." This principle was supposed to apply not only with respect to armed force, but also to any kind of interference or threat. But the new addition specified that some "measures" could be "taken for the maintenance of peace and security in accordance with existing treaties."

Obviously, with this addition, the CFR conspirators who control the U.S. government were guaranteeing their right to intervene at will in Latin America, and this was not to the liking of the Latin American delegates to the Conference. But the experience of seeing mob violence in the streets, destruction of buildings, and indiscriminate killing proved more persuasive than Marshall's arguments in favor of these measures. On the last day of the Conference, the delegates not only unanimously approved the Charter creating the OAS, but also a declaration condemning international communism.[69]

However, even after they had been coerced into approving the creation of the OAS, some of the delegates still had the audacity, or the naiveté, to ask Marshall if there was a possibility of creating a "Marshall Plan" for Latin America. But, having achieved his goal, Marshall demonstrated his disrespect and contempt for the delegates when he replied that financing such a plan was beyond the means of the United States. The capital required for such a plan, Marshall added, "must come from private sources."[70]

The OAS Charter provided the legal mechanism for the application of the Monroe Doctrine in Latin America. Since the U.S. controlled the majority of votes in the OAS, as well as the votes of some of the Latin American delegates, this guaranteed the right of the U.S. to legally intervene militarily in the internal politics of member countries. But, in the event that the vote was not in their favor, with the addition of the above mentioned measure, the U.S. would in one way or another have the right to intervene militarily in Latin American countries.

7. Intelligence Analysis of the Bogotazo

Most intelligence services share the view that the most important thing in the field of intelligence and espionage is not the accumulation of information, but the interpretation and analysis of the information in order to convert it into intelligence that can be used to arrive at a correct estimate of the situation and issue a prognosis.[71] Unfortunately, this is precisely what is conspicuously absent in most studies on the Bogotazo, especially that of Alape.

Almost all authors who have studied the Bogotazo agree that what sparked the riots was the assassination of Colombian leader Jorge Eliécer Gaitán, head of the Popular Party, at the hands of Juan Roa Sierra, a mentally unstable young man. But just a cursory analysis of the events from a counter-intelligence point of view shows that, on the contrary, the Bogotazo was a false flag operation planned by the CFR conspirators, and implemented according to operational principles established by the OSS and the newly created CIA.

In reality, the Bogotazo was a key element of a major psychological warfare operation (psyop),[72] the ultimate goal of which was to frighten the American and Latin American peoples with fear of communism - an artificially created enemy to replace the artificially created enemy that the conspirators had just lost with the end of the war: Nazi Germany.[73] It was therefore not by chance that the first mission assigned to the organization that would later become the CIA's Office of Special Projects was an operation directed against the American people to condition their minds in fear and hatred of the country that would shortly thereafter become the main enemy of the U.S.: the Soviet Union.[74]

The propaganda and sabotage techniques employed in the Bogotazo —transmission of false messages by clandestine radio stations inciting the revolters, distribution of leaflets implicating the Communists, etc.— appear to have been taken directly from one of the psychological warfare operations manuals produced by the Morale Operations Branch of the OSS.[75] The primary objective of the Morale Operations Branch of the OSS was to create unfounded panic, intimidate, demoralize, and create confusion and distrust in both the civilian population and the enemy armies. A secondary objective was to stimulate resentment and rebellion among the occupied populations,[76] primarily by using "black" propaganda,[77] in which the source of information is concealed or disguised as something it is not.[78]

An important fact, but totally ignored by authors who have studied the Bogotazo and which adds weight to the theory that the event was a secret CIA operation, is that only two weeks before the assassination of Gaitán and the riots, the Federal Bureau of Investigation (FBI) office at the U.S. embassy in Bogotá was dismantled. According to a secret document, declassified a few years ago, all FBI agents (FBI agents work in U.S. embassies under the name of "legal attachés") were ordered to return to the U.S. and it was reported that they would not be replaced.[79]

To understand the importance of this information it is necessary to study a little the tortuous relations of FBI Director J. Edgar Hoover and the Wall Street conspirators.

Prior to the creation of the CIA, the FBI was the U.S. government agency in charge of espionage and counterespionage activities in Latin America, and most who have studied the subject assert that the FBI had been doing an excellent job. Despite his personal limitations, Hoover was a true patriot who, contrary to the CFR conspirators, always worked for the benefit of his country. Proof of this is that the FBI was one of the few U.S. government agencies that the conspirators had not managed to penetrate and control. Even more important is the fact that one of the greatest opponents to the creation of the CIA had been precisely Hoover.

Therefore, the elimination of the FBI office in Colombia must have been a precautionary measure to prevent people with inquisitive minds, who were not under the control of the CFR, from witnessing events that, given their professional training, they would have immediately discovered to be a covert CIA operation. The CFR conspirators knew that, had they discovered it, Hoover would have created a scandal that would have been difficult to ignore. That is why they ordered the FBI office at the embassy in Bogotá to be closed.

Fidel Castro's role as agent provocateur during the Bogotazo is obvious and has been amply documented. However, most authors who have studied the Bogotazo and the assassination of Gaitán have made an effort to ignore it and do not mention it. It is difficult to explain why these authors have not seen what is readily apparent once the events are analyzed with a critical eye.

In example, shortly after the riots, the Colombian government asked the British Scotland Yard to conduct an investigation into the events. To that end, the British authorities sent a team of investigators to Colombia, consisting of Chief Inspector Peter Beveridge, Chief Inspector Albert Tansil, and Sir Norman Smith, former head of the British Police in India. Despite certain inaccuracies due mostly to lack of support from the Colombian authorities, poor knowledge of the language and the country, as well as the short time in which the investigation was carried out, the report remains a valuable source of information on the Bogotazo and the assassination of Gaitán.

When Dr. Ricardo Jordán, Chief Investigator of the Colombian Ministry of Justice, first met with Scotland Yard investigators, he mentioned to them a summary he had written detailing what he considered to be the most important facts of his investigation, as well as his initial conclusions. According to Jordan, the summary mentioned first-hand information implicating the Communists in the Gaitán assassination. However, when after some delay Jordán finally handed the document to the British investigators, they found that it "consisted of only two folders, containing only a few sheets of paper, in which there was no opinion or anything" that would prove in the least the participation of the Communists in the events.[80]

Despite Dr. Jordán's efforts to implicate the Communists in the assassination of Gaitán, the British investigators categorically concluded that, "We are fully convinced that no political party, as such, had any part in the assassination."[81] They therefore expressed their definite opinion that no political party could have been connected with the assassination.[82]

Proof that Jordan was selective in the information he provided to Scotland Yard investigators, however, is the fact that nothing is mentioned in his investigation about the involvement of two Cuban nationals in the events. By pure chance, the British investigators discovered this information by studying some documents provided to them by the Colombian Ministry of Foreign Affairs, which contained a report by a Colombian police detective mentioning the two Cubans.[83]

Based on the detective's report, the British investigators mention the fact that,

> Two Cubans, del Pino and Castro, were prominently noticed [emphasis added] when they disseminated from a balcony of the Colon Theater loose sheets with strong Communist overtones, in which they denounced foreign

powers maintaining colonies in the Western Hemisphere, and culminated in an attack on American "imperialism." They did so at 10:30 p.m., while a function attended by the President of Colombia was taking place.[84]

The British also mention that the Bogotá police detective's report stated that, according to what the manager of the Claridge's hotel told him,

> "On the night of the 9th [of April], the Cubans [Castro and del Pino] returned to the hotel armed with rifles or shotguns and revolvers, and with a good load of objects they had looted. The administrator added that that night Castro spoke in English [emphasis added] on the telephone with several people."[85]

In an obvious effort to discredit the information provided by the Claridge's administrator, one author has mentioned the fact that, on that date, Castro did not speak English."[86]

But this author failed to mention that del Pino, who was a U.S. citizen and a former member of the U.S. armed forces, spoke fluent English. Now, since KGB officers do not communicate in English with their Spanish-speaking agents, with whom did Castro or del Pino speak English?

The detective added in his report that a guest at the Claridge's had informed him that on the night of April 9 he heard the Cubans comment on the "effectiveness of the coup" and the "total success of the part they had been given to play." [emphasis added] According to the detective, that eyewitness was convinced that the Cubans were the well-paid instruments of those who had planned the political assassination [of Gaitán].[87]

It could be argued that the behavior of Castro and del Pino described above is not consistent with that of two agents entrusted with a secret mission. But it should not be forgotten that both agents were under 21 years of age and, at least Castro, had not taken a training course in such matters. Therefore, it is most likely that both were carried away by the strong emotions of the day.

For their part, Scotland Yard investigators made a similar mistake. Based on the information they had collected, the British concluded that the behavior of the two Cubans, who, as the investigators themselves stated, made themselves conspicuous, "was not that which might be expected of persons who were part of a dangerous conspiracy to commit murder."[88]

In their analysis, however, the investigators lost sight of the main element. One of the objectives of Castro and del Pino as agents provocateurs during the Bogotazo was precisely to be noticed in their supposed role as agents of communism in order to distract the attention of the authorities from the real agents involved in the operation.

Operation Bogotazo was the pretext used by the CFR conspirators to initiate in the United States what later became known as "the War Scare of 1948."[89] As such, Bogotazo was a limited psychological warfare operation that marked the beginning in the Western Hemisphere of a large-scale psychological warfare operation: the Cold War.

The Cold War soon proved to be extremely lucrative for oil tycoons, Wall Street bankers and top executives of transnational corporations. Just as they had done during the days of Nazi Germany, the bankers and corporations now padded their bank accounts by making handsome profits from lending money and selling armaments and military technology to both sides of the Cold War conflict.

All indications are that the Bogotazo riots, which were apparently a spontaneous outbreak of violence provoked by the assassination of Gaitán, had in fact been planned and prepared in advance. Gaitán's assassination was just a smokescreen that the conspirators used to hide their real causes.

8. The Assassinationof Gaitán

Although his true motives are still disputed, most who have studied Gaitán's assassination agree that the assassin was Juan Roa Sierra, an unemployed 25-year-old from a family of poor workers. What little information there is about Roa indicates that he was an introverted, lazy young man with delusions of grandeur. Although he sometimes got temporary jobs, he supported himself by cohabiting with a woman much older than him, who gave him some money for his subsistence. According to some of those who knew him, Roa's opinions were violently right-wing, but he was not known to have any political affiliation.[90]

On April 9, around 1:30 in the afternoon, on his way to have lunch with some friends, Gaitán was about to leave the Agustín Nieto building where he had his office when someone fired several shots at him. Several witnesses have recounted the event in considerable detail, but some of the versions contradict each other.

According to Guillermo Pérez Sarmiento, director of the United Press in Colombia,

> "I was in the Bar Tívoli, on the corner of San Francisco,
> in the company of Alberto Merino-Arquila and Armando
> Moyse, when we heard the shots, three one after the other,
> and the last one after a brief interval."[91]

Pérez Sarmiento continues his account of the event by adding that, a few minutes later, he went to the Granada drugstore, where the police had momentarily detained the suspect, and saw him, "between two policemen; he had turned his face greenish and seemed possessed by panic." [92]

Another eyewitness, Plinio Mendoza Neira, a close friend of Gaitán's who was with him at the time of the assassination, gave similar testimony:

> 'Suddenly I felt Gaitán pull back, as he tried to cover his
> face with his hands and tried to return to the building.
> Simultaneously I heard three consecutive shots and then
> another."[93]

For his part, Bogotá Police Detective No. 6, who was also near the scene of the events, adds a key piece of information about Roa Sierra. According to the detective, shortly before the murder,

> "I saw del Pino standing in the doorway of the Café Co-
> lombia, while talking with a poorly dressed individual
> whose photograph later appeared in the newspapers as
> that of Gaitán's assassin."[94]

Other sources confirm the detective's statement, and indicate that Castro and del Pino had met with Roa Sierra on several occasions in the days leading up to the assassination. A United Press report published in El Tiempo de Bogotá stated that, "A few days before the assassination, Roa was seen in the company of some people who looked like foreigners."[95]

Police officer Carlos Alberto Jiménez Díaz, who happened to be near the scene, stated that when he heard the shots he approached the alleged assassin from behind with the intention of stopping him. When he felt him, Roa spun on his heels, raised his hands and did not resist when the policeman took the gun he was still holding in his hand and disarmed him.[96]

Just after the policeman disarmed him, Roa exclaimed, "Don't kill me, corporal."[97] Shortly thereafter another policeman arrived at the scene of the crime and, in order to avoid the possibility of a lynching, the two made their way through the small group of people that had already formed and led Roa toward the Granada pharmacy, where they managed to enter a moment before a frightened employee lowered the iron grille.[98]

An employee of the pharmacy, Elías Quesada Anchicoque, then mentioned he had asked Roa, "Why have you committed this crime, to kill Dr. Gaitán?" to which the latter replied in a plaintive tone, "*Ay señor*, powerful things that I cannot tell you. *Ay, Virgen del Carmen*, save me!" The employee asked him again, "Tell me, who sent him to kill [Gaitán], because you at this moment are going to be lynched by the people." To which Roa replied, "I cannot."[99]

One of the authors who has most thoroughly investigated the details of Gaitán's assassination is Rafael Azula Barrera.[100] According to what he was told by an eyewitness who saw the alleged assassin a few moments after committing the crime, Juan Roa Sierra was a small, insignificant individual with a pale, angular, weak face. He had not shaved for several days and was wearing a gray overcoat and a blue tie with red stripes. He was trying to hide behind the iron grille of the Ganada pharmacy.[101] When a policeman asked him why he had fired the shots, Roa Sierra only replied: "The highest motives."[102]

Azula Barrera mentions how police efforts to save Roa were futile. The angry mob in front of the pharmacy soon grew and their threats forced the employees to raise the metal fence. They then began to beat Roa furiously and, a few moments later, had turned him into a wreck.

The mob killed the alleged murderer mercilessly and quickly. Demonstrating great cruelty, or a precise attempt to make him difficult to identify, they beat him to death, then kicked his face into a bloody, formless mass, unrecognizable. Then they stripped the corpse of its clothes and dragged it through the streets until they left it in front of the Presidential Palace.

However, Azula Barrera mentions that, from the first moment, there were doubts that the man killed by the mob was the real assassin. According to Azula Barrera, who at the time was Secretary General of the Colombian Presidency, shortly after the events, President Ospina Pérez and his top advisors discussed and analyzed the assassination, and came to the conclusion that Roa had been killed to silence him.[103]

But Azula, President Ospina and his advisors were not the only ones who had doubts about Roa Sierra's true role in Gaitán's assassination. Two weeks after the assassination, Milton Bracker of the *New York Times* wondered if Roa had had accomplices who had promised to protect him, but were actually there to silence him forever.[104]

Years later, Willard Beaulac, the U.S. ambassador to Colombia during the events, expressed a similar doubt in his memoirs:

> Did Roa act on his own, or was he an instrument of others? Was his action an ordinary crime, or was it politically motivated? These questions have yet to be answered.

Roa Sierra was beaten to death by witnesses to his crime a few minutes after he committed it. Was Roa killed by people so enraged by the crime he had committed that they were not afraid to take revenge at that very moment? Or was his death instigated or caused by people anxious that he would not live to state the reasons why he committed the crime?[105]

With time and the appearance of more trial elements, the doubts, far from disappearing, have increased. Among other things, there is the fact that Roa Sierra had never had military training, to the point that, when he bought the revolver with which he allegedly committed the murder, a friend of his named Luis Enrique Rincón Pardo was the one who tested it by firing a single shot. However, Alejandro Vallejo, who witnessed the murder, later testified that the assassin, still leaning against a stone edge, was "with his legs bent in a shooting position, revolver in hand."[106]

Jorge Padilla, another eyewitness, corroborated the above. According to Padilla, the murderer "had in his right hand the revolver with which he fired another shot. His left hand was resting against the door frame and his knees were bent."[107]

Plinio Mendoza Neira, one of Gaitán's companions who followed him a few steps behind, later stated that an individual he had seen when entering the building a short time before, was still in the same place and,

> "When Dr. Gaitán took his first step onto the street, in a northerly direction, the individual in question, moving quickly towards the northern bastion of the street, standing on the threshold, brought his arm forward and fired three consecutive and very rapid shots, the detonation of which I heard perfectly well."[108]

Mendoza Neira also stated he saw "clearly the body of the attacker and the movements of his arm in three different positions." However, he added, due to his position in relation to the assassin, he could not "perceive neither the weapon, nor the hand, nor the person he was shooting at", because a wall obstructed his vision.[109] Mendoza Neira continues his account of the events by stating how he lunged at the assailant, but the latter jumped onto the platform,

"When I stepped over the threshold, the man was a few steps away from him [Gaitán?], toward the north, with his back turned toward the northwest and his right arm extended forward and downward, firing a new shot at a human body lying on its back on the ground. That shot fired, the individual raised the weapon, a nickel-plated revolver, threatening us and then quickly ran north about twenty paces, after which he turned his body to face us again and again pointed the weapon at us. At that point a police officer grabbed him from behind."[110]

What is most interesting about Mendoza Neira's statement is that, although he was an eyewitness to the murder, he does not claim that the professional killer who fired the first three shots was the same person who, before the police officer grabbed him, had fired a shot at someone lying on the ground.

However, Julio Enrique Santos Forero, another eyewitness, reported that he heard several shots in a row and then saw "a man backing up and who fired a fourth shot, which I did see him fire" in the direction of the group of people leaving the building.[111]

For his part, Mendoza Neira added that the individual,

"When he fired, he appeared serene, impressively serene. ... The vision of seconds that I had of him, but that I remember with absolute precision, was that of shooting with serenity, with perfect tranquility, absolutely conscious of the situation."[112]

But Pascual del Vecchio, another eyewitness, offers a version that differs quite a bit from the above. According to del Vecchio, "the assassin had a hard face. He was pale and transfigured with emotion."[113]

However, another eyewitness, Alejandro Vallejo, adds several interesting details,

"The man I saw was a guy charged with passion in whose eyes shone a look of intense hatred. At that moment I thought he was a fanatic and that idea and the memory of this guy has not been erased from my imagination since then. The aggressive way he looked and the defiant attitude he retained after the fall of Dr. Gaitán, in the fact that he aimed at us, possibly shooting at us as well, in the serene way he stepped back and in the calm way he surrendered as soon as he saw a policeman."[114]

Pascual del Vecchio mentions that, when he arrived at the Nieto building where Gaitán's office was located, he saw an individual whom he thought was an employee. He then adds details about the rapid and inexplicable transformation that the individual manifested: When I entered [the building] that individual was in the most peaceful state. Then in the street he was already absolutely transformed, as if with a look of rage, exalted to the highest degree.[115]

The instantaneous change of the alleged killer also caught the attention of British investigators. According to the Scotland Yard report,

"The impression gained by some witnesses is that, at the moment of the murder, Roa was burning with passion, but all agree that, a moment later, he made no effort to try to escape, and appeared to surrender almost voluntarily."[116]

Two eyewitnesses, Alejandro Vallejo and Jorge Padilla, mention something interesting. According to Vallejo, "I heard three shots that did not seem to me to be from a revolver but from some artificial gunpowder fire."[117] Padilla confirms Vallejo's statement, "I heard two faint detonations that initially I did not take for two revolver shots but for totes."[118] It is also good to remember that another witness states that he saw Roa pointing his revolver at Gaitán after he lay prostrate on the ground.

But this is where things get a little more complicated. Other eyewitnesses claim that it was not one, but two individuals who participated in Gaitán's assassination.

According to statements by Pablo E. López, elevator operator of the Nieto building, since mid-March he had been struck by the presence of an individual "tall, dark, pale, with rather brown eyes, sprouting, rather than sunken, with a restless look, aquiline nose, about twenty-eight years of age." This individual visited the building about twenty times, sometimes going up by elevator and sometimes by stairway. When he used the elevator he went to the fourth floor, where Gaitán's office was located.[119]

The elevator operator added that on the day of the assassination, after half past twelve, this individual went up the stairs and then, when it was a quarter to one o'clock, he went down the elevator. On his way down he met another individual who was in the hallway of the building, smoking a cigarette which he was holding in his left hand, while the other was in the corresponding pocket of his pants. This individual, the one who went down the elevator, "joined the one who was downstairs, whom I had been seeing in that place since I entered to render my services as an elevator operator, and left with him."[120]

Another witness, Daniel Salomón Pérez, mentioned that on the day of the murder he was in the *Gato Negro* café having a glass of red wine and, as he was leaving the café, he passed two individuals entering the café. One of them aroused his curiosity because he was so nervous.[121]

Jorge Antonio Jiménez Higuera, another eyewitness, confirmed the presence of two individuals. According to Jiménez Higuera,

> "At about seven minutes past one o'clock ... I was able to observe the presence of two individuals at the door of the Agustín Nieto building, below the doorjamb, on either side of the gate. The individual who was on the south side, on fourteenth street, nodded his head to the one on the north or right side, as if indicating the exit of Dr. Gaitán."[122]

Jiménez Higuera added that the assassin was "a young guy, rather short in stature; slightly pale brownish", but the other guy was "a little taller and thinner than the assassin, older than the assassin", that was "the one who made the signal to the assassin."[123] Another witness, Julio Enrique Santos Forero, describes the second individual as "a tall man, not stocky, rather sinewy."[124]

Santos Forero, who witnessed Roa's death, stated that when he saw the individual the mob was beating for killing Gaitán, he noticed that this was not the assassin he had seen shot, and he told his friends: "That's not him, this is another one."[125] According to Santos Forero, "this individual was much shorter than the one I had seen being held by the police. Jorge Padilla also confirmed the fact that the alleged assassin and the one he saw in action were two different people.

Santos Forero added that, when he heard the cries of the mob clamoring to kill the assassin, he shouted to them, "No, this wretch serves us well alive, let's not kill him, this is not him", because it seemed to him that this individual was totally different from the one he had previously seen held by the policeman, who was dark and taller, and he believed him to be the real assassin of Gaitán.[126]

Pascual del Vecchio, another witness who managed to enter the pharmacy, thought the same as Santos Forero. When he saw that two strange men entered the pharmacy and began to furiously hit the presumed assassin in the head with a blunt object, he thought that what they were trying to do was to eliminate him so that he would not talk. That is why he approached the crowd and shouted to them, "Don't kill him, so that he will confess and hand him over to justice."

But del Vecchio recalled that his friend Antonio Izquierdo Toledo, governor of Cundinamarca and friend of Gaitán, called him aside and told him, "Pascual don't be crazy. They could assassinate you. Those are agents of the plot."[127]

Another witness who was present in the pharmacy, Carlos Alberto Jiménez Díaz, observed that the presumed assassin, "He seemed very frightened to me. He did not protest the blows he was receiving, but rather seemed resigned to his situation, that is to say, he accepted the fact that caused the public to protest."[128] Luis Eduardo Ricaurte, another witness, confirmed the above, and added: "The man was with a fixed gaze, livid, mute."[129]

A few days before the murder, Roa Sierra had told his mother and some relatives and friends that he was trying to obtain a driver's license to work as a driver and bodyguard for some foreigners, who had offered him a trip to Los Llanos to explore the possibility of exploiting a gold mine there.[130] Those same foreigners had given him the money to buy a revolver, because Los Llanos was a region where there were many wild animals and Indians.[131]

Roa's mother also revealed that, shortly before the events, her son had been very interested in the Rosicrucian organization, as well as that he had been consulting with a German hand reader.

9. Gaitán's Assassin: A Manchurian Candidate?

Two essential things can be inferred from the witness statements. First, that at least two individuals participated in the assassination of Gaitán. One of them, probably Roa Sierra, is described as short, dark-skinned, poorly dressed, nervous, hateful and out of control. The other was taller, thin, light-skinned, well-dressed, fully in control of his actions, and acted like a professional assassin.

Secondly, that only seconds after the murder was committed, Roa Sierra immediately and without transition went from an agitated and violent emotional state to one of depression and inaction - in a second, the individual transformed from a raging tiger to a meek dove. But, although seemingly inexplicable, such rapid and radical behavioral changes are easy to explain if we have the key: mind control.

My interpretation of the Gaitán assassination is that Roa Sierra was a Manchurian Candidate, a predecessor of Lee Harvey Oswald, Sirhan B. Sirhan, James Earl Ray, Mark David Chapman and John Hinckley, Jr. the patsies who, years later, had similar involvement in the assassinations of U.S. President John F. Kennedy, his brother Robert, Martin Luther King, Jr. and John Lennon, as well as the one who tried to assassinate President Ronald Reagan and brought George H.W. Bush within a whisker of becoming president. Bush one step away from becoming President of the United States.

True to the saying that he who speaks much is wrong, Fidel Castro himself exposed years later, perhaps unwittingly, his suspicions, or knowledge, of the use of a Manchurian candidate in the Gaitán assassination. According to Castro,

> "The oligarchy kills because it organizes a conspiracy to kill someone or because it organizes a whole campaign and creates *psychological conditions* for someone to kill a political figure." [emphasis added][133]

The term "Manchurian Candidate," [133] used to designate a killer who has been hypnotically conditioned to commit a crime under mind control, came into use in 1959, when author Richard Condon used it as the title of his successful novel, which was later made into a movie with Frank Sinatra as the main character. Although in the novel the hypnotically conditioned person is the one who commits the murder, in the cases of Roa, Oswald, and Sirhan, all indications are that these Manchurian candidates played the dual role of decoys and scapegoats who drew attention to themselves while the real killers committed the crime.[134]

This is essentially my theory of Roa Sierra as a Manchurian candidate
.

Nevertheless, the idea of hypnotically conditioning an individual to commit criminal acts that he would not consciously do is not new. It is known that as early as September 1942, the Office of Special Services (OSS) had begun mind control experiments in search of a drug that would force prisoners under interrogation, such as captured German U-boat crewmen, to reveal military secrets.[135] In May 1943, OSS officers began using THC acetate (tetrahydrocannabinol, a derivative of marijuana) to elicit information from individuals who refused to cooperate with interrogation. OSS officials referred to THC acetate simply as "TD", a cryptonym for "truth drug."[136]

However, it was not until after the CIA was created in 1947 that the U.S. Navy began the secret CHATTER project, which was the first serious experiment to try to obtain a truth serum. In 1949 the CIA began a similar project, which it called BLUEBIRD, involving some Nazi scientists that the conspirators had managed to bring secretly from Germany through what they called Operation Paperclip.

According to Roa Sierra's mother, in the weeks prior to the assassination, her son had visited no less than nine times the office of Johan Umland Gert, a German astrologer living in Bogotá.[137] Gert not only predicted Roa's future based on the stars, but also gave him money.[138] It was also Gert who first told Roa about the Rosicrucian organization.

Roa's mother also said that, shortly before the events, her son had begun to behave strangely: he had quit his job, had become pensive, as if daydreaming, and sometimes laughed by himself for no reason. Lately he had begun to complain of severe headaches, and that "his head felt as if he were frying corn."[139]

But it is difficult to explain how Roa, who had no job and no source of livelihood, could get money to pay for the consultations of an astrologer. Even more difficult to explain is that it was the astrologer who paid Roa for his visits. Therefore, one has to try to find an explanation for the Gert-Roa relationship from a totally different perspective.[140]

It is quite possible that it was Gert who conditioned Roa under hypnotism to commit the crime (or acted as if he had committed the crime), or that he collaborated with a CIA psychiatrist in the process. It should not be forgotten that Umland Gert was German and that, through Operation Paperclip, the CIA had brought many Nazi scientists to the United States, including many who had been working on secret mind control experiments in Nazi Germany.

In fact, Roa Sierra's mother found that visits to Umland's office had greatly affected her son's behavior. Umland had apparently been suggesting to her son that he was the reincarnation of Gonzalo

Jimenez de Quesada, the founder of the city of Bogotá. This worried her so much that she visited Umland to complain, but the German made such a good impression on her that she dismissed the possibility that Umland was trying to harm her son. Roa's last visit to Umland's office was on April 7, two days before Gaitán's assassination.[141]

William Turner, an author who analyzed the assassination of Robert Kennedy, mentioned the possibility that his alleged assassin may have been a Manchurian candidate who acted programmed under hypnotic suggestion.[142] Turner studied in detail the symptoms of hypnotic conditioning. According to Turner, the main symptoms are, a dramatic change in the personality of the individual and a state of total concentration at the moment of committing the murder, which is manifested mainly in the subject's eyes.

Then, only a moment after the crime is committed, the subject manifests symptoms of leaving the hypnotic state: the individual appears disoriented, with no clear idea of what has just happened. This state is the result of posthypnotic amnesic barriers implanted in the subject's mind by the hypnotist.[143] If we go by eyewitness accounts, Roa evidenced all the symptoms of hypnotic conditioning mentioned by Turner.

Another interesting detail is that in *Mind Control: America's Secret War*, the first part of DVD number 2 of *Inside the CIA: Secrets Revealed*, a documentary produced by the History Channel, an uncle of Sirhan B. Sirhan, the alleged assassin of Robert Kennedy, mentions that, in the months prior to the assassination, his nephew had become a member of the Rosicrucians. This may be just a coincidence - or maybe not.

In April 1943, Dr. Albert Hofman, a scientist working for Sandoz Laboratories in Switzerland, discovered by chance the psychedelic properties of LSD, a substance he himself had succeeded in synthesizing five years earlier.[144] Hofman had unknowingly opened the door to chemical mind control.

It is now known that, at the same time that Hofman was conducting his experiments in Switzerland, several OSS scientists, including Dr. Winfred Overholser, director of St. Elizabeth's Hospital in Washington, D.C., were conducting similar experiments using cannabis indica, a drug popularly known as marijuana.[145] At the same time, Nazi doctors in the service of the Gestapo were conducting similar mind control experiments using prisoners from the Dachau concentration camp as guinea pigs.[146]

When the CIA was created in 1947, the OSS mind control experiments continued, and were made official in April 1950 by CIA Director Admiral Roscoe Hillenkoetter when he approved a new secret project called BLUEBIRD.[147] A few years later BLUEBIRD was renamed ARTICHOKE and, in April 1953, with the creation of MK-ULTRA, a super-secret project dedicated to the study of psychological warfare, ARTICHOKE became part of it.

The person appointed to head MK-ULTRA was Dr. Sidney Gottlieb, who later gained some notoriety when it became known that he had been the person who produced the poison to assassinate African leader Patrick Lumumba. The MK-ULTRA project had a much broader perspective and, while maintaining its emphasis on the study of ways to achieve mind control of experimental subjects, was not limited to psychedelic drugs. MK-ULTRA's experiments included hypnosis, lobotomy, electroshock, sensory deprivation, drug use and sexual abuse.[148]

All indications point to the possibilty that Roa Sierra was not only a Manchurian candidate but also a scapegoat —the patsy whose role was to take the blame for Gaitán's assassination. Most likely, the assassin was a professional assassin in the service of the CIA, whose weapon was fitted with a silencer —which explains the mystery of the muffled sound of the initial shots that caused Gaitán's death.

As in the case of the assassination of Lee Harvey Oswald, the alleged assassin of President Kennedy, Roa's murder was part of a plan to prevent the authorities from being able to interrogate Gaitán's alleged assassin. If Roa fired any of the shots, which is debatable, it was most likely the last one, as Gaitán's body lay face down on the ground.

It is a common saying among the military that the first time is a coincidence, the second a coincidence and the third an enemy action. But in the field of intelligence and espionage there are no coincidences. Intelligence officers, and especially counterintelligence officers, do not allow for coincidences or coincidences. For them, all coincidences and coincidences are potentially misleading, and are seen as enemy action.

In example, the fact that Castro and del Pino had an interview with Gaitán scheduled to take place only a few hours after the assassination occurred could be just a coincidence. However, a number of facts must be taken into account.

First, Castro had been recruited by the CIA a few weeks earlier. Second, that in the days leading up to the Bogotazo Castro made himself conspicuous by drawing the attention of the authorities by acting as an obvious agent provocateur.[149] Third, that in the days leading up to the Bogotazo Castro made himself conspicuous by acting as an obvious agent provocateur.

Third, that in the days prior to the assassination Castro and del Pino had been seen in the company of the alleged assassin. Fourth, that it appears that Castro and del Pino were the ones who gave Roa the idea to buy a firearm and supplied him with the money to buy it. Finally, the fact that Castro and del Pino were so close to the scene when the crime occurred would make even the most naive intelligence officer suspect that they had a hand in the murder.[150]

It is impossible to know with certainty what role Fidel Castro played by his presence so close to the scene of Gaitán's assassination. According to a secret U.S. Embassy report, Fidel Castro had acted as a watcher or finger-man for the assassins of Manolo Castro.[151] That may have been one of the tasks given to him by his handlers in the CIA in the Gaitán assassination. However, knowing Castro's psychopathic nature[152] and his penchant for assassination, I am inclined to believe that, in violation of his orders, he did it just for show.

With the assassination of Gaitán the CFR conspirators killed several birds with one stone. First, they got rid of a nationalist leader and a potential enemy they feared. Gaitán had played an important role after the "banana massacre" in the Magdalena region, when United Fruit workers went on strike in 1928 and were eventually massacred by army troops.

Gaitán took up the defense of the workers and accused the government of being a puppet of the North American capitalists, and this brought him national fame. Obviously, his intervention in the events earned him the enmity of some important members of the Council on Foreign Relations who had close ties with United Fruit, among them David and Nelson Rockefeller, as well as Allen and John Foster Dulles.

In a report dated March 16, 1946, John C. Wiley, U.S. Ambassador to Colombia, commented to the State Department that, regarding Gaitán, at the Embassy, "We view his political triumphs with considerable apprehension. Those who know him assure us that he does not love the United States."

Second, if Gaitán had become president of Colombia, he would have created countless headaches for the CFR conspirators. Amparo Jaramillo, Gaitán's widow, recounts that, upon learning of the assassination, she went to her husband's office to try to save some documents on the role of President Ospina Pérez and Shell in relation to the exploitation of Colombia's oil, which Gaitán intended to expose to the people, only to find that the office had been ransacked.[153]

Thus, the conspirators used Gaitán's assassination to incite the masses to join a riot they had prepared in advance. Finally, by blaming the local Communists and, by extension, the Soviet Union, they created an excellent ideological pretext to force Latin American countries to create the OAS, an instrument of imperial domination, and to justify the beginning of the Cold War they had so carefully planned.

However, I will not make the mistake of the leftists of blaming the CIA and insinuating that the KGB and local Communists were innocent bystanders to the events. We cannot ignore that the Soviet Communists also have their long list of dirty tricks carried out against the peoples of the world and the Russian people themselves.

Nor do I rule out the possibility that the Communists had their own plans to harass the Conference. But everything indicates that the assassination of Gaitán and the magnitude of the disturbances took them by surprise. This was evidenced by the state of confusion displayed by the Colombian Communists, as well as their inability to gain political advantage from the Bogotazo.[154]

A secret report produced by the Intelligence Division of the U.S. General Staff, dated May 13, 1948, reached similar conclusions. According to the report,

> "There is abundant evidence that the Communists had devised various methods of interfering with the conduct of the Conference, including mass demonstrations, a general strike, inciting a student group, and possible sabotage. However, while there is no doubt that they were well prepared to take advantage of the situation, and did so, it does not seem possible that they would have succeeded in inciting more than minor disturbances (which would probably have been controlled by the police) had it not been for the spontaneous reaction of the Bogotá mobs as a result of [Gaitán's] assassination."[155]

So everything indicates that, at least in this operation, the CFR conspirators were much more efficient than the KGB.

In his interview with Fidel Castro, Arturo Alape asked him: "Comandante, why do you think they killed Gaitán? Castro's long answer is highly revealing, so I am going to quote it in detail:

"Imagine, I cannot make a categorical statement. Gaitán could have been killed by the CIA, for example, imperialism could have killed Gaitán as an exponent of a progressive movement. ... Gaitán could have been killed by a fanatic, it is possible. ... I repeat, Gaitán could have been killed as a result of an imperialist plan, of an oligarchic plan, or it could have been the result of the individual action of a fanatic. ... I have no elements of judgment to tell you that it was the CIA or imperialism who killed him, although knowing all the activity and all the policy of the CIA and imperialism, a popular leader like Gaitán could have been assassinated by the CIA."[156]

Castro's response, in which he mentions several times the possibility of CIA involvement in Gaitán's assassination, could be mistakenly interpreted as evidence that Castro had no involvement in the assassination. However, it is good to remember that one of the uses to which the conspirators have put the CIA is as a scapegoat: to take the blame for the crimes committed by their hidden masters.

What is most remarkable about what Castro says about the CIA is that he portrays the Agency as an autonomous entity or as a dependency of an abstract "U.S. imperialism." But he does not mention that the CIA is a creation of the oil tycoons and Wall Street bankers and that, like himself, it has always worked for them.

10. New Pieces of the Puzzle

As a confirmation of the forensic principle that every contact leaves a trace,[157] many years after the events of April 9, 1948, an important piece of this historical puzzle called the Bogotazo appeared in the most unexpected place: a prison in Cuba.

In late 1980, General José Abrahantes, at the time head of Cuba's Ministry of the Interior, ordered one of his officers, intelligence captain Carlos Cajaraville, later in exile in Florida, to interrogate a prisoner who had asked to be released in exchange for valuable information.[158] The prisoner was an American citizen named John Mepples (or MacMepples) Spiritto, who was serving a sentence in a Cuban prison for having collaborated in the early 1960s with some anti-Castro guerrilla groups in the Escambray mountains, in central Cuba.[159]

According to Spiritto, who claimed to have worked for the CIA, in 1947 he had been sent to Colombia as part of Operation PANTO-

MIME, a plan aimed at neutralizing or, failing that, physically eliminating Gaitán. Apparently, the intelligence officers who interrogated
Spiritto concluded that the information he had provided was true,
because shortly thereafter he was released and the Cuban government provided him with a modern apartment in Havana's beautiful
Vedado neighborhood.

Some years later, several Cuban counterintelligence officers
working on a documentary film thought of the propaganda potential
of the information Spiritto had provided and decided to exploit it.
Their plan was to use Spiritto in the documentary, which they had
titled Pantomima,[160] to discredit the CIA.

Spiritto, who spoke fluent Spanish, mentions in the documentary how in 1947 the CIA sent him on a top secret mission to Colombia. His orders were to try to buy Gaitán by making him an offer so
tempting that he could not refuse. This consisted of offering him a
large sum of money and a professorship at a university in Rome or
Paris.

But, to his surprise, Gaitán rejected the offer. Spiritto reported
the failure to Thomas Elliot, his senior CIA chief in Bogotá. Elliot
then ordered him to try to neutralize Gaitán by other means, including his physical elimination.

Two years after Spiritto was interviewed, Major Manuel Piñeiro
(Barbarroja), head of the America Department, the section of Cuban
intelligence in charge of counterintelligence operations against the
United States, contacted Gloria, Gaitán's daughter, and invited her
to come to Havana and watch the interview with Spiritto for the
documentary. Piñeiro wanted to know if what Spiritto had stated
matched what Gloria remembered about her father.

Shortly thereafter, Gloria traveled to Havana and watched the
film. To her surprise, she discovered that what Spiritto had mentioned about trying to bribe her father by offering him money and a
professorship at a European university, as well as a luxurious apartment in the city of his choice, coincided perfectly with what her
father had told his family privately in 1947, and that only they knew
about it. Gloria Gaitán was not the only one who corroborated the
veracity of the information provided by Spiritto. According to
Cajaraville, who participated in Spiritto's interrogations, "the details he gave [about Gaitán's assassination] were astounding. Some
of them we confirmed with our friends in Colombia."[161]

In the interview, Spiritto "confesses that he had organized the
assassination of Gaitán, with U.S. embassy officials in Bogotá, using Roa Sierra as the physical assassin."[152] According to what Gloria

Gaitán herself later stated in an interview,

"On a trip to Cuba, in the years of 1961 or 1962, Comandante Piñeiro, whom everyone called Red Beard, invited me to see a film of a statement by a CIA agent who claimed to have been part of the plot to assassinate my father, Jorge Eliécer Gaitán.

"In the original, unedited version, which was the one I saw, the agent went into details about the first stage advanced by Tomás Elliot to try to bribe my father to abandon politics. I suffered an attack of tachycardia that forced the temporary suspension of the projection, since the CIA agent was relating a fact that I had known directly from my father's mouth.

"In fact, in 1947, Dad came home for lunch one day and told Mom, in my presence, he had been offered a professorship in criminal law at the Sorbonne in Paris or at the University of Rome, guaranteeing him the ownership of a splendid apartment in one of the most luxurious neighborhoods of those cities. They would also give him an immense estate in the Sabana de Bogotá and another in the Eastern Plains, and would grant him the necessary financing so that his children could, for the rest of their lives, study in the colleges or universities of their choice in Europe. This last part was the one that did not allow me to forget the matter, because I insisted on insisting to my father to abandon politics so that I could go to study in the Old Continent. Mom, sometimes, told me that it was a pity that my father had not let himself be tempted, because that would have saved his life.

"The shock I received was tremendous, when I began to hear from that man's lips the description of each and every one of the bribery proposals that I already knew. The agent, instead of talking about the Llanos, referred to "the Colombian pampas", but the rest was identical, in the same words, as my father had related it. I asked Piñeiro for a copy and we agreed that he would give it to me before my return to Colombia."[163]

As she expressed in her interview, Gloria asked Piñeiro to give her a copy of the film, but then, most likely after having consulted with Castro, Piñeiro refused to give it to her, arguing that it could cause them political problems with the Colombian government.

For his part, journalist Arturo Alape mentions that when he was in Cuba in 1982 researching for his book on the Bogotazo, Gabriel García Márquez mentioned to him the existence of the documentary, which had now been titled Operation Triangle. In 1983 Alape visited Havana again, and managed to get the documentary shown to him. Although the Cubans refused to provide him with a copy, Alape claims he managed to secretly make a copy of the audio, which he then transcribed. Alape provided a copy of the transcript to Gloria Gaitán, who donated it to the archives of the Centro de Documentación de la Casa Gaitán in Bogotá.[164]

By this time, however, the production of the documentary had encountered some unexpected problems. Apparently, the Cuban intelligence officers in charge of making the documentary, who like all intelligence officers around the world have been trained to spot inconsistencies and anomalies, had noticed that Castro was mentioned over and over again in the documentary, most of the time doing things that were difficult to explain. Therefore, knowing how things are in Castro's Cuba, they decided that, in order to avoid problems, it was best not to go ahead with the production of the documentary.

According to Cajaraville, the intelligence officers working on the production of the documentary feared that it would not be to Castro's liking[165] —something in Cuba has proven to be extremely damaging to your health. So the documentary was declared secret for national security reasons and permanently shelved.

Several years later, while visiting Havana, Alape was invited by a Cuban intelligence officer to visit Spiritto at his apartment in Vedado. During the visit, Spiritto denied the information he had given in the documentary interview, claiming that he had simply lied to get out of prison. This was the excuse Alape later offered when someone criticized him for not including Spiritto's confession in his *book El Bogotazo: Memories of Oblivion.*[166]

Alape recounts that when he was finishing his book, "García Márquez told me personally that Spiritto's document was not reliable for the Cuban authorities, that for that reason he was warning me about its publication." According to Alape, that was the reason why "having the transcript of such a document at hand", the Spiritto interview was never published.[167] But what Alape does not explain is why he published in its entirety the interview he did with Fidel Castro, which, as I have shown above, is totally uninformative and false.

Moreover, Alape's explanation does not fit the facts, because he knew perfectly well that Gloria Gaitán, based on the confidential information of the offer that the CIA agent had made to her father, had come to the conclusion that what Spiritto had stated was true. Therefore, a more plausible explanation that is more in line with the reality of the facts is required.

Most likely, Alape, who belonged to the legion of Latin American journalists[168] and intellectuals who admired Castro because they believed he has strongly opposed U.S. imperialism, did not want to hurt the feelings of his admired tyrant. Moreover, his book was published by Casa de la Americas, an institution controlled by Castro's intelligence services, and not following García Márquez's advice (or veiled threat?) would have meant that his book would not have been published.

Therefore, one must conclude that Alape, showing opportunism of the worst kind, did not include Spiritto's interview in his book out of pure political expediency. In doing so, he committed not only an act of unforgivable intellectual dishonesty, but, by concealing a key document in this history, he also betrayed the memory of Gaitán and the thousands of Colombians who lost their lives in the Bogotazo and the Violence that followed.

Because of his desire to serve as a megaphone to spread Fidel Castro's falsehoods, Alape's book is one of the books that has done the most damage to the Colombian people and the peoples of Latin America. That book, which has circulated widely, has contributed like no other to present Fidel Castro as an anti-imperialist hero and not as what he really is: a traitor at the service of the worst imperialist interests of the oil tycoons, the Wall Street bankers and the executives of the transnational corporations that control U.S. policy.

In 1994, taking the opportunity of Castro's visit to Colombia, Gloria Gaitán met with him and asked him to give her a copy of the documentary. But, to her surprise, Castro flatly denied the existence of the documentary, the confession and even the existence of Spiritto. When Gloria rebutted him, telling him that she had a copy of the soundtrack of the documentary, Castro became angry and, according to Gloria, they got into a rather heated argument.[169]

But that was not the end of this convoluted real-life espionage novel.[170] According to Gloria Gaitán, in 1993 she was contacted by Dr. Yesid Castaño and informed that Dr. Antonio Robayo, owner of the Kokorico restaurant chain, possessed certain information that a close friend, CIA agent Thomas Elliot, had left him before he died of cancer. This is the same Thomas Elliot that Spiritto mentioned in his confession as his superior CIA boss who had ordered him to try to bribe Gaitán or, failing that, to physically eliminate him.

Castaño assured Gloria that the information, which contained photos of the surveillance they had subjected Gaitán to, included all the documentation on the preparation of the assassination of her father. Castaño assured Gloria that Dr. Robayo was willing to provide the documentation. However, Gloria claimed that it was impossible to reach Robayo, and that he never responded to her calls.[171] Unfortunately, shortly after Dr. Castaño contacted Gloria, Dr. Robayo was killed in an assassination attempt on him at the El Nogal Club.

However, there is one important fact that does not appear in most of the information that has been published about Spiritto. According to other sources, in the early 1950s, Spiritto began working on ARTICHOKE, a top-secret CIA project dedicated to the study of mind control methods.[172]

After learning of Spiritto's active participation in the Gaitán assassination, in which Roa Sierra was used as a Manchurian candidate, it is logical to conclude that it was his first-hand experience that influenced his superiors to put him to work on the ARTICHOKE project, a program whose objective was precisely the creation of psychologically programmed assassins.

But this is where things get a little more complicated.

In his autobiography *Vivir para contarla*, Colombian writer Gabriel García Márquez states that he was an eyewitness to the murder of Roa Sierra at the hands of the angry mob. According to García Márquez,

"Fifty years later, my memory is still fixed on the image of the man who seemed to instigate the crowd in front of the pharmacy, and I have not found him in any of the countless testimonies I have read about that day. I had seen him up close, with a classy dress, an alabaster skin and a millimetric control of his actions. So much did he catch my attention that I kept my eye on him until he was picked up in a too-new car as soon as the killer's corpse was taken away, and from then on he seemed erased from historical memory. Even from my own, until many years later, in my time as a journalist, when I was struck by the idea that the man had managed to have a false assassin killed to protect the identity of the real one."[173]

Memory does not fail García Márquez, because Gaitán's widow remembers something very similar. According to Amparo Jaramillo de Gaitán,

"It was not the people, it was not Juan Roa Sierra who assassinated him, but a guy who was divinely dressed (sic) in front of the office. It was not Roa Sierra, and it was from a café in front of the office that the shots came from."[174]

This version of events, expressed repeatedly by Gaitán's widow, also coincides with the testimony of Yesid Castaño. Gloria Gaitán collected Castaño's testimony and presented it in April 1998 at a press conference at the Instituto Colombiano de la Participación Jorge Eliécer Gaitán. According to Gloria Gaitán, Yesid Castaño told her that Dr. Robayo had received from a CIA agent photographs of the crime scene showing the elegantly dressed man mentioned by García Márquez and Amparo Jaramillo, who was shouting to the rioters to lynch the alleged perpetrator of the assassination.[175]

11. The Mysterious James Jesus Angleton

As of today no one has been able to discover who the mystery man was, but the suspicion of García Márquez and Gaitán's widow that the elegant mystery man took part in the assassination makes perfect sense.

Azula Barrera expressed the suspicion that the elegant mystery man was Enrique Ovares, president of the Student Federation of the School of Architecture and Secretary General of the University Student Federation.[176] Ovares was one of the legitimate leaders of the University of Havana who traveled to Bogotá to counter the presence of Fidel Castro, who had illegitimately appropriated the representation of the FEU. In fact, photos of Ovares taken at the time bear some resemblance to the description that has been offered of the individual who inflamed the mob with his shouts to kill Roa.

However, the mere fact that Ovares is pictured to the right of Castro in one of the best known photos of the Bogotazo eliminates that possibility. Garcia Marquez must have seen that photo, and he would have immediately recognized Ovares, and the elegant mystery would have ceased to be a mystery. Therefore, that possibility must be ruled out.

For my part, I have a suspicion —and so far it remains just that: a suspicion, albeit based on circumstantial evidence, some of which I have so far been unable to corroborate directly— that the mysterious elegant individual who incited the mob to kill Roa Sierra was none other than James Jesus Angleton, a former OSS officer who had begun working for the CIA, and a personal friend of Allen Dulles - and, therefore, a confidant of the CFR conspirators. A few years later, Angleton was appointed head of CIA counterintelligence.

Without a doubt, James Jesus Angleton is one of the most colorful personalities in the world of intelligence and espionage. His life and career have been chronicled in several books and articles,[177] as well as in a novel.[178] To paraphrase Churchill's well-known description of Soviet foreign policy,[179] Angleton's life is a classic mystery wrapped in an enigma. Richard Helms, one of the CIA's senior executives, called him "a strange man; very strange."[180]

But it seems that, despite so much scrutiny by brilliant minds, CFR undercover agent James Jesus Angleton outwitted everyone. Behind his deceptive facade of mystery, intellectualism, and patriotism, Angleton was not only a traitor, but also a common criminal - one more among the many professional criminals that the CFR conspirators used time and again to carry out their secret plans to implement their treacherous domestic and international policies.

I base my suspicion that Angleton was the mysterious elegiac mentioned by Garcia Marquez on several different pieces of information:

First, in 1947 Angleton physically closely matched the description mentioned by several witnesses of the individual who incited the rioters to kill Roa. He also fit the description given by Gaitán's secretary of the unidentified individual who, in the days leading up to the assassination, twice accompanied Roa on his visits to Gaitán's office. According to Gaitán's secretary, Roa was accompanied,

By another man, tolerably well dressed, of somewhat aggressive appearance and bulging eyes. On these occasions, it was the latter, not Juan Roa Sierra, who spoke in an attempt to obtain an interview [with Gaitán][181]

The description of the mysterious individual offered by Gaitán's secretary is very close to the physical description of Angleton at the time given by one of his biographers.[182] It also fits the description of the elegant mystery man offered by García Márquez and Gaitán's widow.

Second, because it is clear that the mystery man played an important role in this top-secret operation, and Angleton was one of the few men trusted by Allen Dulles, who was himself an agent of the Rockefellers. During World War II, Angleton was one of the OSS's top counterintelligence officers in Italy, taking direct orders from Allen Dulles. One of the few known photographs of Angleton,[183] shows him carrying the urn containing Dulles' ashes, an honor that would only be bestowed on one of the deceased's closest friends.

Although most biographies and articles about Angleton portray him as a hero of American counterintelligence, the truth is that he was nothing more than a common criminal with no moral or ethical principles. Angleton played a cardinal role in laundering Nazi money, as well as, in collusion with the Vatican, creating an escape route for the rats escaping from the sinking Nazi ship.[184]

Third, because his mother was Mexican, and although Angleton was not fully fluent in Spanish, he at least spoke it fluently enough to pass himself off briefly as a native speaker of the language. Angleton was the son of an American cavalry officer, James Hugh Angleton, who participated in the invasion of Mexico with General Pershing's troops in an attempt to capture Pancho Villa. In Mexico, James Hugh fell in love with Carmen Mercedes Moreno,[185] a beautiful Mexican woman he met in the border town of Nogales. Shortly thereafter they were married, and, demonstrating his Catholic faith, he gave his son the name Jesus, pronounced "Jesús" as in Spanish.

In an interview she gave to Tom Mangold for his biography of Angleton, Carmen mentioned that, as a child, her son had been very attached to his maternal grandmother Mercedes, who did not speak English. This is evidence that, from an early age, Angleton had some command of the Spanish language.[186]

Fourth, because there is a period in Angleton's life when it is not clear where he was and, strangely, this period coincides with the events of the Bogotazo. According to his biography, during World War II Angleton, who was an OSS officer in Europe, remained separated from his wife Cicely and their newborn son, to the point that she had begun divorce proceedings. But in 1947, Angleton began writing to her again, returned to the U.S., and they resumed their marital relations.[187]

In early 1948, Angleton moved to Tucson, Arizona, to live with his wife and son. From January to June he lived with them at his wife's parents' home. In July, Angleton accepted an important position in the CIA, as senior assistant to the director of the Office of Special Operations, and Angleton and his family moved to Washington, D.C.[188] However, the only source for this information is his wife, Cicely Angleton, in an interview she gave to Jeff Goldberg on March 3, 1989.[189]

But there is something that does not fit this version of events. Angleton's personnel file at the CIA indicates that, although he officially began working for the Agency on December 30, 1947, he was granted a seven-month leave with pay to stay with his wife in Tucson before he assumed his new position at the CIA.[190]

However, there is evidence that during the leave time that the CIA had theoretically granted him, Angleton was in charge of performing important duties for the Agency. According to some sources, Angleton played an important role in a CIA covert operation in Italy aimed at preventing the Communists from winning the elections that were to take place on April 18, 1948.[191]

So Angleton secretly traveled to Italy to do counterintelligence work when he theoretically had a CIA permit to stay with his family in Tucson. Consequently, Angleton also had the time and opportunity to travel secretly to Colombia under a false identity and passport, carry out a much more secret mission than the one in Italy, the assassination of Gaitán, and return to Italy or Tucson without anyone missing him before moving to Washington, DC.

Fifth, because as an OSS officer who had actively participated in the war, Angleton had the military training necessary to have been the professional assassin who, using a gun fitted with a silencer, fired the first shots that caused Gaitán's death.

Sixth, because first in the OSS and then in the CIA, Angleton was directly involved in two secret projects studying mind control techniques: BLUEBIRD and ARTICHOKE.

Moreover, the Gaitán assassination was not the only time Angleton participated in a secret operation to assassinate an enemy of the Wall Street bankers. He also played a major role in the assassination of U.S. President John F. Kennedy.[192] In 1964, a few hours after Mary Pinchot was murdered near her Georgetown home, Angleton forced a window and broke into her home like a common criminal and stole her personal diary. Pinchot, a 43-year-old artist, was one of Kennedy's secret lovers, and the CFR conspirators feared that her diary might contain some incriminating reference connecting them to the assassination. That is why they sent a person of their absolute confidence to destroy the evidence: James Jesus Angleton.

As payment for his work on behalf of the Wall Street bankers, in 1954 CIA Director Allen Dulles had appointed Angleton head of the Agency's counterintelligence section. But the CIA's counterintelligence chief was also a criminal of the worst kind, which is why the CFR conspirators trusted him and continued to use him on sensitive and compromising missions.

But there is another, much more important element that connects, at least indirectly, Angleton to the Gaitán assassination: Angleton played a role similar to the one I have described above, in the Kennedy assassination.

According to well-informed sources, long before Kennedy's assassination, Angleton was in contact with Lee Harvey Oswald, the President's alleged assassin.[193] According to these researchers, Angleton sent Oswald to the Soviet Union on a super-secret mission to demonstrate to the Soviets how easy it was to shoot down a U-2 spy plane.

As a member of the U.S. military, Oswald had worked for some time at Atsugi Naval Air Base in Japan, used by some of the U-2s flying over the Soviet Union. Possibly Oswald explained to the Soviets that the U-2 was nothing but a sophisticated glider, with huge balsa wood wings, and that only by exploding anti-aircraft missiles 100 to 150 meters away would the plane be shot down. Proof that no missile detonated directly against the plane is that the pilot, Francis Gary Powers, did not perish and the wreckage of the plane showed no signs of having been shot down by an explosive.[194]

One might ask, why did the Americans themselves want their enemies to shoot down one of their planes? Simply because, as I have explained above, the Cold War was a hoax, and the CFR conspirators who control American politics needed to keep it hot. But Nikita Khrushchev, with his new policy of peaceful coexistence, threatened to cool it down. To that end, the Soviet Premier was preparing for a meeting in Paris with American President Dwight Eisenhower. Everyone hoped that the meeting would result in a cooling of tensions between the two countries.

But the downing of the U-2, and Eisenhower's admission that his mission was to spy on the Soviet Union, prompted Khrushchev to cancel his participation in the meeting. This was used by the conspirator-controlled press to inflame the gullible American public and as a justification for increased war budgets, which directly benefited the U.S. military-industrial complex controlled by Wall Street bankers.

However, that was not the only mission Angleton gave Oswald. It seems that Lee Harvey Oswald was the American version of Juan Roa Sierra.

Several authors have provided evidence of the involvement of the CIA, and specifically of Angleton, in the assassination of President Kennedy. Some sources claim that Angleton was in Dallas, Texas, on the day of the assassination.

Today, most scholars who have investigated the assassination of the American president agree that Oswald was nothing more than a scapegoat, a patsy who did not even fire his rifle at the president.

According to some authors, like Roa Sierra, Oswald was a Manchurian candidate, who had been psychically conditioned to believe that he committed the assassination, while other expert snipers, placed at strategic points, fired the shots. According to the plan, once the assassination was committed, other controlled agents would assassinate Oswald, exactly as happened with Roa Sierra. But it seems that, at the last moment, Oswald managed to come out of his hypnotic state, became aware of the situation and tried to escape.

There is testimonial evidence that, once captured by the police, Oswald claimed several times that he had not shot at the president. Shortly thereafter Jack Ruby, a mobster who owned a prostitute bar in Dallas, managed to get close to Oswald despite the police siege and shot him at point-blank range. As in the Roa Sierra case, Oswald's death silenced the alleged killer.

In conclusion, Angleton had the motive, the ability, the means and the opportunity to have participated in Operation Bogotazo. Moreover, like any experienced criminal, Angleton created an alibi for himself, backed up by a respectable if not entirely impartial witness: his wife. Of course, only a very gullible person could think that someday the memo in which Dulles ordered Angleton to assassinate Gaitán would be found among declassified CIA documents. Such orders are never put in black and white, but rather, to avoid leaving compromising traces, they are given verbally, and sometimes only hinted at. A word to the wise is a word to the wise.

I first expressed my theory that Roa might have been a Manchurian candidate in my novel *The Mother of All Conspiracies,* published in 2005.[195] But the fact that Roa may have been an early case of a Manchurian candidate is so obvious that others have already independently come to the same conclusion.

Some years ago I found on the Internet a long article written by an independent Australian researcher, Greg Parker, entitled "Bogota Ripples, Was Sierra a 'false assassin'?", in which he provides an excellent analysis of the Gaitán assassination and comes to a conclusion similar to mine. According to Parker, [Roa] "Sierra was the first CIA assassin to be 'brainwashed'"[196] —i.e., a Manchurian candidate-which is consistent with my own conclusion.

Another researcher who has independently reached a very similar conclusion is researcher Allan Weberman. In an article published on the Internet on February 16, 1999, Weberman asserts that the Bogotazo was an early CIA operation.197 Cuban exile journalist Andrés Rivero also came to a similar conclusion.198

12. The Bogotazo: the Mystery Remains

The Bogotazo is a key event in understanding how the CFR conspirators have used the CIA to achieve their ultimate goal of turning
the U.S. into a totalitarian Communo-Fascist dictatorship. This explains the continuing efforts of key CFR members aimed at muddy-
ing the historical waters as well as sabotaging attempts by uncon-
trolled researchers to uncover the truth about the events of the
Bogotazo. Evidence of this is the CIA's efforts to block Paul Wolf's
attempts to obtain the declassification of certain secret CIA documents.

Wolf, a tireless and meticulous private investigator turned successful lawyer, has devoted long hours to researching the events of
the Bogotazo and the assassination of Gaitán. Through his efforts,
he has compiled what is undoubtedly the most complete archive of
documents on these events and has selflessly placed them at the service of other investigators. Not surprisingly, Wolf has come to the
inevitable conclusion that the CIA must know more than it admits
about the Gaitán assassination.

In an effort to find evidence to corroborate his hypothesis, Wolf
availed himself of a law stateing that secret U.S. government documents must be declassified and made available to the public 25 years
after they were written.[199] But the CIA, in violation of the law, blocked
all his attempts.

Finally, after all persuasive efforts had been exhausted, Wolf went
a step further and legally demanded that such documents be made
public. But this was only the beginning of a long legal battle. Finally, on October 12, 2002, Wolf and his attorney appeared before a
U.S. District Judge to state their case. The CIA was represented by
one of its attorneys.

At the hearing, Wolf's attorney explained that the Bogotazo coincided with the Ninth Conference of Latin American States, "the
meeting that ushered in the Cold War. The Conference was the first
attempt to create an alliance in connection with the Cold War in the
Western Hemisphere." He also mentioned the inexplicable fact that,
despite the provisions of the Freedom of Information Act (FOIA),
documents related to the Bogotazo, written more than 60 years ago,
are still classified as secret.

For her part, the CIA's lawyer justified the CIA's lack of interest
in making these documents public, in case they exist - something the
CIA neither confirms nor denies - because it would reveal sources
and methods that could cause damage to the national security of the
United States. This argument was repeated several times by the CIA's

lawyer during the hearing of the case.

But what the CIA's legal representative claimed makes no sense. Today, the intelligence and espionage methods used by the CIA in 1948 have changed so radically that disclosing what the Agency used in 1948 is totally irrelevant. Therefore, if we discard the methods, the only reason that could be alleged would be that the CIA is protecting its sources, i.e., its secret agents who participated in the Bogotazo.

However, more than 60 years after the events of the Bogotazo, it is logical to think that most of the CIA secret agents who participated in the events have passed away. Therefore, what source or secret agent still living played such an important role in the Bogotazo that, if revealed, would harm not the national security of the U.S. but the interests of the CFR conspirators?

At present, one of the few people who actively participated in the Bogotazo and is still alive is Fidel Castro. Therefore, one must conclude that the CIA, or those who control it, do not want anything in the CIA's secret files about Castro's participation in the Bogotazo and the assassination of Gaitán to be made public.

n conclusion, everything indicates that the assassination of Gaitán and the Bogotazo were the result of a psychological warfare operation carefully planned by the CFR conspirators and carried out by intelligence officers of the defunct OSS and the newly created CIA. This explains the fact that a large majority of the key participants in the operation were former members of the OSS, members of the CIA and members of the CFR.

Among those mentioned are,

> General George C. Marshall (CFR), U.S. Secretary of State, Head of the U.S. Delegation to the Ninth Conference.
> General Matthew B. Ridgway (CFR), Military Advisor to the U.S. delegation to the Ninth Conference.
> Averell Harriman (CFR), U.S. Secretary of Commerce.
> John McCloy (CFR), President of the International Bank for Reconstruction and Development, attended the Conference.
> William Wieland, protégé of Sumner Welles (CFR), probably in the State Department intelligence service, later accused of supporting Castro before and after he took power in Cuba in 1959.
> Roy Rubbotom, State Department official, accused of being pro-Castro.
> William Pawley, a friend of Allen Dulles and connected to the

CIA. According to a witness, Pawley was present at the meeting at Mario Lazo's house.[200]

Willard Beaulac, U.S. Ambassador to Colombia and former U.S. Ambassador to Cuba. It is suspected that he also attended the meeting at Lazo's home.

Norman Armour (CFR, OSS), U.S. Under Secretary of State. U.S. delegate to the Ninth Conference.

Richard Salvatierra, CIA officer. Attended the meeting at Lazo's home.

John Mepples Spiritto, CIA officer who later worked on the project. ARTICHOKE. Tried to bribe or assassinate Gaitán.

John C. Wiley (CFR, OSS), former U.S. Ambassador to Colombia.

Robert Lovett (Skull & Bones), substitute U.S. Secretary of State, closely linked to the CFR.

Rafael del Pino Siero, former member of the U.S. armed forces with possible links to the CIA. He attended the secret meeting at Lazo's house.

Fidel Castro Ruz, was also present at the meeting at Lazo's house, where it is suspected that he was recruited by the CIA and later became a secret agent of the Rockefellers.

Apart from the information I have provided above, the activities during the Bogotazo of such a large group of people connected with the U.S. intelligence services and the CFR indicate that the Bogotazo was not a spontaneous explosion of violence, but a false flag operation; a key element of a large-scale psyop later known as the Cold War.

However, it should not be forgotten that all intelligence and espionage activities, and especially covert operations, are carried out under the strictest rules of compartmentalization and need-to-know, which, translated into good romance, means that the left hand does not know what the right hand is doing. Therefore, it must be assumed that most of the people mentioned above did not know exactly what the whole operation they were participating in consisted of.[201] Most likely, some of them mistakenly thought they were doing patriotic work, in defense of the interests of the American people.

For example, Ramón Conte, who was one of the lowest in the chain of command during Castro's recruitment, mentioned that another CIA agent had told him that U.S. intelligence services had received information that during the Ninth Conference someone was going to make an attempt on the life of a high political leader.

According to Conte, one of the tasks assigned to Fidel Castro in

Colombia in his work for the CIA was to investigate whether there were any plans for a personal attempt on the life of U.S. Secretary of State George Marshall.[202] Of course, whoever told Conte this simply misinformed him, just as other participants in the operation may have received different misinformed versions of the operation to be carried out in Bogotá.

So it is most likely that only Allen Dulles, Frank Wisner and James Angleton, and perhaps George Marshall, Averell Harriman and Robert Lovett, as well as their masters, Nelson and David Rockefeller, had a clear idea of the true purpose and scope of the operation.

El Bogotazo was the first large-scale psychological warfare operation carried out by the newly created Central Intelligence Agency on the orders of its real masters, the CFR conspirators. The CIA has always been one more instrument of the conspirators in their long struggle against the American people and the peoples of the world to achieve their goal of creating a Communo-Fascist New World Order under their total control.

The methodology used in Operation Bogotazo conformed to a variant of the Hegelian principle of thesis-antithesis-synthesis,[203] The Bogotazo was the terrible antithesis which the conspirators presented as a covert operation of the new enemy, Soviet communism, and used it as a threat to convince the American and Latin American peoples to accept as a lesser evil what appeared to be a bad, but more acceptable alternative: the Cold War.

The Bogotazo marked the great beginning of the Cold War in the Western Hemisphere. A few years later Nelson Rockefeller, one of the CFR's chief conspirators, was desperately trying to sell the whole world on the idea of building nuclear shelters in every building[204] and American schoolchildren were rehearsing every day how to take shelter under their desks in case of nuclear attack. For the American people, the times of living in constant fear of a surprise nuclear attack had begun.

13. The CIA, the CFR Conspirators and the Bogotazo

A few weeks after theBogotazo, Council on Foreign Relations undercover agent Allen Dulles was commissioned to make a study of why the CIA had not alerted the U.S. government in time to the possibility of the riots. Dulles used the CIA's alleged failure to predict the riots as a pretext to get rid of the then CIA Director, Admiral

Roscoe Hillenkoetter, who was not a CFR agent, whom he blamed for the failure.[205]

Shortly thereafter, Hillenkoetter returned to his Navy post and Allen Dulles was appointed CIA Director. However, contrary to Dulles' claim, the CIA's Directorate of Intelligence had in fact previously informed the U.S. authorities about the possibility of unrest during the Ninth Conference, but, as is always the case, the CIA's report was totally ignored.

In his memoirs, Willard Beaulac, U.S. Ambassador to Colombia, gave a lie to Dulles' accusations that the CIA had failed to warn of the possibility of riots, when he mentions,

> Reliable reports had given ample warning that the Communists were planning to demonstrate against the Conference and, if possible, would cause riots and even civil war to obstruct it.[206]

Contrary to Dulles' assertion, several detailed reports supplied by the CIA's Directorate of Intelligence, warning of the possibility of Soviet instigation of riots in Colombia, were blocked at the American embassy and were not made available to Secretary Marshall.[207] For example, a report dated in Colombia two months before the Bogotazo, stated,

> January 29. - Mr. G., [probably Antonio Garcia] a Colombian Communist leader who had been given the task of overthrowing the (Conservative) government of [Ospina] Perez , has boasted that, if necessary, he has planes and artillery. It is claimed that this group has stored arms and explosives in 17 houses in Bogotá.[208]

The reader may not understand how it is possible that the CIA, which planned and carried out Operation Bogotazo, also informed the government about the possibility of the riots. The confusion comes from the fact that in reality the CIA is not a homogeneous organization, but consists of two parts, one dedicated to the gathering and analysis of information and the other dedicated to covert operations. In the first one work honest Americans who believe they are fighting for the defense of their country. These were the Intelligence Directorate analysts who warned about the possibility of unrest. In the other work secret agents of the CFR who are fighting to defend the interests of the oil tycoons and Wall Street bankers.[209]

It should therefore be noted that, as a result of a common simplification, when someone says "a CIA report", they really mean "a report written by someone at CIA." This is important when you consider that, as I explained earlier, since its inception, the CIA has never been a homogeneous entity. The only department of the CIA that is of interest to the CFR conspirators who created it, and which is totally under their control, is the one that conducts covert operations. This department works under the strictest rules of compartmentalization and need-to-know. This ensures that neither the American people, nor members of the government, nor even employees of the other branches of the CIA, know about the covert activities that these CIA officers carry out.

But the CIA officers who alerted about the possibility of riots, worked in the intelligence analysis branch and were not part of the Bogotazo operation, therefore, they were unaware of the CIA's role in it. The Bogotazo was most likely carried out mostly by a group of former OSS officers in the State Department's Office of Policy Coordination (OPC), headed by CFR undercover agent Frank Wisner.[210]

After conducting an exhaustive study of why CIA reports warning of the possibility of unrest in Bogotá had been ignored, a Senate Internal Security Subcommittee came to this conclusion,

> Admiral Hillenkoetter [CIA Director], directly accused the State Department Assistant in Bogotá O.J. Libert, and Ambassador Willard L. Beaulac of failing to send the reports to the State Department in Washington. In particular, Mr. Libert prevented the reports from reaching Secretary Marshall's security officers because, according to him, the protection offered by the Bogotá police was "adequate", and he did not wish to "unnecessarily alarm the delegates."[211]

Beaulac's activities in blocking CIA reports warning of possible unrest, as well as his possible participation in the secret meeting at Mario Lazo's residence, indicate that the ambassador probably played an active role in the operation. Moreover, all indications are that, as an active member of the CFR, Secretary of State Marshall also played an important role and had been informed in advance of the operation.

In his 15 April 1945 testimony before the Congressional Subcommittee investigating the CIA's "failure" to predict the Bogotazo riots, CIA Director Admiral Hillenkoetter refuted his critics when he asserted that, on the contrary, the CIA had reported in time the "possibility of an eruption of violence" during the Conference, and that this information had been passed on to State Department executives.[212] Hillenkoetter also reported that certain State Department employees had blocked the transmission of a key CIA report dated March 23, which alerted the State Department to the possibility of unrest during the Conference.[213]

Moreover, according to a State Department Bureau of Intelligence Research Report dated October 14, 1948, the theory that Colombian Communists were involved in the riots was based on the fact that they had already planned well in advance to sabotage and discredit the activities of the Conference, as well as to hinder the activities of the attending delegates, particularly the Americans.[214]

As is evident, not only the CIA's intelligence analysis branch, but also the State Department's intelligence section, had previously warned about the possibility of disturbances in Bogotá during the Ninth Conference. However, due to compartmentalization and the need to know,[215] essential characteristics of any intelligence service, intelligence analysts were unaware that it was the CIA's covert activities section that had planned and then carried out the Gaitán assassination and the riots.

An important key to understanding the disinformation techniques used by the CIA in Operation Bogotazo is the fact that, although CFR undercover agents in Bogotá prevented CIA and State Department reports from reaching their intended recipients, those same CFR agents kept the Colombian press well informed about the danger of riots. Francisco Fandiño Silva, a well-known Colombian journalist, later recalled that "The American Embassy informed me that they had been alerted that a bomb attack was being plotted against General [Marshall]."[216]

As part of the same pattern of disinformation, Gaitán received a message from Ambassador Beaulac on March 24, informing him that the Communists were planning to disrupt the Conference and that, if they succeeded, they would most likely blame it on Gaitán's Liberal Party.[217]

Only a few hours after the riots broke out, Secretary of State General Marshall, CIA Director Admiral Hillenkoetter, U.S. Ambassador Willard Beaulac, Colombian President Dr. Mariano Ospina, Secretary of the Presidency Rafael Azula Barrera, as well as other important witnesses, concluded that the riots were the result of a Communist operation instigated by the Soviet Union.

However, apparently intrigued by the first "failure" of the CIA's intelligence branch, one of its officers, Russell Jack Smith, telephoned one of his personal contacts in Secretary Marshall's office in the State Department and asked, "How did Secretary [Marshall] get the information that the riots were part of a Communist plot?" "Oh", his contact replied, "he just looked out the window of his villa six or seven miles away and said, 'The Communists did it'."[218]

A few days later, the *Philadelphia Inquirer* published an article entitled "Marshall Accuses International Communism for Bogotá Revolt", which provided even more fraudulent facts to convince the gullible American public that the assassination of Gaitán and the riots had been carried out by Colombian Communists with the support of the Soviet Union.[219]

In an effort to terrorize the American people with fear of communism, Secretary of State Marshall declared to the press that the riots had been instigated by the Soviet Union, and that they were but an extension into the Western Hemisphere of the tactics of subversion and violence the Soviets were using in Europe.[220]

The next day, Marshall continued his disinformational task, but, unbeknownst to him, he made a mistake that gives us a clear clue as to who actually instigated the riots. According to Marshall, "the riots conformed to the same pattern established in the riots in France and Italy.[221] What Marshall conveniently did not say was that the April 1948 riots in Italy had also been provoked by American intelligence agents under the direction of Frank Wisner and the collaboration of James Jesus Angleton. This explains why they fit the same pattern as the Bogotazo riots.

Two days later, on April 14, the *New York Times* published an editorial continuing the campaign aimed at terrorizing Americans with the fear of communism. According to the *NYT*,

In support of the outcome of the Colombian government's investigations, Secretary of State Marshall and other delegates to the Inter-American Conference have accused the Soviet Union and its instrument, international communism, of instigating the revolt that destroyed Bogotá and cast a shadow over the entire Western Hemisphere. Based on first-hand information and personal observations, [Marshall and the delegates] see behind the tragic events that disrupted the deliberations the same forces that tried to provoke insurrections in France and Italy. And that makes Bogotá, as Mr. Marshall said, not just a Colombian or Latin American incident, but a world problem, and a clear demonstration of what Russia is capable of in its (no longer cold) war against democracies.

The most curious thing is that this furious "anti-Communist" is the same George Marshall who in December 1945 traveled to China as a special envoy of the American president to try to reconcile the anti-Communist Chiang Kai-Shek with the Communist Mao Tse-Tung. At the time, all indications were that Chiang's troops would be victorious in their fight against the Communists, but Marshall succeeded in getting Chiang to agree to a cease-fire. Predictably, the reconciliation efforts of CFR agent George Marshall soon thereafter guaranteed victory for Mao and the Communists.[222]

Efforts to convince the American public that the Bogotazo had been a Communist operation continued for many years. With the Bogotazo, the Cold War, which proved so beneficial to Wall Street bankers, oil tycoons, and the military-industrial complex, had moved to the forefront of American foreign policy.

The defeat of Nazi Germany[223] marked the end of World War II, but also the fact, well hidden first by the mass media and then by unscrupulous historians, that the conspirators had lost the enemy they had worked so hard and so much money to create. Therefore, they needed to find as soon as possible the new enemy they so badly needed to fill the vacuum left by the Nazis in order to justify their aggressive imperial policies and their unbridled militarism. That is why, long before the war came to an end, they had already decided to assign that role to the Soviet Union and international communism.

As a result of secret talks at the Yalta conference in February 1945, the conspirators, through their secret agents Franklin D. Roosevelt (CFR) and his adviser Alger Hiss (CFR), reached a secret agreement with Stalin for the Soviet Union to occupy parts of eastern Germany, as well as Czechoslovakia, Hungary, Poland, Bulgaria, Romania, Yugoslavia and the Baltic countries - what later became known as the so-called "Soviet bloc." To that end, President Roosevelt ordered General Dwight Eisenhower (CFR), to halt the advance of American troops until the Red Army occupied those territories.[224] This ensured that the new enemy the plotters had created would be seen as an empire eager to expand its borders by aggressive means. But they also had to convince the American people of the existence of a new threat from what they had always considered their backyard, and to that end they carried out Operation Bogotazo.

Since the beginning of 1948, when he was recruited, the destinies of Fidel Castro and the Council on Foreign Relations have been intimately linked. Just a brief analysis of the relations between Fidel Castro and the United States shows that almost every American who has supported Castro in one way or another has been related, directly or indirectly, to the CFR and, although the conspirators have made an effort to conceal these relations, some people have suspected it.

Possibly one of the first to suspect it was Earl E.T. Smith, who was U.S. Ambassador to Cuba when Castro was fighting his guerrilla war against Batista. Smith was totally convinced not only that Castro was a Communist, but that he had managed to come to power in Cuba in 1959 thanks to the efforts of some important people in the U.S. State Department, especially William Wieland and Roy Rubbotom.[225] These two shady characters, particularly Wieland, were often accused of being pro-Castro because they were covert Communists. What neither Ambassador Smith nor anyone else apparently suspected was that both Wieland and Rubbotom supported Castro not because they were Communists, but because they were controlled agents of the CFR.

For many years, the State Department was the focus of attention of many American patriots who watched this government department fall into the hands of individuals who consistently acted to the detriment of their country. Some of these patriots, such as Senator Joseph McCarthy,[226] Ambassador Earl E.T. Smith,[227] and FBI Director J. Edgar Hoover, were firmly convinced that the State Department had been infiltrated by a conspiracy of Communists who were using it to advance their secret anti-American agenda.

McCarthy had discovered that the State Department was controlled by a fairly extensive group of individuals who were working tirelessly behind the scenes to destroy their country and aid their enemies. In a speech he delivered in Wheeling, West Virginia, on February 9, 1950, McCarthy mentioned that he had compiled a list of 205 State Department employees who were working hard against the interests of the American people.

Unfortunately, McCarthy had come to the erroneous conclusion that the secret CFR agents who had infiltrated the State Department must necessarily be Communists. Among the enemy agents on McCarthy's list were top State Department executives Alger Hiss (CFR) and Owen Lattimore (CFR). But the traitors had not only infiltrated the State Department. The list included Harry Hopkins and Laughlin Currie, who worked directly for President Roosevelt in the White House, as well as Harry Dexter White in the Treasury Department. The list also included General George Marshall, whom McCarthy accused of treason against the U.S..

All as one, President Eisenhower (CFR), Secretary of State Dean Acheson (CFR) and well-known journalist Edward Morrow (CFR) joined forces in their defense of the defendants and in a blistering attack on McCarthy. The result was that, although most of the people McCarthy indicted were eventually proven to be traitors,[228] his grievous error cost him his political career and possibly even his life.[229]

Nevertheless, it would be unfair to blame McCarthy for his mistake. As Professor Carroll Quigley has explained, the modus operandi of the CFR conspirators closely resembles the way the Communists act. Quigley, one of the scholars who studied the CFR and the activity of the conspirators in detail, found,

> "There is, and has been for a generation, an international Anglophile network that operates very much in the way the radical Right believes Communists act. In fact, this network is not averse to cooperating with Communists, or any other group, and frequently does so."[230]

Another who made a mistake similar to McCarthy's in identifying traitors was Robert Welch. In his book *The Politician*,[231] Welch accused both President Dwight Eisenhower and his brother Milton of being Communists.

> "However, in truth, neither of these individuals accused by McCarthy and Welch were Communists in the strict sense of being followers of Marxist-Leninist doctrines and certainly were not secret agents of the Soviet Union. Nevertheless, in a sense they were partly Communists,[232] but only in the sense that they were secret agents of the only true Communo-Fascist party in the United States: the Council on Foreign Relations."

On the other hand, any effort to find a connection between the CFR conspirators and a particular political ideology is a total waste of time. The fact that they have at one time supported and financially aided Fascist and Communist regimes only means that they have done so to advance their secret plans of deindustrialization and population reduction as stepping stones to the implementation of the New World Order.

In particular, two mysterious characters who actively participated in Operation Bogotazo, William Wieland and Roy Rubboton, have topped the list of pro-Castro "Communists" infiltrating the U.S. State Department. However, the truth is that none of them were Communists, but secret agents in the service of the CFR conspirators. It should not be forgotten that, since the end of 1941, the State Department had fallen completely under the control of the conspirators.[233] Therefore, everything indicates that Castro's real promoters were never in the Kremlin but in the Harold Pratt House in Manhattan, headquarters of the CFR.

14. The Caribbean Magnicide

Little has been said about Fidel Castro's real role in the assassination of Gaitán, but there is incontrovertible evidence that assassinating political leaders, particularly presidents, has always been one of Fidel Castro's strongest obsessions.

It is possible, and his later life seems to confirm this, that Jesuit preceptors familiarized their favorite pupil with Father L'Amy's Theology, which sets out the principle by which the Order grants its members the right to physically eliminate their adversaries.[234] It is also probable that, as a student of the Jesuits at the Colegio de Belen in Havana, the young Fidel heard from the mouths of his Jesuit preceptors the principle of the legitimacy of assassinating tyrants, as well as of "committing, without sin, acts considered criminal by the ignorant masses."[235]

Proof of this is that, in his impassioned self-defense during the trial for the attack on the Moncada barracks in 1953, Castro mentioned the theory of the Spanish Jesuit Juan Mariana who, in his book *De Rege et Regis Institutione*, comments that when a ruler usurps power, even if he has been democratically elected, but governs in a tyrannical manner, it is licit for a citizen to commit tyrannicide.[236]

However, although some of Castro's Jesuit preceptors still profess great admiration for their former student, it would be unfair to blame them entirely for his later conduct. For some unknown reason, assassinating heads of state became one of Fidel Castro's many obsessions, which he began to put into practice at a very young age. Hugh Thomas himself, one of the most serious scholars of Castroism, noted Castro's apparent desire to perpetuate "a student tradition of tyrannicide."[237]

The first person Castro assassinated was Leonel Gómez, his rival in the elections for president of the Law School, whom he shot in the back in 1947. In 1948, he participated in the assassination of Manolo Castro. That same year he assassinated Oscar Fernández Caral, sergeant of the university police. In 1949 he assassinated Justo Fuentes and Miguel Sáez, other student leaders.

But if Castro proved to be skillful in eliminating his enemies, he has been even more so in getting rid of his friends when they are no longer useful to him. Among those who lost their lives due to trusting Fidel Castro too much are: Frank País, principal leader of the 26th of July Movement; Comandante Camilo Cienfuegos, first figure in importance in the Rebel Army; Rafael del Pino Siero, his youthful friend; Osvaldo Sánchez, leader of the traditional Communist Party; Comandante Manuel Piñeiro (Barbarroja), Chief of the America Department of the intelligence services; Commander René Rodríguez, Director of the Institute of Friendship with the Peoples; Commander Arnaldo Ochoa, hero of the war in Angola; Colonel Antonio "Tony" de la Guardia, his man of confidence and personal assassin; Commander José Abrahantes, former Director of the intelligence services, and many more, including Che Guevara,[238] which would make this list endless.

However, what Fidel Castro has excelled at most in his long criminal career is assassinating heads of state. Unfortunately, the deep hatred Castro has always felt for democratically elected heads of state overcame any tyrannical sentiments he might have felt.

In 1947, when he was only 21 years old, Castro joined a group of university students visiting President Ramon Grau San Martin at the Presidential Palace. Grau was a politician who had been democratically elected by popular vote. During the visit, the President and the students approached one of the large windows on the second floor of the Palace. At that moment Castro suggested to one of them that they assassinate the President,

> "I have the formula to take power right now and get rid of this son of a bitch forever. We grab him and throw him over the balcony. Oncw he is dead, we will speak to the people on the radio and proclaim the triumph of the student revolution."[239]

It is pertinent to remember that Grau was a prestigious surgeon and university professor. In addition, he was a nationalist politician who always opposed U.S. control over Cuban politics and sovereignty. Grau had earned the hatred of the CFR conspirators when he began to fight for the elimination of the Platt Amendment from the Cuban Constitution. The Amendment authorized the U.S. to intervene militarily in Cuba at will.[240]

In the summer of that same year, Castro joined a group of adventurers who planned to invade the Dominican Republic, assassinate President Rafael L. Trujillo, and stage a coup d'état to seize power. Castro participated in the military training, which took place on Cayo Confites, a small island north of Oriente province. But the authorities discovered the plot and arrested most of the participants. Castro managed to escape.[241]

Eyewitnesses claim that on April 9, 1948, during the Bogotazo riots, shortly after 4 p.m. that day, they saw Castro at the front of a mob shouting "To the palace." According to witnesses Castro was carrying a rifle and hysterically shouting that they were going to the palace to kill Colombian President Mariano Ospina Pérez.[242]

In August 1951, the coffin containing the mortal remains of Cuban populist leader Eduardo "Eddy" Chibás was taken to the University of Havana for students to pay homage to him. José Pardo Llada, at the time a friend of Castro's, tells that Fidel approached him and said, "Pepe, let's take the dead body to the Palace and take power. You will be the President and I will be the Chief of the Army."[243] The President of Cuba at that time was Carlos Prío Socarrás, elected by popular vote.

Pardo Llada does not mention whether Castro told him how he planned to get rid of President Prío, but an earlier incident may give us an idea of what Fidel had in mind.

In 1949, while Castro was making preparations for a trip he planned to make to the United States, he visited almost daily the apartment of his friend Max Lesnick, located on Morro Street, very close to the Presidential Palace. Lesnick told Tad Szulck that one day, while looking out from the balcony towards the Palace, Fidel took a broom and, pointing it as if it were a rifle, told Lesnick's grandmother: "Look, if Prío comes out to the terrace of the Palace to make a speech, I will kill him from here with a single bullet from a rifle with a telescopic sight."[244]

In March 1953, Fidel Castro and a group of conspirators plotted to assassinate President Fulgencio Batista. The opportunity presented itself when Batista decided to attend a meeting of veterans of the War of Independence, to be held in July in Santiago de Cuba, in the province of Oriente. Castro and some of the conspirators obtained false documentation, army uniforms and official car license plates, and traveled to Santiago to make an attempt on Batista's life. But Batista apparently suspected something was wrong and cancelled the visit. The police had suspicions that Castro was up to something and arrested him. But soon after he was released for lack of evidence.

There are rumors that the attack on the Moncada Barracks, which Castro and his group carried out a few months later, on July 26, 1953, was to coincide with a visit Batista was to make to the barracks. But again Batista cancelled the visit at the last moment. There may be some truth to the rumors, because the ploy Castro and his men used to get the guards to open the entrance door was to shout, "Open the door. General [Batista] is here!"[245]

Castro's obsession with assassinating presidents did not end when he took power in Cuba in January 1959. On April 26 of that year, shortly after his victory, Castro infiltrated a group of 84 Cubans and Panamanians living in Cuba into Panama. The objective of this group was to assassinate President Ernesto de la Guardia and ignite the spark of a revolution in that country. But, a few hours after landing, the Panamanian military forces neutralized the invading force.[246]

Castro denied his participation in the invasion. Nevertheless, the fact gives us an idea of his true political affiliation. The Panamanian government was not a dictatorship and its president had been democratically elected by popular vote, so the attack had no ideological justification.

Shortly after the frustrated Panamanian adventure, another military group secretly left Cuba on June 1, 1959, bound for Costa Rica, from where they intended to infiltrate into Nicaragua to assassinate President/Dictator Anastasio Somoza, Castro's sworn enemy. The invasion failed and, of course, Castro denied his participation in it, but it fits Castro's modus operandi in such an operation.

Less than two weeks later, on June 14, 1959, Castro sent a similar group to the Dominican Republic, with the mission to assassinate President Rafael L. Trujillo. Castro's animosity toward the Dominican dictator dated back to his days at the University of Havana, when, in 1947, he joined a group of Cubans training at Cayo Confites to invade the Dominican Republic and assassinate Trujillo.

Both operations, in Nicaragua and the Dominican Republic, failed, and Castro was quick to deny that he had personally ordered them. But, given his affinity for such action, it is not unreasonable to think that it was Castro himself who ordered them.[247]

Just a couple of months later, in mid-August 1959, Castro sent a military group to Haiti. Their mission was to assassinate François "Papa Doc" Duvalier, the Haitian dictator. The group was composed of 30 Cubans, had been organized by Che Guevara, and was commanded by an Algerian who had fought in Castro's forces in the Sierra Maestra. But, as had happened with the operations against Panama and the Dominican Republic, this one also turned out to be a disaster, and most of the attackers perished. Castro never responded to the Duvalier government's accusations of his complicity in the operation.[248]

On July 26, 1960, during a speech he gave in celebration of the attack on the Moncada barracks, Castro declared his commitment to "liberate" the rest of Latin America.[249]

In 1962, Castro attempted to assassinate the democratically elected president of Panama, Roberto Chiari. According to an FBI report dated October 25, 1962, Humberto Rodríguez Díaz, one of the assassins sent by Castro, in complicity with a former Cuban ambassador to Panama, tried to make an attempt on the life of the Panamanian President.[250]

The next year, in the spring of 1963, Castro sent several tons of arms and ammunition to a revolutionary group to assassinate President Rómulo Betancourt.[251] Castro's obsession with assassinating Betancourt, who initially supported him, has been amply documented.

It is highly revealing that Castro's attempts to overthrow the Venezuelan government were not directed against a tyrannical or undemocratic government. On the contrary, they were aimed at preventing the establishment of democracy in Venezuela. The main objective of the revolutionaries Castro supported was to sabotage the 1963 presidential elections. Castro's plan was to provoke the Venezuelan military into staging a coup d'état and thereby discredit the democratic process in Venezuela. But Betancourt and the democratic reformists were firmly determined to carry out the elections and, finally, Castro apparently lost interest in the Venezuelan process.

That same year, Colombian newspapers published reports that the planes that had transported a group of assassins from Cuba to Colombia's Guajira peninsula had been provided by Fidel Castro. The mission of this group was to assassinate President Leon Valencia and overthrow his government. This information was corroborated on October 17, 1963 by President Valencia himself, in a note he sent to all diplomatic missions in Bogotá in which he held Castro responsible for the operation.

A few months later, on February 26, 1964, a new plot was uncovered on the occasion of a visit Valencia planned to make to Cali. The next year, Valencia again singled out Castro as the instigator of both assassination attempts.[252]

In July 1979, Nicaraguan dictator Anastasio Somoza was overthrown by members of the Sandinista National Liberation Front, which had Castro's support. Somoza managed to escape the country and became a political exile in Paraguay. A few months later, Somoza and his bodyguards were assassinated on a street in Asuncion by a group using machine guns and bazookas. Some members of Castro intelligence publicly boasted that the assassination team had been trained in Cuba.[253]

According to a source in the U.S. Department of Justice, for some time the CIA and FBI investigated the possibility that Castro was planning to use his U.S. resident agents to try to assassinate President Gerald Ford and his presidential election opponent, Ronald Reagan, in 1976. One of their informants alerted the FBI office in San Francisco that members of the radical terrorist group Emiliano Zapata, in coordination with Castro operative Andres Gomez, were planning to assassinate both leaders.[254] It should not be forgotten that the conspirators detested Reagan, who was not a member of the CFR. That is why they then tried to assassinate him when he was president, so that Vice President George H.W. Bush (CFR) would take over the presidency. Bush (CFR) to take over the presidency.

In the slimy documentary *Fidel*, directed by Estela Bravo, an American very close to Castro's intelligence services, he tells an anecdote about what happened when he visited the Soviet Union in 1963 at the invitation of Nikita Khrushchev. The Soviet Premier wanted to smooth things over with Castro after the events of the 1962 missile crisis, in which he had reached an agreement with President Kennedy behind Castro's back.

According to Castro, Khrushchev invited him to go hunting and, during the hunt, an animal jumped a few meters in front of the Soviet Premier and Castro shot it with his shotgun. The projectiles crossed dangerously close to Khrushchev's face. "And do you know what went through my mind at that moment?" asked Castro in the documentary to his interlocutor, "What happens [laughs] if in a hunt, in one of these accidents, I shoot Khrushchev?"

The very fact that Castro so vividly recalled the event, and recounted it in minute detail, including what went through his mind, indicates that he has a pathologically convoluted mentality. But, in reality, what possibly went through his mind was to assassinate Nikita Khrushchev who, according to Castro, had betrayed and humiliated him during the missile crisis. Everything indicates that Khrushchev never realized how close he was to being one more victim in the long list of heads of state assassinated by the Caribbean assassin.

Although most of Castro's initial assassination attempts failed, it would be wrong to think that they were just the lucubrations of a feverish youthful mind. On the contrary, Fidel Castro has had long experience in the assassination profession, both directly and indirectly, and the evidence indicates that he has sometimes succeeded in his endeavors - not only in committing murder, but in doing so with impunity. The greatest proof of his skill in that field is probably his role the assassination of U.S. President John F. Kennedy which, for some strange reasons, most of the people who have studied it have made an extraordinary effort to ignore.

15. Fidel Castro: Kennedy's Assassin?

Shortly after assuming the presidency in 1963, President Lyndon B. Johnson told some close friends that he had suspicions that the assassination of President John F. Kennedy had been "influenced or directed" by Fidel Castro as revenge.[255] As time went on, far from diminishing, Johnson's suspicions increased. A few years after Kennedy's assassination, Johnson confessed to his friend Howard K. Smith, "I'm going to tell you something that will shake you up: Kennedy was trying to assassinate Castro, but Castro assassinated him first." [256]

It seems that Robert Kennedy, the President's brother, harbored similar suspicions. When in January 1971 journalist Jack Anderson reported the story of the Kennedy brothers' plans to assassinate Fidel Castro, he also reported that Robert Kennedy had been emotionally devastated after his brother's death. Robert believed that his attempts to assassinate Castro might have provoked his brother's assassination.[257]

But President Johnson and Robert Kennedy were not the only ones who harbored suspicions about Castro's involvement in the assassination of President Kennedy. Another who had the same suspicions was Supreme Court Justice Earl Warren. Warren privately told friends that "one of the prime suspects" in Kennedy's assassination was Fidel Castro.[258]

Former U.S. Ambassador to Mexico Thomas Mann also had the same suspicions. As he put it,

Castro is the kind of person who would take revenge in this way. He is the kind of extremist who reacts emotionally rather than intellectually, and without much concern for the risks. His life story demonstrates this.[259]

Senator Robert Morgan, a member of the Senate Intelligence Committee (also called the "Church Committee"), was even more categorical. According to him, he was not only suspicious, but totally convinced that Castro had been the assassin of President

Kennedy. Morgan said,

There can be no doubt in my mind that Fidel Castro, or someone on his orders, assassinated John F. Kennedy in revenge for our attempts to assassinate him."[260]

President Johnson and the rest of those like him who were suspicious of Castro's role in the Kennedy assassination may not have been far from the truth, for Castro had ample reason for revenge. On the very same day Kennedy was assassinated in Dallas, Desmond Fitzgerald, a senior CIA intelligence officer and personal friend of Attorney General Robert Kennedy, held a secret interview with Rolando Cubela to plan the assassination of Fidel Castro.[261] But many people suspect that Cubela was acting as a double-agent, following orders from Castro himself.

As his close collaborators could have attested, Castro was a very vindictive person. He never forgave an offense, real or imagined, particularly when he believed someone has humiliated him. And there is no doubt that Castro was very humiliated by the outcome of the 1962 missile crisis. Some eyewitnesses have recounted in great detail the pique he took when he was given the news that Khrushchev and Kennedy had reached an agreement to solve the crisis behind his back, ignoring him completely. According to Che Guevara's account, Castro kicked a wall with such force that the impact dislodged a mirror which shattered into a thousand pieces.[262]

I myself was an eyewitness to one of Castro's angry outbursts when, a few days after the crisis ended, he told a group of students at the University of Havana that Nikita Khrushchev was "a faggot" and John F. Kennedy was a "shit-eating millionaire" and a "son of a bitch."

In truth, Castro had every reason to feel humiliated. Theodor Sorensen pointed out that some of the measures that Ex-Comm (Executive Committee of the National Security Council) advisors suggested Kennedy take during the crisis, such as low altitude reconnaissance flights over Cuba, were not only aimed at better aerial reconnaissance, but also at harassing and humiliating Castro.[263]

American presidents are surrounded at all times by a tight security ring of highly skilled Secret Service agents. Although a lone assassin always has the advantage of initiative and surprise, there is incontrovertible evidence that shortly before the assassination, Secret Service agents received orders to remove the security ring protecting Kennedy. A few minutes later the assassination was carried out.

Obviously, neither the Mafia, nor the anti-Castro Cubans in Miami, nor the South Vietnamese, nor any of the other groups that have been mentioned as possible culprits in the assassination, had the authority to order the Secret Service to leave the President alone. Only a few high-ranking U.S. government officials had that authority.

Lee Harvey Oswald, the alleged assassin, was just a patsy: a Manchurian candidate similar to Roa Sierra. As in the case of Roa Sierra, the plan was to eliminate him once the real assassins had killed Kennedy. But everything indicates that at the last minute Oswald smelled that something was afoot and managed to escape. Once in custody, another agent of the conspirators, Jack Ruby, assassinated Oswald. Shortly thereafter Ruby was himself assassinated.

But few know that, shortly before the assassination, Ruby had been in Cuba on two occasions. According to him, the reason for his visit was to meet with Santo Trafficante, his Mafia friend who was imprisoned in Cuba. However, many suspected that Trafficante was actually working for Castro.

I am not going to go into a detailed explanation here, which would be too long, of the facts that point to Fidel Castro as a participant in the assassination of John F. Kennedy. Suffice it to say that there are already authors who have pointed out that possibility and provided irrefutable evidence of that participation. See, for example, Gus Russo's book *Live by the Sword*,[264] Wilfried Huismann's documentary *Rendezvous with Death*, and my own book *The Secret Fidel Castro*,[265] in which I devote an entire chapter to this subject. But, as you will see below, in my case I have gone a step further, and I am now convinced that the assassination of Kennedy, Gaitán, Allende, and possibly Che Guevara, were joint operations executed by Castro and the CIA following orders from Wall Street bankers and oil magnates ensconced at the Council on Foreign Relations.

16. Fidel Castro: Allende's assassin?

The death of the constitutional president of Chile, Salvador Allende, on September 11, 1973, is higly reminiscent of *Rashomon*, the famous novel by Riunosuke Akutagawa, later immortalized in a film by Akira Kurosawa. As in *Rashomon*, the alleged eyewitnesses give different and contradictory versions of the events, which are in turn denied by others who claim to know the truth.

The most widespread version, expressed by Fidel Castro and immediately and unreservedly adopted by Allende's close collaborators, is that the President of Chile died as a hero fighting against the coup plotters. In a speech he delivered at the Plaza de la Revolución in Havana on September 28, 1973, Fidel Castro made this idealized version of events official. But, as we will see below, little by little versions have been appearing that differ radically from that initial history of the events.

Inexample, even among the President's close collaborators who were in La Moneda at the time of the events, the versions are contradictory. In his book The Deaths of Allende,[266] Hermes Benítez presents several hypotheses about how Salvador Allende died. One of the best known is the version of Dr. Patricio Guijón, according to which Allende committed suicide with his own AK-47 rifle given to him by Fidel Castro. This version was accepted and spread by the military coup perpetrators.

However, the only person who testified that Allende had committed suicide was Dr. Guijón himself, who was part of the presidential medical team. Dr. Guijón declared that Allende had committed suicide because when he was coming down from the second floor of La Moneda, shortly after the coup plotters occupied the building, he heard a shot, went back upstairs, and found Allende in a pool of blood.

It is good to clarify that Guijón was not an eyewitness of Allende's death, therefore he did not see him commit suicide. Moreover, to date, there is not a single eyewitness to this alleged suicide.

For their part, from the beginning, Chilean leftists did not accept the suicide version. According to them, Allende died heroically in the battle of La Moneda, firing his rifle against the assailants until the last moment. This was the version offered by his daughter Beatriz "Tati" Allende and by Fidel Castro.

Without going into details, since most of this information is in the public domain and is available to everyone on the Internet, there are several versions of how many shots were heard. On the other hand, some claim that, after his death, Allende's corpse was placed on a divan, with the rifle between his legs. Several bullet impacts are also mentioned in the gobelin that upholstered the wall behind the divan.

In an article entitled "The Sacrifice of a Latin American Citizen", Hugo Guzmán, one of the bodyguards, offers interesting details about what happened in the last moments of the assault on La Moneda,

"We, as escorts, cannot attest that Allende eliminated himself. ... The first ones to enter the place where Allende's body was, were a reporter supposedly from El Mercurio who, as far as we know, was a CIA agent. He was the only one who took all the photos. Officer Fernandez Larios, from Army Intelligence, who is now in the United States as a protected witness because he helped them to blame the DINA for the assassination of Foreign Minister Orlando Letelier in Washington, D.C., also enters. He is a CIA man. And General Pedro Espinoza, head of Intelligence, came in. In the only two photos that have been seen, Allende appears with a completely clean shirt. The collar of the shirt also appears white, clean, without stains. A person who shoots himself in the head, what bleeds is a lot. He had a clean collar and shirt. That is one thing that contradicts with the version of self-immolation with the AK rifle."[267]

By the way, there are reports that the soldiers, in addition to taking the photos, put the corpse on the floor, undressed him, searched him and then dressed him again with his clothes. Furthermore, another of Allende's bodyguards says that the two photos testify to even more confusion. In one, Allende appears half reclining with the AK rifle above his legs, and in the other photo he is sitting on the couch, not reclining, and with the AK standing on the floor, between his legs, with the butt resting on the floor.

The above description coincides with versions published in 1974 and 1975, which indicated that Allende had fought after firing his collaborators, together with members of the escort, until he was shot down by a burst of gunfire. Two bodyguards would have carried him to the presidential chair and left him there after placing the rifle on his legs. These could have been some of the members of Allende's personal security, wounded and killed later.

On the other hand, the autopsy performed on Allende is far from definitive. Everything indicates that the forensic doctors' report was made under duress. Hortensia Bussi, Allende's widow, was not allowed to see the body. Less than 24 hours after his death, Allende had already been buried in a cemetery in Viña del Mar.

In an article published on September 11, 2003, the author narrates how in February 1986, Hortensia Bussi, Allende's widow told him:

"To this day I do not know what happened to him, To this day I do not know whether or not Allende's corpse was in the coffin presented to me by the military. ... I saw nothing but a white canvas, under which there was supposed to be a body, and a soldier grabbed me by the wrist and forced me to close it. I do not know, I never knew, if that was Allende."[268]

As if all this were not enough, in 2005, Juan Vivés, pseudonym of Andrés Alfaya, a former Castro intelligence officer living in exile in France, gave the world a new and diametrically different version of the facts. According to Vivés, the Chilean President did not commit suicide or die in combat, but was assassinated, following Castro's orders, by the Cuban Special Troops General Patricio de la Guardia, who in practice was the real head of Allende's personal security.

Vivés claims that he heard this from his uncle, former Cuban President Osvaldo Dorticós, who in turn had heard it from the highest levels of the Cuban government. Although surprising, Vivés' statement simply added veracity to a persistent rumor that has circulated in Cuba for many years.

Moreover, according to other sources in Chile, the story that Allende committed suicide with the Kalashnikov rifle given to him by Castro simply cannot be true. In the first place, because Allende's body had four bullet wounds: two in the abdomen, one in the thorax, and one in the head, which penetrated through one eye and destroyed a large part of the back of his skull on its way out. This totally negates the possibility of suicide.

Secondly, because the projectiles found in Allende's corpse were 9 mm, a different caliber than the 7.62 mm used by the AK-47. However, it is known that Patricio de la Guardia usually carried a UZI submachine gun, which fires 9 mm bullets.

Some of those present at La Moneda deny that Patricio de la Guardia was there when the President died, but others claim that both de la Guardia brothers, Tony and Patricio, were there when Allende died. In fact, a sort of conspiracy theory has begun to circulate in which it is alleged that the rest of the photos taken by the photographer were made to disappear because Patricio de la Guardia appeared in some of them.

In an interview conducted somewhat later, Vivés elaborated on the subject. According to Vivés, several weeks after the coup, he was at the Las Cañas bar of the Habana Libre Hotel (former Havana Hilton), where he met Patricio de la Guardia and the head of Fidel's bodyguard, known as "El Chino." During the conversation, el Chino asked Patricio how the men of Allende's bodyguard that he [el Chino] had trained had behaved. Vivés assures that Patricio's answer when referring to Allende was categorical: "I shot him and killed him for being an asshole. Downstairs I had to kill a journalist who was nicknamed 'El Perro'".

But Vivés is not the only one who affirms that Patricio de la Guardia was the one who killed Allende. Dariel Alarcón Ramírez ("Benigno"), one of the three survivors of Che Guevara's guerrillas in Bolivia, now in exile in France, has confirmed Vivés' statement. According to Alarcón, he was also present when on another occasion, on his return from Chile, Patricio de la Guardia confessed to a group of friends that he had killed Allende.[269]

However, the version of events told by Vivés and confirmed by Alarcón is not new. An AFP cable dated September 12, 1973, the day after the events, had reported that,

According to Chilean right-wing sources, President Allende was killed by his personal guard just as he was asking for a five-minute cease-fire to surrender to the military who were about to enter the La Moneda palace.[270]

On the other hand, the only thing that explains why Castro did not shoot Patricio de la Guardia when he shot his twin brother Tony, is that Patricio possessed information that, if disclosed, would be highly damaging to Castro.

Every intelligence officer discovers, sooner or later, that he works for a corrupt organization, whose sole purpose is material gain and the survival of its leaders. When they realize this, intelligent intelligence officers prepare for a betrayal coming from within their own organization and put in a safe place compromising documents that, in case of emergency, they can use against their employers. These are usually the intelligence officers who manage to retire and die in their beds. Many of those who do not suffer the consequences, some paying with their own lives. In this case, Patricio proved to be much smarter than his brother Tony.

In every crime, the first thing an investigator does is to check whether the alleged perpetrator had the motive, skill, means, and opportunity to commit it, as well as whether he was a repeat offender; that is, whether he has a tendency to commit that particular type of crime.

A cursory analysis of the facts shows that Fidel Castro had the motive. There are many who affirm that Allende's triumph demolished Castro's theory of armed struggle as the only way to implement socialism in a Latin American country. Castro therefore had every reason to derail the democratic process in Chile and get rid of Allende. Moreover, and this is very important, as we will see later, Castro must have been very offended when, in his eyes, Allende humiliated him.

Castro also had the skill, that is, he was skilled in political assassinations. From the time he entered the University of Havana, he joined the gangster groups that swarmed at that time. There Castro discovered that there was a quick way to get rid of his enemies.

Castro also possessed the means. In the months following Allende's seizure of power, Castro had managed to infiltrate thousands of his agents, many of them members of his special forces, into Chile. Some of these agents ended up swelling the ranks of the GAP (Group of Friends of the President), a sort of personal guard for Allende's protection.[271] Through diplomatic pouches sent to the Cuban embassy in Santiago, Castro managed to smuggle hundreds of weapons and ammunition of various types into the country.

Castro also had the opportunity to commit Allende's assassination. This opportunity was provided by the military coup itself. The chaos prevailing in La Moneda at the time when the attackers were preparing for the final assault created the right conditions to commit Allende's assassination and to cover it up behind a fake death in combat or a fake suicide.

The globalist conspirators at the Council on Foreign Relations and military-industrial-complex have always sought to create enemies of the United States to justify that country's arms race, from which they alone benefit, not the American people. Castro's task was to make Allende yet another enemy of the United States —just as he did years later with the sub-agent Hugo Chavez. But the Chilean President was not an uneducated gorilla like Chávez, but an educated, intelligent person, a lover of his country's laws and, apparently, he had a very different idea about Chile's future than Castro.

Late in 1971, Castro visited Chile for a week at Allende's invitation, but extended his visit for almost three weeks. According to comments made to his close collaborators, some expressed during the flight back to Cuba, during the visit Castro came to the conclusion that Allende was not going to be a docile instrument for his purposes. Castro commented again and again on his skepticism about the possibility of a peaceful path to socialism in Chile under Allende's leadership.

On the other hand, Allende also seems to have come to the conclusion that friendship with Fidel Castro was not in his best interest. Proof of this is his refusal to appear at the final farewell ceremony for Castro at the National Stadium and the fact that, contrary to protocol, he did not sign a joint declaration with Castro at the end of his trip.

When Castro informed his Wall Street masters of the failure of his attempts to incite Allende to take the path of violent revolution, they decided that they had to get rid of the President of Chile. To do so, they made use of their department specialized in subversion and psychological warfare, the CIA, and two of its most valuable agents: Henry Kissinger and Fidel Castro.

Kissinger's experience with the Allende assassination served him well in planning the assassination of Prime Minister Aldo Moro in 1978. Incidentally, it is likely that some of the members of the Red Brigades who assassinated Moro on CIA orders were trained in Cuba.

Several Kissinger aides have mentioned that Kissinger was much more concerned about Allende in power in Chile than Castro in Cuba, because, according to Kissinger, "Allende was a living example of democratic social reform in Latin America", and because Allende's success within the democratic process could "trigger" results like those in Europe, where Eurocommunism, operating within parliamentary democracy, worried him and also "frightened him."[272]

The overthrow of Allende was the final blow that totally and definitively discredited the theory of "peaceful coexistence" formulated by Soviet Premier Nikita Khrushchev. Shortly after the overthrow of Allende, Boris Ponomarev, Head of the International Department of the Communist Party of the Soviet Union (CPSU), expressed in a report on the events in Chile, that communism should prepare "to answer with revolutionary violence the reactionary violence of the bourgeoisie."[273] This statement indicated that Leonid Brezhnev's regime had abandoned Khrushchev's doctrine of peaceful transition to socialism in the Third World in favor of a policy of aggressive military strategy —just as Castro, Kissinger and their CFR masters wanted.

Another author has mentioned that, as a result of the military coup of Allende, "Soviet tactics underwent major innovations" during this period, such as the official declaration that "political-military fronts" modeled after Castro's M-26-7 would assume the revolutionary vanguard role previously ascribed to the traditional Communist parties.[274]

It becomes clear that there was an overlap between the objectives of Kissinger and the Castros - both key agents of the CFR conspirators - in keeping the Cold War as hot as possible.

As for Castro, he not only carried out the order to the letter, but did so with gusto. First, because of his irrational hatred for any head of state. Secondly, because of the humiliation to which Allende subjected him when he refused to attend the event at the stadium. We must not forget that Castro is a person who never forgives a humiliation, real or imaginary.

Fidel Castro played a decisive role in undermining Allende's government. First, because he organized, financed and armed the Revolutionary Left Movement, MIR, a radical leftist group that tried to
implant socialism in Chile through violent criminal activities, such
as terrorism, bank robberies and assassinations. Secondly, because
Castro also collaborated and gave weapons and military training to
the extreme leftist members of Allende's own party.

At the time of the coup, there were about 13,000 foreigners in
Chile, most of them Cubans, who had entered the country illegally.
These foreigners were creating a parallel army that could oppose the
regular Chilean military forces. Many of these Cubans managed to
occupy important administrative positions in Chilean state offices.

The Cuban embassy in Santiago had accredited 42 diplomats, in
contrast to only six in the Chilean embassy in Havana. During the
year of the coup, 987 Cubans visited Chile on diplomatic or commercial missions. It is known that many of them intervened in political and economic activities of the Chilean government, particularly
those related to the presidency of the Republic. Most of the instruc-
tors and leaders of the paramilitary groups were Cuban or had been
trained in Cuba.

Later, with his week-long official visit to Chile that lasted 21
days, precisely at the critical moment when the Popular Unity government was facing strong opposition from the center-right, the un-
welcome and interfering guest caused even more problems. For three
weeks, in an effort to cause as much damage as possible to the Allende
government, Castro strolled around Chile praising in rallies the radical measures of his own regime, criticizing parliamentary democracy, teaching how to make a Marxist revolution, and earning the
animosity of conservatives and the military.[275]

In bidding farewell to the Chilean people during his speech at a
rally at the National Stadium —which Allende as a sign of his displeasure did not attend - Castro declared, in an obvious criticism of
Allende, "I return to Cuba more revolutionary and extremist than I
came."

In reality, what Castro was doing was what he has always did with
great success on behalf of his CFR masters: acting as an agent provocateur, pushing others down undesirable paths. While publicly
expressing his support for Allende, behind the scenes he was ma-
nipulating Cuban-trained militant extremists to pressure Allende from
the far left.

The immediate result of Castro's work as an agent provocateur in the service of Wall Street bankers in close coordination with the CIA was not long in coming. On the very day of his farewell, thousands of opposition women took to the streets in protest, furiously banging their pots and pans in protest of the growing lack of supplies. For their part, some members of the Revolutionary Left Movement (MIR) tried to repress the women by throwing stones at them.

Castro had destroyed in a few days the precarious peace between the divergent groups that Allende had worked so hard and so long to achieve.

Not content with having harassed and conspired against Allende while he was alive, Castro also tried to manipulate him for his hidden ends after his death. In a speech he delivered in Havana on September 28, 1973, Castro told the world the false story that Salvador Allende had fallen in La Moneda fighting with the rifle he himself had given him.

But it seems that Fidel Castro's hatred for the Allende family was not limited to the President. Shortly thereafter, it became known that Beatriz "Tati" Allende had committed suicide in Havana by shooting herself with the pistol of her husband, Luis Fernandez de Oña, a Cuban Security officer. It was not long before Allende's sister Laura also committed suicide by throwing herself from the 16th floor of the apartment where she lived in the Vedado neighborhood.

A fact that highlights the hidden evil side of Fidel Castro is his behavior in relation to "Tati" Allende.

Beatriz Allende, "Tati", was the president's closest collaborator, and headed the private secretary's team at the La Moneda Palace. In order to use her for his purposes, Fidel Castro appointed the handsome Cuban Luis Fernández de Oña (alias "Demid") to pose as a diplomat, seduce her, and marry her in order to control her and obtain information. After the military coup, Beatriz went into exile in Cuba with her husband. But, once there, Fernández de Oña returned to his first wife, and explained to Beatriz that he had never loved her and that he had married her following superior orders.

As can be seen, Castro's treatment of Allende's daughter, which began long before the first differences between Castro and Allende, was not friendly, but treacherous and hostile. However, this is not surprising, but marks a style of behavior typical of Fidel Castro. Many who have known him closely affirm that Castro has no friends, and that he uses those around him as chips in his secret game, and then discards them when it suits him without even a hint of scruples.

After knowing the cardinal role that Fidel Castro played in the destabilization, overthrow, and possibly physical elimination of Salvador Allende, it would be a mistake to think that his motives were only personal. It is true that the Chilean model of socialism was in contradiction with the Castro model of the violent way. It is also true that Allende humiliated Castro, and Castro does not forgive humiliations. But it is more likely that Fidel Castro received the orders to eliminate Allende from his real masters: the Wall Street bankers who have always been the real secret promoters of the violent revolution.

In reality the overthrow and assassination of Allende had been dictated on September 16, 1970, 12 days after Allende won the elections and was waiting for the confirmation of the Chilean Congress. The order was mentioned by the international criminal agent Henry Kissinger, spokesman for the bankers, in a press conference he gave in Chicago as special assistant to the White House on national security matters. According to Kissinger, if Allende was confirmed, a Communist regime would emerge in Chile, and soon Argentina, Bolivia and Peru would follow suit.

Of course, one should not be fooled by Kissinger's language. The creation of a "Communist" regime in Chile, and that the example would spread throughout Latin America, was precisely the golden dream of the bankers and the U.S. military-industrial complex, always on the lookout for enemies.

However, to the globalist conspirators' surprise, and despite the efforts of their agent Fidel Castro, Allende refused to implement in Chile the Communist regime dreamed of by the CFR conspirators. It is suspected that the CIA's destabilizing operations in Chile were authorized by the super-secret "Committee of 40" headed by Kissinger in the National Security Council. It is good to remember that the National Security Council (NSC) and the CIA were created in 1947 by the bankers for their own secret purposes. By getting their hands on control of the CIA, the NSC, and the State Department —which they had already taken over for many years— the bankers were able to establish almost total control over the U.S. government.

In a honeyed letter she wrote to Fidel Castro in 2007,[276] Gloria Gaitán expressed her deep love for the murderous Caribbean tyrant. In her obtuseness, Gloria has gone to great lengths to ignore the multiple indications that point to Castro as an active participant in her father's assassination. Moreover, she has ignored Fidel Castro's possible involvement in the assassination of her lover, Salvador Allende.[277]

But Gloria Gaitán is not an isolated case. Paradoxically, Fidel Castro has always had the support not only of Wall Street imperialist conspirators, but also of the unwary anti-imperialists who oppose so-called "U.S. imperialism" —which is nothing but the imperialism of the oil magnates and Wall Street bankers who control the U.S.. This goes some way to explain why these tinpot "anti-imperialists" have lost every battle. For them, Sun Tzu's book *The Art of War278* should be required reading.

According to Sun Tzu, only he who knows his enemy and knows himself will win every battle. Unfortunately, most of those who fight against "American imperialism" do not know who their real enemy is and who their secret agents are.

17. More on the Bogotazo

On the morning of April 11, word spread that the rioters had laid down their arms after reaching an agreement with the government. Because the situation was chaotic, Castro, del Pino and the rest of the Cubans took refuge in a hotel in downtown Bogotá and contacted the Cuban embassy with the ambassador, Guillermo Belt, who was also attending the Ninth Conference, to give them asylum and try to get them out of the country. Belt promised to send an embassy car to pick them up.

But since it was almost 5:30 in the afternoon, and the curfew began at six o'clock, the hotel owner threw them out on the street. It was then when, according to Castro, by pure chance, they ran into an Argentine embassy official driving a car with diplomatic plates, and Castro convinced him to take them to the Cuban embassy.

The next day, Castro, del Pino and the other Cubans were able to return to Cuba in a cargo plane, which in theory had gone to pick up some bulls that had been taken to Bogotá to be exhibited at an agricultural fair.

Upon their arrival in Havana, Castro told the press that they had escaped from Colombia on their own using fictitious names. Some sources claim that Castro used his pseudonym "Alejandro."

But there are some elements of this story that do not fit the reality of the facts.

First, the animosity between Fidel Castro and the then president of Cuba Ramon Grau San Martin was well known, especially by Belt, who was a personal friend of Grau. Secondly, in Castro's version of events given to Tad Szulc, the Cubans at the embassy received them very well because they had become famous. Therefore, the fictitious names were not used to deceive the Cubans at the embassy, but the Colombian authorities. In other words, they left the country with false documents. But, as such documents are not produced overnight, everything indicates that they had been prepared beforehand.

Thirdly, due to the riots, the Colombian authorities had suspended all commercial flights from Bogotá. It is therefore difficult to explain why the flight taking Castro and del Pino back to Cuba was allowed to take off.

It is pertinent to add that the Cuban ambassador and delegate to the Ninth Conference, Guillermo Belt, was a high-ranking politician in Cuba, who maintained close relations in the upper echelons of Washington with important figures in the U.S. government and armed forces. Belt was Cuba's ambassador to the U.S. from 1944 to 1949. He had also been head of the Cuban delegation to the San Francisco meeting where the United Nations Organization was created. From 1945 to 1949 he also represented Cuba at the UN. Moreover, Belt was linked to several Wall Street banking organizations.

But most importantly, according to the information I copy below, at one point Belt gave an explanation as to why he played a key role in helping agents provocateurs Castro and del Pino escape from Colombia. This help was not due to personal sympathy for Castro, because in 1957, Belt had told the U.S. ambassador to Cuba, Earl E.T. Smith, that Castro "had been accused of committing various crimes during the Bogotazo."

On May 9, 2012, Cuban journalist Antonio Llano Montes mentioned on his morning show on Miami's Radio Mambí that he had been a close friend of President Ramón Grau San Martin. According to Llano Montes, in a private meeting with Grau in which Guillermo Belt was participating, Llano Montes took the opportunity to ask Belt, "why did you take Fidel Castro out of Colombia in a plane after his participation in the Bogotazo", and he answered with a big smile: "Orders from above" and, with a nod of his head, he pointed north. Since these orders had obviously not come from President Grau, Llano Montes interpreted this response to mean that the orders had come from Washington.

In a telephone conversation on May 15, 2012, Llano Montes confirmed to me the accuracy of this information.

Interestingly, once again, both the U.S. and Perón governments seem to have played an important role in helping Castro and del Pino escape from Colombia after they had done their job as agents provocateurs in the service of the Wall Street conspirators.

Epilogue

The Bogotazo and September 11, 2001

Just a cursory analysis of the tragic events of September 11, 2001 shows that the methodology followed was a carbon copy of that used in the Bogotazo in 1948. Therefore, one must conclude that both events were planned and carried out by the same group of conspirators: oil tycoons, Wall Street bankers and other CFR conspirators.

The list of similarities between the Bogotazo and the events of September 11, 2001 is extensive, and it would require a long treatise to point them out in detail. However, just citing a few of these is enough to prove it. Let us see:

2. Motive

Bogotazo: Defeat and end of the main enemy: Nazi Germany. The Bogotazo is used as a pretext to start the Cold War against the new enemy: the Soviet Union.

9/11/2001: Collapse and disappearance of the main enemy: the Soviet Union. The attacks of September 9, 2001 are used as a pretext to start the War on Terror against the new enemy: the Muslim terrorists.

3. Use of scapegoats

Bogotazo: Roa Sierra, the assassin of Gaitán, was just a scapegoat, the scapegoat who would take the blame for the crime. Since Roa did not have the skill or training to fire a gun the way the assassin did, everything indicates that he was not the one who killed Gaitán.

9/11/2001: The Muslim fanatics, who allegedly flew the planes that crashed into the buildings, were just the scapegoats to take the blame. Since this group of Muslims did not have the training, much less the experience, to fly such planes, all indications are that it was others who were in control of the planes and directed them to their targets.

3. Use of Manchurian candidates

Bogotazo: Juan Roa Sierra, the alleged assassin of Gaitán, presents many of the characteristics of having been a Manchurian Candidate; a hypnotically conditioned individual who, under mind control, commits a crime without being aware of it.

9/11/2001: Several of the Muslims who allegedly hijacked the planes that later crashed into the World Trade Center and the Pentagon were evidently not fully aware of what they were actually doing. Some of them had been living on a U.S. military base in the southern United States.

4. Warnings from intelligence agencies are ignored.

Bogotazo: Despite attempts by General Marshall and other CFR agents to cover it up, the intelligence branch of the CIA warned in advance that something was afoot, but their warnings were ignored.

9/11/2001: Several intelligence agencies, including Russian and Israeli intelligence services, warned the CIA in advance that something serious was being plotted against the U.S., but their warnings were ignored.

4. Prior knowledge of the facts

Bogotazo: A Venezuelan newspaper published news of the riots before they had broken out.

9/11/2001: The day before the events, someone called Willie Brown, the mayor of San Francisco, and advised him not to fly that day. Several days before the events, some activity in the futures markets indicated that someone knew that the airlines involved were going to have a sudden drop in their stock prices. The CIA carefully monitors this type of activity, but in this case ignored it.

A tv station mentioned the collapse of building number 7 when the building still looks unscathed on the screen. The building collapsed several minutes later.

A group of so-called "neo-cons" [neo-conservatives, although followeres of Trotskyist ideology] had created the Project For a New American Century (PNAC). One of their initial documents mentions the need for a catastrophic Pearl Harbor-type event that they could use as an excuse to convince the American people to accept the drastic changes that were coming.

6. Creation of false leads

Bogotazo: Castro and del Pino distributed loose sheets of Communist content at the Colon Theater, and then detectives found Marxist literature in his Claridge's hotel room.

9/11/2001: The FBI reported finding a copy of the Koran in one of the cars abandoned at the Boston airport by the alleged hijackers of the planes. The nearly intact passport of one of the alleged hijackers was found among the pulverized ruins of the World Trade Center (WTC) buildings.

7. Destroyed buildings

Bogotazo: Witnesses reported that flammable materials had previously been placed in several of the buildings that the rioters then destroyed.

9/11/2001: Several witnesses reported that powerful explosives (probably thermite) had previously been placed in the twin towers of the WTC and were detonated to coincide with the planes crashing into the skyscrapers.

8. Disinformation techniques

Bogotazo: False radio reports with Communist overtones were broadcast to the Colombian population.

9/11/2001: Fake videos of Osama bin Laden taking the blame for the attacks were shown to the U.S. population.

9. Subsequent disinformation analyses of the events

Bogotazo: Secret CFR agents in the U.S. government produced a report blaming local Communists and international communism for the riots.

9/11/2001: An investigative commission controlled by CFR agents produced a report blaming Muslim terrorists for the events.

10. Ideological justification

Bogotazo: The year before the Bogotazo, CFR member George Kennan had published an alarming article in Foreign Affairs stoking fear of communism and Soviet expansionism.

11/9/2001. In the summer of 1993, CFR member Samuel Huntington published an article in Foreign Affairs in which he warned of the growing danger of a clash of civilizations between the Judeo-Christian and Muslim worlds. In 1996, the topic "The Danger of Muslim Fundamentalism" was discussed at the World Economic Forum in Davos, Switzerland. In 1997, Zbigniew Brzezinski (CFR, Trilateral Commission), published his book The Grand Chessboard in which he warned about the growing Muslim terrorist threat.

11. Beginning of . . .

Bogotazo: A long, unwinnable war against international communism.

11/9/2001: A long, unwinnable war against international terrorism.

12. Direct beneficiaries

Bogotazo: Oil maagnates, Wall Street bankers, transnational corporations and the U.S. military-industrial complex.

9/11/2001: Oil magnates, Wall Street bankers, transnational corporations and the U.S. military-industrial complex.

13. Use of agent provocateurs

Bogotazo: Fidel Castro visits several Latin American countries, and recruits dupes for the coming struggle against U.S. imperialism.

11/9/2001. Fidel Castro visits several Muslim countries, and recruits dupes for the coming struggle against U.S. imperialism.

14. Objective of the psychological warfare operation (PsyOp)

Bogotazo: Terrorizing the Latin American and North American peoples with fear of communism so that they will accept as a lesser evil changes that would otherwise be unacceptable.

9/11/2001: Terrorizing the American people with the fear of terrorism so that they accept as a lesser evil changes that would otherwise be unacceptable.

15. PsyOp type

Bogotazo: PsyOp based on the Hegelian principle of thesis-antithesis-synthesis, in which the assassination of Gaitán and the riots played the role of false flag type antithesis.

11/9/2001: PsyOp based on the Hegelian principle of thesis-antithesis-synthesis, in which the attacks on the WTC and the Pentagon played the role of false flag antithesis.

16. Long-term results

Bogotazo: The period known as La Violencia, which reduced the freedoms of the Colombian people, and the Cold War, which reduced the freedoms of the American people.

9/11/2001: The so-called War on Terror, which has greatly reduced the freedoms of the American people and most of the peoples of the world.

The Hegelian PsyOp technique used in the 9/11/11 operation has been so successful that other governments have also used it. For example, the "terrorist" attack that destroyed four trains at the Atocha station in Madrid in 2004 and the bomb scare on the London subway in 2005, have all the characteristics of having been operations of this type.12

Appendix

According to the *U.S. General Staff Dictionary of Military Terms*, intelligence is the end product resulting from the collection, processing, integration, analysis and interpretation of available information.[1] In fact, the official definition of the term "intelligence" accepted by the U.S. intelligence services is "information that has been evaluated."

In a 1955 report to the U.S. Government, *the Herbert Hoover Commission, a U.S. Congressional study group dedicated to analyzing intelligence activities*, concluded that: "Intelligence is that which has to do with all the things that must be known before a course of action can be initiated." [2] A similar definition was given by a true expert in the field more than 2000 years ago. According to Sun Tzu, "The reason why the enlightened prince and the wise general always succeed in defeating the enemy is because of their foreknowledge."[3]

Therefore, although the term intelligence encompasses something much more complex, we can accept the shorter definition that intelligence is only information after it has been properly evaluated.

Although the definition of intelligence is very simple and straightforward, most authors dealing with the subject confuse it. Some of them use the terms information and intelligence as synonyms, when it is obvious they are not. Others have even used the term "raw intelligence" as a synonym for information, but, as we will see below, contrary to information (which can contain misinformation and disinformation), intelligence is a very elaborate product, and there is nothing "raw" about it.

The U.S. intelligence services use a conventional classification to determine the degree of credibility, reliability, importance and accuracy of an information. The intelligence services of other countries use similar rankings. This analysis is based on both the analysis of the source and the information itself. The system is relatively simple.

1. The evaluation of the information

According to an undated secret CIA manual, information evaluation, also called assessment or validation, is concerned with the analysis of specific information in terms of credibility, veracity, accuracy and relevance, and the use of this information once it becomes intelligence. The evaluation or assessment of information is achieved in several stages and is indicated by a conventional system of letters and numbers.

Reliability of the source   Truthfulness of the information

A. Completely reliable   1. Confirmed by reliable sources
B. Generally reliable   2. Probably true
C. Acceptably reliable   3. Most likely true
D. Generally unreliable   4. Doubtful
E. Unreliable   5. Unlikely true
F. Unverifiable   6. Unverifiable

As can be seen, the evaluation of information is simultaneously concerned with both the veracity of the information itself - a lengthy process that involves meticulously verifying new information and how it integrates with existing information that has been verified - and the reliability of the source supplying the information. Both aspects must be considered independently, because the reliability of the source alone does not guarantee that the information is true, nor does the veracity of the information alone guarantee that the source is reliable. In general, however, most people, including intelligence officials, tend to believe what they suspect or expect to be true.

It should be emphasized that the two assessments must be completely independent of each other, which is indicated according to the system shown above. For example, information considered "probably true" from a "generally reliable" source would be designated as "B2."

As can be inferred, intelligence analysts are similar to meteorologists in that they never categorically affirm or deny anything, but only issue criteria of probabilities that something is true or not. For example, the information about the events of the Bogotazo that Fidel Castro provided to Arturo Alape could be classified as "E4", i.e., doubtful information from an unreliable source.

Many aspects are taken into consideration when evaluating the reliability of the source: Did the agent see or hear the information with his own eyes and ears or through other sources? What was his access to those sources? Is the agent characterized by always telling the truth or does he tend to lie or exaggerate? Is he a good observer? Does he have a good memory? Is he rigorous in the verification or transcription of his data?

Keep in mind that the authority of a source is very relative. A source of great authority may produce reliable information, but the intelligence officer must always ask himself, why, what is his motivation? The greater the authority of the source, the greater the possibility that it may be biased or compromised and, therefore, the greater the danger of disinformation.

Very authoritative sources in totalitarian governments do not always tell the truth, but very authoritative sources in democratic countries are not always very reliable either. There is evidence that the CIA has been involved in recruiting professors and students at the most prestigious American universities and journalists in the most influential American media. In addition, there are suspicions that the KGB, the Mossad, and even the Cuban intelligence services, among others, have done a good job penetrating American universities and media.

From the point of view of intelligence and espionage, a document stolen from the enemy is more valuable than a secret offered for free by any source, since the stolen one diminishes, but does not totally eliminate, the risk that it is deliberately misleading information. The source must also be questioned, even one whose good faith is beyond doubt. The danger facing intelligence services, like most investigators, is believing what they want to believe, a problem that has affected all intelligence services around the world at one time or another. The problem of assessor bias is unavoidable in intelligence, and extends to even the most complete information from the most reliable sources.

Bias in the evaluation of information cannot be totally eliminated in an intelligence service, and especially in high government circles, and is exacerbated by the creation of evaluators to evaluate evaluators. Within intelligence services, the only effective safeguard lies in the individual competence and quality of its members, as well as in their intellectual honesty and personal courage to stand up to pressures from above.

It must always be kept in mind that no source can be considered infallible and no piece of information can be accepted as totally accurate. In any case, the possibilities of error, misinterpretation, misunderstanding and deception are too high to blindly trust any information.

Super-patriots, doctrinaires, court historians, bureaucratic climbers, people of provincial vision and, above all, opportunists, are potential dangers to the correct evaluation of information. Perspective, insight, worldly experience, a philosophical point of view, knowledge and sense of history, and perhaps even a little skepticism and a sense of humor, are the qualities of an intelligence analyst that minimize error in his or her interpretation and evaluation of information.

2. Assessing the September 11, 2001 events

To properly assess the events of 9/11/2001, one must keep in mind that all of the initial information about the events that the American people received came from a single source: the U.S. government. With the sole exception of Congresswoman Cynthia McKinney, who from the beginning questioned the version of events offered by the U.S. government, no one in either major party questioned it.4

However, the U.S. Government, like all governments in the world, is composed of politicians and politicians have never been a source of truthful information.5 Moreover, it is a proven fact that at present the U.S. Government has completely fallen under the control of the CFR conspirators, whose goal they have openly expressed on many occasions: the destruction of the U.S. as a sovereign country and the creation of a New World Order. Therefore, I will evaluate the sole source of the information about the events of September 11, 2001, i.e., secret CFR agents infiltrating the U.S. government, with an E: Unreliable.

We will now evaluate the accuracy of the information itself.

The main characteristic of truthful information is that it fits perfectly with previous information that has proven to be true. Of course, there is a first time for everything, and the fact that something has never happened is not a sure proof that it will not happen someday. But a piece of information that constitutes an exception to the rule must be evaluated much more carefully than one that represents yet another in a series of similar events.

The evaluation of the information itself is a process involving a check against intelligence already in hand about similar events that occurred prior to the one we are evaluating, as well as a guess as to the accuracy of the information related to the event on the basis of how well or how poorly it fits with this prior intelligence.

However, in the analysis of historical events we have the advantage that we can add to the evaluation of the information not only the existence (or non-existence) of similar events that occurred before the event we are evaluating, but also the existence (or non-existence) of similar events that have occurred after the event in question.

In the case of the events of 9/11/2001, the evidence shows, first of all, that never before that date had a skyscraper with or without a steel structure collapsed as a result of a fire of any kind.

For example, on July 28, 1945, a twin-engine B-25 bomber lost its path in the fog and crashed into the 78th, 79th, and 80th floors of the Empire State Building, at the time the tallest skyscraper in New York City. However, although the fire spread over several floors and firefighters had to struggle for several hours to extinguish it, the building did not collapse.

On the other hand, evidence shows that, more than ten years after the events of September 11, 2001, no skyscraper has collapsed as a result of fire. Examples abound.

In October 2004 a raging fire broke out in one of the tallest skyscrapers in Caracas. Although the fire destroyed 20 of the upper floors, the building did not collapse.

In February 2005 a violent fire broke out in a skyscraper in Madrid. Firefighters spent more than a day fighting to extinguish the blaze, which completely consumed the 30 upper floors. However, the building did not collapse.

In November 2010, a 28-story apartment building in Shanghai, China, was totally consumed by fire. But the structure remained intact and the building did not collapse.

In April 2012, the Russian Federation's skyscraper under construction in Moscow fell prey to a raging fire that consumed much of the upper floors. However, firefighters were able to bring the blaze under control. The building did not collapse.

Second, the evidence shows that never, before or after September 22, 2001, has a skyscraper, steel-framed or not, collapsed on its own footprint except as a result of controlled demolition. There have been a few cases where tall buildings have collapsed as a result of earthquakes or construction failures, but they always collapse unevenly, causing damage to other buildings around them. This is precisely the reason why controlled demolition companies charge large sums of money to do their highly specialized work.

If buildings, especially tall buildings with a steel structure, would normally collapse in their own footprint when demolished, the work of these companies would be superfluous, but it is not. However, CFR agents in the U.S. government would have us believe that, unusually, on September 11, 2001, not one, or two, but three6 steel-framed skyscrapers collapsed on their own footprint as a result of fires.

Therefore, after assessing the veracity of the information and the reliability of the source, any intelligence analyst would conclude that the accuracy of the very information provided by CFR agents in the U.S. Government could be assessed as a 5, i.e., unlikely. Never before or since September 11, 2001 has a skyscraper collapsed in its own footprint as a result of a fire.

Therefore, any intelligence assessment of the events of 9/11/ 2001 would produce something close to an E5, i.e., unlikely information from an unreliable source. For the same reasons, based on the above analysis, the intelligence services of other countries must have assessed the information on the events of 9/11/2001 provided by CFR agents in the U.S. Government as a clumsy attempt to pass disinformation disguised as real intelligence. This includes the report produced by the official Commission that studied the events - almost all of whose members were CFR agents.

Moreover, the fact that the events of September 11, 2001 served as a pretext for implementing policies decided long in advance is a sure indication that it was an operation carried out by CFR conspirators infiltrating the U.S. government. Just as the Bogotazo was used as a pretext for the beginning of the Cold War, the events of September 11, 2001 were the pretext to justify the beginning of an endless war against terrorism, which has become a war against the American people and the peoples of the world.

Beginning with the explosion of the battleship Maine in 1898 in Havana Bay, and ending with the events of September 11, 2001, U.S. foreign policy has been based on lies created by the CFR conspirators and implanted in the minds of gullible citizens by a complicit press. Lies are the most powerful weapon used by governments around the world to keep their people terrorized and subjugated. Unfortunately, the U.S. government is no exception.

Notes

Foreword

1. Several years before Karl Marx wrote the *Communist Manifesto* in 1872, Clinton Roosevelt had already published in 1841 his treatise The *Science of Government based on Natural Law,* in which he expounds exactly the same principles that Marx copied in his Manifesto. In turn, in 1912, when Benito Mussolini was still a farm hand in the fields of Italy and Hitler an altar boy at Lambach Abbey, Edward Mandell House published under a pseudonym his novel, *Philip Dru: Administrator*, in which he describes in detail the basic principles of a Fascist coup d'état as a preliminary step to the seizure of political power. On the other hand, some researchers claim that both Clinton Roosevelt's *Science of Government* and Marx's *Communist Manifesto* are plagiarized from a collection of documents written by Adam Weishaupt in the 18th century.

2. The most notorious psychopaths in recent human history have been Vladimir Lenin, Adolf Hitler and Fidel Castro, but some second rate ones, such as Henry Kissinger, Dick Cheney and Hillary Clinton, have tried to emulate them.

3. See, Servando Gonzalez, "Fidel Castro Supermole", http://www.intelinet.org/sg_site/articles/sg_castro_supermole.html.

4. Forrestal quoted in Phoebe Courtney, *The CFR: Part II* (Littleton, Colorado: *The Independent American*, 1975), p. 24.

5. *Project for the New American Century*, "Rebuilding America's Defenses: Strategy, Forces and Resources For a New Century", September, 2000, p. 51.

6. Alex Callinicos, "The Grand Strategy of the American Empire", *International Socialism Journal* No. 97 (Winter 2002), http://pubs.socialistreviewindex.org.uk/isj97/callinicos.htm.

7. James Petras, *Rulers and Ruled in the U.S. Empire: Bankers, Zionists and Militants* (Atlanta, Georgia: Clarity Press, 2007).

8. Proof of this is that in a relatively recent article, Petras made the mistake of criticizing Castro and, to his surprise, earned the ire of the Caribbean tyrant. See, James Petras and Robin Eastman-Abaya, "Cuba: Continuing Revolution and Contemporary Contradictions", *Dissident Voice,* August 13, 2007, http://dissidentvoice.org/2007/08/cuba-continuing-revolution-and-contemporary-contradictions/.

9. Dr. Locard's forensic principle is quoted in Zakaria Erzinclioglu, *Every Contact Leaves a Trace: Scientific Detection in the Twentieth Century* (London: Carlton, 2001), p. 10.

10. For a critical analysis of the National Security Archive see,

Servando Gonzalez, *The Nuclear Deception: Nikita Khrushchev and the Cuban Missile Crisis* (Oakland, California: Spooks Books, 2002), pp. 210-215.

Introduction

1. A notable exception is a short article, published on April 19, 1948 in the Cochabamaba newspaper *Voz Obrera*, under the title, "The shot that assassinated Gaitán was directed from Wall Street". An editorial entitled "An assassination and a riot", published in the same issue, mentions the activities of the North American intelligence services in Latin American countries and the possibility that an agent provocateur in their service may have been the real author of the crime.

2. It is known as false flag recruitment when an agent is recruited by an intelligence service posing as a different one. Modernly, the term has been extended to indicate a covert operation whose executor hides behind a false identity. False flag operations are very old, ranging from Nero burning Rome and blaming the Christians, to the Nazis burning the Reichstag and blaming the Communists.

3. Jack Davis, "The Bogotazo", *Studies in Intelligence*, Vol. 13, Fall 1969. According to Davis, "Thorough investigations indicated that he [Castro] had had minimal involvement [in the Bogotazo]".

4 John Loftus and Mark Aarons, *The Secret War Against the Jews: How Western Espionage Betrayed the Jewish People* (New York: St. Martin's Press, 1994), p. 8.

Part One: The CIA

1. See, Peter Grose, *Continuing the Inquiry* (New York: Council on Foreign Relations, 1996), p. 1.

2. Lawrence E. Gelfand, *The Inquiry: American Preparations for Peace, 1917-1919* (New Haven: Yale University Press, 1963), pp., 44, 317.

3. Ibid. pp. 5, 316.

4. Ibid., p. 212.

5. To understand the difference between information and intelligence, see Appendix.

6. Cover story: (1). A fictitious, but plausible, story used to disinform about the visible evidence of a covert operation. (2). A false, but relatively plausible, explanation used to explain a covert operation gone wrong. (3). A false, but plausible, story used by an intelligence

officer to conceal his real mission. Also called a "legend.

7. See, Grose, *op. cit.*

8. On page 58 of his book *The Rockefeller File* (Seal Beach, California: '76 Press, 1976), Gary Allen cites page 42 of the CFR 1952 Annual Report, which mentions the fact that, because they hold high government positions, some CFR members hide their membership for a time. It also mentions that, during an investigation of the CFR conducted by a Congressional Committee (Reece Congressional Committee) in 1953, it was learned that the CFR also had secret members. Two of these, businessman Cyrus Eaton and Senator William Fulbright, were later found to be Communist agents.

Today, one of these secret members could be Barack Hussein Obama, because he follows the treacherous political line of the CFR to the letter.

9. Talent spotter: An intelligence officer or operational agent whose primary function is to locate and evaluate individuals who could be recruited as agents for intelligence and espionage work.

10. Grose, *op. cit.*, p. 11.

11. *Ibid.*, p. 10.

12. Members of the Democratic Party believe that conservatives control the press, while Republicans think it is controlled by liberals. In reality, both are right. Liberal members of the CFR control the press, but the owners are conservative (rather reactionary) members of the CFR.

13. Carroll Quigley, *op. cit.*, pp. 1247-1248.

14. Among the main ones are the Consejo Mexicano de Asuntos Internacionales, the Consejo Colombiando de Relaciones Internacionales, the Consejo Nacional de Relaciones Exteriores de Panamá, the Consejo Argentino para las Relaciones Internacionales, the Consejo Chileno de Relaciones Internacionales, the Consejo Uruguayo para las Relaciones Internacionales and the Instituto Peruano de Estudios Internacionales.

The fact that Enrique Krauze, editor of Letras Libres, gave a lecture at the headquarters of the Council on Foreign Relations in New York, in which he criticized in harsh terms one of the candidates for the presidential elections in Mexico, is evidence that the CFR not only controls U.S. policy, but also interferes rudely in that of Mexico.

15. The members of the English Fabian Society are supporters of communism as conceived by Karl Marx. However, contrary to traditional Communists, the Fabians believe that the correct way to conquer political power is gradually, by infiltration, capturing the institutions of government from within. Appropriately, the symbol of the Fabians is the wolf disguised as a lamb. The Italian Marxist Antonio Gramsci advised using a technique similar to that of the Fabians.

16. The fact is mentioned in Joseph J. Trento, *The Secret History of*

the CIA (Roseville, California: Forum, 2001), p. 44. In a book he published a few years later, *Prelude to Terror* (New York: Carroll & Graf, 2005), Trento places Dulles' secret office on Wall Street.

17. For a detailed study of the Federal Reserve Bank, see G. Edward Griffin, The Creature from Jekyll Island: A Second Look at the Federal Reserve (Westlake Village, California: American Opinion, 1994).

18. General Butler enlisted in the U.S. Marine Corps at the outbreak of war with Mexico. During the 34 years he served in the Marines, Butler was twice awarded the Congressional Medal of Honor, the first for the capture of Veracruz in 1914, and the second for the capture of Fort Riviere, Haiti, in 1917.

19. Smedley D. Butler, *War is a Racket* (Los Angeles: Feral House, 2003), p. 10.

20. Operation Keelhaul executed after the end of World War II, Operation Phoenix in Vietnam, the murder of thousands of civilians during the invasion of Panama, as well as the unnecessary killing of thousands of Iraqi soldiers during the Gulf War on the so-called "highway of death", are some of the most notorious crimes committed by American intelligence organizations and armed forces following orders from the Wall Street Mafia, but they are not the only ones.

21. For example, the president of La Raza, an anti-American leftist organization that exploits Mexican patriotism for its secret purposes, was for many years Raul Yzaguirre, a member of the CFR.

22. It was John D. Rockefeller, the man most associated with free enterprise capitalism, who said, "Competition is a sin. What most people ignore is that monopoly capitalism is not really capitalism, but socialism manifested in either of its two extreme forms, communism or fascism.

23. William Engdahl's *A Century of War: Anglo-American Oil Politics and the New World Order* (London: Pluto Press, 2004), p. 32.

24. *Ibid.*, p. 33.

25. Daniel Yergin, The Prize: The Epic Quest for Oil, Money and Power, Part I (New York: Pocket Books, 1991), p. 59.

26. John Christian Ryter, "The Secret Life of AIC", *NewsWithViews.com*, March 31, 2009.

27. In 1841, many years before Marx published his Communist Manifesto, Clinton Roosevelt, an ancestor of President Franklin D. Roosevelt, had published his book The Science of Government Founded on Natural Law, in which he expressed before Marx the basic tenets of communism.

28. Antony C. Sutton, *Wall Street and the Bolshevik Revolution* (New Rochelle, New York: Arlington House, 1974).

29. G. Edward Griffin, *The Creature From Jekyll Island: A Second Look at the Federal Reserv*e (Appleton, Wisconsin: American Opinion,

1994).

30. Ryter, *op. cit.*

31. *Western Technology and Soviet Economic Development* (Three volumes) (Stanford, California: Hoover Institution Press, 1968-1973), *Wall Street and the Bolshevik Revolution* (New Rochelle, New York: Arlington House, 1974); and *The Best Enemy Money Can Buy* (Billings, Montana: Liberty House Press, 1986). These rigorous academic studies cost Professor Sutton his job at the Hoover Institution of Stanford University.

32. Most likely, the Rosenbergs, true Communist fanatics, were unaware that their real role was to pay with their lives as scapegoats in a psyop devised by the conspirators to misinform the American people.

33. For a detailed history of the betrayal, see George Racey Jordan, *From Major Jordan's Diaries* (Boston: Western Islands, 1965), pp. 72-106. The events recounted by Major Jordan were largely confirmed in 1980 in a novel written by James Roosevelt, son of President Franklin Delano Roosevelt. See, James Roosevelt *A Family Matter* (New York: Simon & Schuster, 1980).

34. Sutton, *The Best Enemy Money Can Buy,* pp. 101-111.

35. See Antony Sutton, *Wall Street and the Rise of Hitler* (Seal Beach, California: '76 Press, 1976); also, Charles Higham, *Trading With The Enemy: An Exposé of the Nazi-American Money Plot,* 1933-1949 (New York: Delacorte Press, 1983).

36. See, Joseph Borkin, T*he Crime and Punishment of I.G. Farben* (New York: The Free Press, 1978), p. 1.

37. Sutton, *op. cit.*, p. 33. I.G. Farben was the company that produced Ziklon B, the lethal gas used to murder prisoners in Nazi extermination camps.

38. Carroll Quigley, *Tragedy and Hope: A History of the World in Our Time* (New York: Macmillan, 1966), p. 308.

Sutton, *op. cit.*, p. 163.

40. Borkin, *op. cit.*, p. 49.

41. *Ibid*, p. 59.

42. Charles Higham, *Trading With The Enemy: An Exposé of the Nazi-American Money Plot, 1933-1949* (New York: Delacorte Press, 1983), p. 59.

43. *Ibid.*

45. Jim Marrs, *The Rise of the Fourth Reich: The Secret Societies That Threaten to Take Over America* (New York: William Morrow, 2008).

46. See, Robert Wilcox, *Target Patton: The Plot to Assassinate General George S. Patton* (Washington, D.C.: Regnery, 2008).

47. Christy Macy and Susan Kaplan, *Documents: A shocking*

collection of memoranda, letters, and telexes from the secret files of the American Intelligence Community (New York: Penguin Books, 1980).

48. *Ibid.*, p. 10.

49. Jeffrey T. Richelson, *A Century of Spies: Intelligence in the Twentieth Century* (New York: Oxford University Press, 1995).

50. *Ibid.*, p. 131.

Black: said of any type of operation whose true source is concealed or falsely attributed to another source. In the case of propaganda, "black" also means that the content is mostly false.

52. R. Harris Smith, *OSS: The Secret History of America's First Intelligence Service* (Berkeley: University of California Press, 1972), p. 1.

53. See, John Prados, *Keepers of the Keys: A History of the National Security Council from Truman to Bush* (New York: William Morrow, 1991), p. 52.

54. *Ibid.*

55. Information on Roosevelt as CFR stooge in Curtis D. Ball, *My Exploited Father-in-law* (Washington, D.C.: Action Associates, 1970), pp. 23-24, 92, 185.

56. Among the books supporting the thesis that the Japanese attack on Pearl Harbor was not only provoked, but not prevented and then used as a pretext to enter the war, are, Robert B. Stinnet, *Day of Deceit: The Truth About FDR and Pearl Harbor*; also, Rear Admiral Robert A. Theobald (USN Retired), *The Final Secret of Pearl Harbor - The Washington Contribution to the Japanese Attack.*

57. John Prados, *Safe for democracy: The Secret Wars of the CIA* (Chicago: Ivan R. Dee, 2006), p. 43.

58. *Ibid.*

59. Smith, *op. cit.*, pp. 15-16.

60. Higham, *op. cit.*, p. 216.

61. *Ibid.*

62. For a detailed study of how the OSS helped Nazi war criminals escape, see Thomas M. Bower, *The Pledge Betrayed: America and Britain and the Degasification of Post-War Germany* (New York: Doubleday, 1982), especially Part 4.

63. Lyman Kirkpatrick, *The Real CIA* (New York: MacMillan, 1968), p. 15.

64. Daniel Yergin, *The Prize: The Epic Quest for Oil, Money, and Power* (New York: Pocket Books, 1993), p. 43.

65. See, Peter Collier and David Horowitz, *The Rockefellers* (New York: Signet, 1977), p. 23.

66. Gary Allen, *The Rockefeller File* (Seal Beach, California: '76 Press, 1976), p. 23.

67. Ida Tarbell, "The Standard Oil Company,' in Earl Latham (ed.), *John D. Rockefeller: Robber Baron or Industrial Statesman?* (Boston: D.C. Heath and Company, 1949.), p. 33.

68. See, Appendix, The Evaluation of Information.

69. Collier & Horowitz, *op. cit.*, p. 5.

70. Fitzhugh Green, *American Propaganda Abroad* (New York: Hyppocrene, 1988), p. 99.

71. See, John Loftus and Mark Aarons, *The Secret War Against the Jews* (New York: St. Martin's Press, 1994), pp. 64-73.

72. Charles Higham, *Trading With the Enemy: An Exposé of the Nazi-American Money plot 1933-1949* (New York: Delacorte Press, 1983).

73. *Ibid.* The story is told in detail in Chapter 3, "The Secrets of Standard Oil".

74. See, Stephen Schlesinger, "Cryptanalysis for Peacetime: Codebreaking at the Birth and Structure of the United Nations", *Cryptologia 19* (July 1995), pp. 217-235.

Black: In the intelligence and espionage lingo, an operation is said to be "black" when its true originator is kept secret or attributed to another. In the case of propaganda, "black" means that its content is false.

76. R. Harris Smith, *OSS: The Secret History of America's First Intelligence Service* (Berkeley: University of California Press, 1972) p. 1.

77. John Loftus, The Belarus Secret (New York: Alfred A. Knopf, 1982), p. 69.

78. See, John Prados, *Keepers of the Keys: A History of the National Security Council from Truman to Bush* (New York: William Morrow, 1991), p.

79. *Ibid.*

80. See, William Greider, *Who Will Tell the People: The Betrayal of American Democracy* (New York: Simon & Schuster, 1992), p. 365-366.

81. Ronald Kessler, *Inside the CIA* (New York: Pocket Books, 1992), p. 85.

82. I never called Barack Obama president because I did not consider him legally so. See, Servando Gonzalez, "Barack Obama, Administrator: A History of Today", http://www.nolanchart.com/article6230.html.

83. Although General James L. Jones does not appear on the list of CFR members, his actions show quite clearly who his real masters are.

84. Jones' statement appears at http://www.infowars.com/nsc-advisor-jones-i-take-my-daily-orders-from-dr-kissinger/, March 23, 2009. Kissinger, Scowcroft and Berger are all members of the CFR.

85. "Hillary Clinton: 'CFR Tells Government What It Should Be Doing,'" PrisonPlanet.com, July 16, 2009, http://www.prisonplanet.com/

hillary-clinton-cfr-tells-government-what-it-should-be-doing.html.

86. A good source for discovering the true causes of most U.S. interventions around the world is William Engdahl's book, *A Century of War: Anglo-American Oil Politics and the New World Order* (London: Pluto Press, 2004). See also, Daniel Yergin, *The Prize: The Epic Quest for Oil, Money, and Power* (New York: Pocket Books, 1993).

87. Trevor Monroe, *The Politics of Constitutional Decolonization* (Kinston: University of the Wrest Indies, 1947), p. 27.

88. Sun Tzu, *The Art of War* - translated by Samuel B. Griffin (London: Oxford University Press, 1963). Sun Tzu was a Chinese general who lived 500 B.C. His book is considered the bible of intelligence and espionage.

89 Dulles quoted in David Wise and Thomas B. Ross, *The Espionage Establishment* (New York: Random House, 19670), p. 290.

90. Michael Parenti, *Dirty Truths* (City Lights: San Francisco, 1996) pp. 185-186.

91. Evan Thomas, *The Very Best Men: The Daring Early Years of the CIA* (New York: Simon and Schuster, 2006), pp. 9, 29.

92. Barton J. Bernstein, "American Foreign Policy and the Origins of the Cold War", in Barton J. Bernstein, ed, *Politics and Policies of the Truman Administration* (Chicago: Quadrangle, 1970), pp. 16-17.

93. H.W. Brands, *The Devil We Knew: Americans and the Cold War* (New York: Oxford University Press, 1993), p. vi.

94. Frank Kofsky, *Harry S. Truman and the War Scare of 1948* (New York: St. Martin's Press, 1993), p. 308.

Part Two: Fidel Castro

1. Although del Pino claimed to be a student at the University of Havana, he was actually a student at the School of Arts and Crafts, which had no relation to the University.

2. The only exception is my book *Psychological Warfare and the New World Order: The Secret War Against the American People* (Oakland, California: Spooks Books, 2010).

3. The psychologist is mentioned in Thomas B. Allen and Norman Polmar, *Merchants of Treason* (New York: Dell, 1988), pp. 65-66.

4. *Ibid.*

5. Talent spotter: An intelligence officer or operational agent whose primary function is to locate and evaluate individuals who could be recruited as agents for intelligence and espionage work.

6. Carlos Franqui, *Vida, aventuras y desastres de un hombre llamado Castro* (Barcelona: Planeta, 1988), p. 51.

7. Confidential, Dispatch No. 336, April 26, 1948. Embassy, Havana. http://www.icdc.com/~paulwolf/Gaitán/archives/mallory26april1948.htm.

8. Confidential, Memorandum for the Files, January 2, 1958, http://icdc.com/~paulwolf/aitan/gringosintherevolution/topping2jan1958.jpg. What is most interesting about this document is that it reveals that Castro may have had a similar role, as a lookout or prompter, in the Gaitán assassination.

9. Ernest Hemingway, "The Shot", *True* the men's magazine. April, 1951. pp. 25-28. See also, Roberto Gonzalez Echevarria, "The Dictatorship of Rhetoric/the Rhetoric of Dictatorship: Carpentier, Garcia Marquez, and Roa Bastos", *Latin American Research Review,* Vol. 15, No. 3 (1980), pp. 205-228, where he states that, "the assassination of Manolo Castro was recreated in Hemingway's story 'The Shot'".

10. Carlos Alberto Montaner mentions the fact in his, *Journey to the Heart of Cuba: Life as Fidel Castro* (New York: Algora, 2001), p. 16.

11. Luis Conte Agüero, *Los dos rostros de Fidel Castro* (Mexico, D. F.: Editorial Jus, 1960), p. 222.

12. *Ibid.*, p. 227.

13. Andrés Suárez, *Cuba: Castroism and Communism* (Cambridge, Mass.: The M.I.T. Press, 1967), p. 14.

14. Ernst Halperin, "Castroism-Challenge to Latin American Communism", in *Problems of Communism*, Vol. XII, No. 5 (September-October 1963).

15. José D. Cabús, *Castro ante la historia* (Mexico: Editores Mexicanos Unidos, 1963), pp. 24-25.

16. Contrary to popular opinion, the real objective of the Bay of Pigs invasion was not to overthrow Castro, but to consolidate him in power. See, Servando Gonzalez, *Psychological Warfare and the New World Order: The Secret War Against the American People* (Oakland, California: Spooks Books, 2008), pp. 193-200.

17. See, Servando Gonzalez, *The Secret Fidel Castro: Deconstructing the Symbol* (Oakland, California: Spooks Books, 2001), and The Nuclear Deception: Nikita Khrushchev and the Cuban Missile Crisis (Oakland, California: Spooks Books, 2002). See also my long article, "Fidel Castro Supermole".

18. See, Ramón B. Conte, *Hidden History of Fidel Castro's Crimes* (self-published, n.p., 1995), pp. 15-30.

19. In his book *Inside the Company: CIA Diary* (New York: Bantam, 1989), p. 396, former CIA officer Philip Agee identifies Isabel Siero Perez, del Pino's aunt, as one of the CIA agents at the Miami station.

20. Both in his book and in the telephone interview I conducted

with him years later, Conte mentions a William Bolieu. However, after much research and conjecture, I came to the conclusion that Conte was actually referring to Willard Beaulac, who shortly thereafter was appointed U.S. Ambassador to Colombia.

21. Ramon B. Conte, *Op. Cit.*, pp. 17-18.

22. The interview with Conte can be listened on my website: www.servandogonzalez.org.

23. Information on Pawley in Mario Lazo, *Dagger in the Heart: American Policy Failures in Cuba* (New York: Twin Circle, 1968), pp. 144-145, 170-171.

24. Intelligence agencies do not call their spies "agents", but "intelligence officers", who have military ranks. The agents are the people recruited in the different countries by the intelligence officers. Those are the ones who carry out the task of espionage. The James Bond character is a farce that has nothing to do with the real profession of intelligence officer.

25. CFR secret agent George Marshall already had some experience in creating the Communist threat: Marshall played a major role in implementing a plan conceived by the CFR conspirators to betray Chiang Kai-Shek and hand China on a silver platter to Mao Tse-Tung and his "agrarian reformers".

26. However, it would be a mistake to conclude that, contrary to the Americans, the Soviets were the good guys in the movie; a dichotomy that occurs in Hollywood movies, but not in real life. But, for purely practical reasons, at that time the had postponed, but not abandoned, their plans for revolutionary conquest through armed subversion.

27. Foy D. Kohler, "Cuba and the Soviet Problem in Latin America", in Jaime Suchlicki, ed.; *Cuba, Castro, and Revolution* (Coral Gables, Florida: University of Miami Press, 1972), p. 121.

28. William Benton, *The Voice of Latin America* (New York: Harper and Row, 1965), p. 83.

29. Sputnik was the name of the first artificial satellite that circled the Earth after being successfully launched by the Soviets. What is not said in any of the official histories is that the U.S. Navy had a missile ready that would launch an artificial satellite before the Soviets did. But CFR agents in the military ordered the Navy not to launch the missile. Sputnik was efficiently used by the CFR propaganda machine to stoke fear of the Soviets and justify the Cold War.

30. Foy D. Kohler, *op. cit.*, p. 121.

31. The existence of a military-industrial complex in the U.S. is not a figment of the left or of Communists. The concept was first mentioned by President Eisenhower in his farewell address to the presidency. One explanation is that Eisenhower, a secret agent of the CFR, may have had

a guilty conscience. Another explanation is that his mention of the existence of the military-industrial complex was a disinformation strategy, because it coincided with its disappearance and its replacement by the military-industrial-financial complex controlled by Wall Street bankers.

32. Robert J. Alexander, "Soviet and Communist Activities in Latin America", in DeVere E. Pentony, ed., *Red World in Tumult: Communist Foreign Policies* (San Francisco: Chandler, 1962), p. 240.

33. William Z. Foster, *Outline History of the Americas* (New York: International Publishers, 1951), p. 375.

34. Meddling in the internal affairs of other countries is a diplomatic norm used by most countries, especially powerful ones. But if the activity is discovered, in general the protest of the affected country never becomes public knowledge, unless the affected country wishes to create a diplomatic incident.

Robert Loving Allen, *Soviet Influence in Latin America* (Washington, D.C.: Public Affairs Press, 1959), p. 86.

36. *Ibid.*

37. Nathaniel Weyl, *Red Star Over Cuba* (New York: Hillman/Macfadden, 1961).

38. Angel Aparicio Laurencio, *Antecedentes desconocidos del nueve de abril* (Madrid: Ediciones Universal, 1973).

39. Alberto Niño, *Antecedentes y secretos del 9 de abril* (Bogotá: Editorial Pax, 1949).

40. *Ibid.*, p. 54.

41. See, for example, Enrique Ros, *Fidel Castro y el gatillo alegre* (Miami: Ediciones Universal, 2003), p.188. Shortly after Castro seized power in Cuba in 1959, del Pino, now residing in the U.S., began plotting to overthrow Castro. But Castro set a trap for him, succeeded in capturing him, and he was sentenced to 30 years in prison. Years later, del Pino died in prison under strange circumstances. Some suspect that Castro ordered his assassination in order to eliminate an eyewitness to his real wanderings during the Bogotazo.

42. Alberto Niño, *op. cit.*, p. 54.

43. Alcides Orozco, "Two Cubans Distribute Arms", Bogotá, Colombia, April 19 (1948), *UPI*, quoted in Nathaniel Weyl, Red Star Over Cuba (New York: Hillman/Macfadden, 1961), p. 92-93.

44. *Ibid.*, p. 92.

45. Francisco Fandiño Silva, L*a penetración Soviética en América y el 9 de Abril* (Bogotá, Nuevos Tiempos, 1949) p. 77.

46. Niño, o*p. cit,* p. 77.

47. José Domingo Cabús, *Castro ante la historia* (Mexico City: Editores Mexicanos Unidos, 1963), p. 35.

48. *Ibid.*

49. Jose Guerra Aleman, *Barro y Cenizas* (Madrid: Fomento Editorial, 1971), p. 29.

50. The Cuban Communist Party —the real one, not the fake one Castro created when he took power— changed its name three times. When it was founded in 1925 it was called the Communist Party of Cuba. Then it took the name Unión Revolucionaria Comunista (Revolutionary Communist Union) in 1940. Finally, in 1944, it was called the Popular Socialist Party. However, Cuban Communists never used that name and referred to it simply as "the Party".

51. For an interesting and detailed analysis of the long-running feud between Cuban Communists and Fidel Castro, before and after he took power in 1959, see F. Lennox Campello, "The Cuban Communist Party Anti-Castro Activities, http://members.tripod,com/~Campello/castro.html.

52. Richard Pattee, "The Role of the Roman Catholic Church", in Robert Freeman Smith, ed., *Background to Revolution* (New York: Alfred A. Knopf, 1966), p. 110.

53. Jules Dubois, *Fidel Castro: Rebel - Liberator or Dictator?* (New York: Bobbs-Merrill, 1959), p. 17.

54. "4 Estudiantes Detenidos, Acusados del Asesinato de Manolo Castro", *Hoy*, February 26, 1948.

55. Due to one of those unexpected twists of fate, Vladimiro Roca, son of Blas Roca, economist and former military pilot of Castro's MIGs, became disenchanted with Castro's "communism" and became one of the most famous Cuban dissidents. In March 1999, after having been imprisoned since July 1977, Roca was sentenced to a long prison term for having written, along with other dissidents, a civic manifesto entitled "La patria es de todos" (The Homeland Belongs to All).

56. Although the action was not mentioned in the press, coinciding with the Moncada attack there was also an attack against a barracks in the city of Bayamo, also in Oriente province.

57. *The Daily Worker*, New York, August 5, 1953.

58. Everything indicates that the Cuban Communists were not mistaken about the true ideology of Fidel Castro. For an analysis of the Fascist roots of Castroism, and why I consider Castroism to be nothing but fascism in disguise, see Servando Gonzalez, *The Secret Fidel Castro: Deconstructing the Symbol* (Oakland, California: Spooks Books, 2001), p. 233-303.

59. Luis Dam, "El grupo 26 de julio en la cárcel", *Bohemia*, July 8, 1956.

60. Fidel Castro, ¡Basta ya de mentiras!", *Bohemia*, July 15, 1956. The article is quoted in Rolando E. Bonachea and Nelson P. Valdés, eds.,

Revolutionary Struggle, 1947-1958 (Cambridge, Massachusetts: The MIT Press, 1972), p. 323. As I could not find the original in *Bohemia* magazine, I translated into Spanish the version that appeared in the book by Bonachea and Valdés, which in turn is a translation into English, therefore the version I offer is not faithful to the letter, but to the essence of the content. *Traduttore, tradittore.*

61. *Ibid.*

62. Theodor Draper, *Castroism, Theory and Practice* (New York: Praeger, 1965), p. 28.

63. Luis Conte Agüero, *Fidel Castro: Psiquiatría y política* (Mexico, D. F.: Editorial Jus, 1968), p. 88.

64. Javier Felipe Pazos, "Cuba -'Long Live the Revolution'", *The New Republic*, November 3, 1962, p. 15.

65. Lionel Martin, *Red Star Over Cuba* (New York: Hillman/Macfadden, 1961), pp. 73-85, 92-97.

66. Ramon Conte is the Cuban CIA agent who witnessed the presence of Castro and del Pino at the secret meeting at Mario Lazo's house I mentioned earlier.

67. Castro's speech is quoted in Andres Suarez, *Cuba: Castroism and Communism* (Cambridge, Mass.: The M.I.T. Press, 1967), p. 94.

68. *Cantinflesco*: adjective created to describe the speech of Cantinflas, a character created by the Mexican comic actor Mario Moreno. Cantinflas was characterized because he talked a lot and said little.

69. José Martínez Matos (ed.), *Antes del Moncada* (Havana: Editorial Pablo de la Torriente, 1986), p. 59.

70. Sun Tzu, *The Art of War* [English translation by Samuel B. Griffith] (London: Oxford University Press, 1963).

71. In truth, I have recently discovered that a few anti-Castro members of the so-called "original exile" have awakened from their slumber and have begun to identify their true enemies. Unfortunately, even these few still refer to Fidel Castro's communism.

72. For a detailed analysis proving that Fidel Castro's political ideology is closer to fascism than to communism, see Servando Gonzalez, *The Secret Fidel Castro: Deconstructing the Symbol* (Oakland, California: Spooks Books, 2001), pp. 233-305.

73 However, while it is true that most of the initial group of Cuban exiles in Florida were members of the Cuban oligarchy, the image that still prevails in large sectors of the American public, which sees pro-Castro Cubans as progressives and revolutionaries and anti-Castro Cubans as extreme right-wing reactionaries, is an invention of Castro's intelligence services disseminated by the American mass media controlled by the CFR conspirators.

On the contrary, as one author has pointed out, "Miami's political culture has been understudied and oversimplified, while Cuba's political culture has been sacralized and frozen in its 1959 colors. But I am of the opinion that the political culture of the exile has incorporated important gradual changes and democratization, while the political culture of the island has been imposed and maintained through repression. The superficial appearance of approval and support [for the revolution] on the island is a veil. The monolithic image of Miami is wrong". See, Holly Ackerman, "Searching for Middle Ground: Cuba's Chronic Dilemma", *Peace Magazine*, www.peacemagazine.org/9703/cuba-ha1.htm.

74 Theodore Draper, *Castroism: Theory and Preactice* (New York: Frederick A. Praeger, 1966) p. 71.

75. The fact that Castro mentioned in his self-defense during the trial for the attack on the Moncada barracks in 1953, the theory of the Spanish Jesuit Juan Mariana, expounded in his book *De Rege et Regis Institutione*, indicates that the idea of assassinating his opponents was instilled in Castro by his Jesuit teachers at the Colegio de Belen.

76. Luis Ortega, "Las raíces del castrismo", *Encuentro de la Cultura Cubana*, No. 22 (Spring 2002), p. 322.

77. Mario Lazo, *Dagger in the Heart* (New York: Twin Circle, 1968), p. 182.

78. According to Alfonso Tarabocchia, an investigator with the Dade County Sheriff's Intelligence Unit in Florida, "The [Cuban] exile community has been penetrated to the highest degree. See, David Corn, *Blond Ghost* (New York: Simon and Schuster, 1994), p. 85. More recently, Juan O. Tamayo of the *Miami Herald* reported that at certain times Castro intelligence is believed to have maintained in Florida some 300 intelligence officers dedicated to spying on the Cuban exile community. See, "Spies Among Us: Castro Agents Keep Eye on Exiles", *The Miami Herald*, April 11, 1999. Reports of Castro's intelligence activities in penetrating exile organizations have been extensively documented. See, for example, Mervin K. Sigale, "Castro's Spies Prowl Miami, Defector Says", *The Miami News*, Dec 18, 1971; "Dead 'Exile' Was My Spy, Castro Says", *The Miami Herald*, February 9, 1987; Liz Balmaseda, "Exile: I Was Mastermind of Mariel", *The Miami Herald*, July 31, 1989; "Cuba: Agents Leading the Anti-castro Opposition", *Intelligence Newsletter* # 28, July 10, 1992, http://www. indigo-net.com/intel.html; Tim Weiner, "Castro's Moles Dig Deep, Not Just Into Exiles", *The New York Times*, March 1, 1996; Charles Cotayo, "Alleged Spies Swam Among a Sea of Organizations", *El Nuevo Herald*, September 16, 1998; Lucia Newman, "In Rare Admission, Castro Says Cuba has Dispatched Spies Across U.S..," *CNN*, October 20, 1998; Associated Press, "Cuban Museum a Tribute to Espionage", *The New York Times*, December 7,

1998; Juan O. Tamayo, "Witness: I Was Castro Spy in Foundation", The Miami Herald, March 12, 1999. See also, Susana Lee, "Lo mejor de la misión: el regreso a Cuba", *Granma*, March 24, 2000; and Rui Ferreira, "Un presunto espía tuvo como tarea lanzar campaña contra la Fundación", *El Nuevo Herald*, December 22, 2000. See also, Servando González, "El extraño "Encuentro" de Jesús Díaz con la muerte", www.cubanet.org/opi/05150201.htm, and, Servando González, "Carlos Wotzkow, espía castrista?" www. intelinet.org/sg_sie/intellience/ sg_wotzkow_spy.html.

79. By way of explanation, some recalcitrant anti-castroCommunists in exile have made their own the far-fetched theory that the fall of the Communist regime in Russia is a farce, and that the Communists are still in power.

80. Salvador Díaz-Versón, "Desde 17 años atrás Fidel Castro Trabajaba para Rusia", *El Mundo en el exilio*, October 19, 1960.

81. See, U.S. Senate Subcommittee on Internal Security, hearing, *Communist Threat to the United States Through the Caribbean*, August 13, 1959, Part 2, Appendix, p.115.

82. Ibid., May 2, 1960, Part 7, p.425. See also, Salvador Diaz-Verson, "When Castro Became a Communist: The Impact on U.S.-Cuba Policy", *Institute for U.S.-Cuba Relations, Occasional Paper Series*, Vol.1, No.1, November 3, 1997, http://www.latinamericanstudies.org/ diaz-verson.htm.

83. Alberto Niño H., *Antecedentes y secretos del 9 de abril* (Bogotá: Editorial Pax, 1949), p. 50.

84. Salvador Diaz-Versón, "When Castro Became a Communist: The Impact on U.S.-Cuba Policy", *Institute for U.S.-Cuba Relations, Occasional Paper Series*, Vol.1, No.1, November 3, 1997, Note 9, http:// www.latinamericanstudies.org/diaz-verson.htm.

85. Luis Adrián Betancourt, "CIA: el capítulo cubano", *Juventud Rebelde*, June 30, 2002.

86. Nathaniel Weyl, Red Star Over Cuba (New York: Hillman/ Macfadden, 1961), pp. 73-85, 92-97.

87. Hugh Thomas, *Cuba: The Pursuit of Freedom* (New York: Harper and Row, 1971), p. 829.

88. Lionel Martin, *The Early Fidel* (Seacaucus: Lyle Stuart, 1978), p. 118.

89. Carlos Franqui, Vida, aventuras y desastres de un hombre llamado Castro (Barcelona: Planeta, 1988), p. 43; Servando Gonzalez, *The Secret Fidel Castro: Deconstructing the Symbol* (Oakland, California: Spooks Books, 2001).

90. The full text of the speech with Castro's confession of Marxist faith was published in the morning edition of *Hoy*, the PSP newspaper, on

December 2, 1961.

91. See, Loree Wilkerson, *Fidel Castro's Political Programs from Reformism to Marxist Leninism* (Gainesville, Florida: University of Florida Press, 1965), p. 81.

92. See, *Editorial Research Reports* July 9, 1967.

93. Hugh Thomas, **Cuba: The Pursuit of Freedom** (New York: Harper & Row, 1971), p. 1489.

94. Gabriel García Márquez, "Fidel Castro: El oficio de la palabra hablada", Prologue to Gianni Mina, *Habla Fidel* (Mexico, D.F.: Edivisión, 1988) p. 17.

95. Graffiti in a Paris subway station in the 1960s: "Je sui Marxiste, tendance Groucho".

96. For many years, Cubans called Fidel Castro "the horse".

97 Luis Conte Agüero, *Fidel Castro: Psiquiatría y política* (Mexico City: Editorial Jus, 1968), p. 18.

98. Jesús Arboleya, *The Cuban Counterrevolution* (Athens, Ohio: Ohio University Research Center for International Studies, 2000), p. 61.

99. Jaime Suchlicki, *Cuba: From Columbus to Castro* (New York: Scribner's, 1974), pp. 143.

Bohemia Libre, December 1961.

101. Daniel James, *Cuba: The First Soviet Satellite in the Americas* (New York: Avon, 1961), p. 34.

102. Peter G. Bourne, *Fidel: A Biography of Fidel Castro* (New York: Dodd, Mead & Company, 1986), p. 29.

103. In truth, Malaparte wrote his book not as a eulogy, but as a critique of fascism. This cost him that Mussolini sent him to prison and exile.

104. Talent spotter: Intelligence officer or operational agent whose primary function is to locate and evaluate individuals who could be recruited as agents for intelligence and espionage work.

105. agent: Someone who has been recruited, trained, monitored, and employed to obtain information from within an organization or country. Agents are the only employees of an intelligence service whose job it is to spy. Intelligence services generally do not recruit citizens of their own countries as agents.

106 Agent of influence: a bribed or ideologically compromised person - not directly under the control of a foreign intelligence service - who occupies a position in his country through which he can influence policy or public opinion.

107 Carlos Alberto Montaner, "Does Castro want to abandon the Soviets?" *La Estrella de Panama*, February 22, 1985.

108. Daniel James, op. cit., p. 31.

109. Although Draper uses the word "cuerpo" in his English

translation, the word used by Castro in the Spanish original is "haz". See, Theodore Draper, *Castroism, Theory and Practice* (New York: Praeger, 1965), p. 8.

110. The word Fascist is derived from the Latin word fasces, a bundle of wooden rods tied with a red string carried by Roman lictors when they appeared before magistrates. The tied rods symbolized unity and authority.

111. Luis Conte Agüero, *Cartas de presidio.* (Havana: Editorial Lex, 1959), p. 60. The Castro principle of the cardinal importance of leadership is also mentioned by Theodore Draper, op. cit., p. 9.

112. Walter Laqueur, *Fascism: Past, Present, Future* (New York: Oxford University Press, 1996), pp. 34-35.

For a typical example of a Fascist attack on capitalism, see A. Grandi, La futura civiltá del lavoro nel mondo (Bologna: Stiassi and Tantini, 1941).

114. Chibas quoted in Daniel James, op. cit., p. 34.

115. Festus Brotherson, Jr. Rapporteur, "Cuba: The New Regime of 1959 and Alternative Revolutionary Outcomes", in *José Martí and the Cuban Revolution Retraced,* Proceedings of a Conference Held at the University of California,. Los Angeles, March 1-2, 1985. (Los Angeles: UCLA Latin American Center Publication, 1986), p. 35.

116. I make this fine distinction between fascism and communism not because I think communism is better than fascism, but to clarify the true essence of Castroism. Although the Soviet gulags were based on a different theory than the Nazi lagers, the result was quite similar.

117. Hugh Thomas, "The U.S. and Castro, 1959-1962", American Heritage, Vol. 29 No. 6 (October/November 1978), p. 34.

118. *The Secret Fidel Castro: Deconstructing the Symbol* (Oakland, California: Spooks Books, 2001).

119. Georgie Anne Geyer, *Guerrilla Prince* (Boston: Little, Brown and Company, 1991), pp. 233-305.

120. A. James Gregor, *The Fascist Persuasion in Radical Politics* (Princeton, N.J.: Princeton University Press, 1974), p. 302.

121. See, Jules Dubois, *Fidel Castro* (New York: Bobbs-Merrill, 1959), p. 83. For an interesting comparison between Castro's words and Hitler's, see "History Will Absolve Me", in F. Castro and R. Debray, *On Trial* (London: Lorringer, 1968), p. 40. See also Konrad Heiden, *Der Führer* (Boston: Houghton Mifflin, 1944), p. 206; as well as William Shirer, *The Rise and Fall of the Third Reich* (Greenwich, Conn.: Fawcett, 1962), p. 118.

122. Hugh Thomas, op. cit. p. 828.

123 . In its November 25, 1959 issue, *El Libertario*, a publication of the Cuban anarchists, mentioned that the militias were reminiscent of

Mussolini's combatini Fascisti or the Falangist "blue shirts". See, Carlos
M. Estefanía, "Liquidación del socialismo libertario en Cuba: ¿final de
una utopía?", Revista *Cuba Nuestra*, http://hem.passagen.se/cubanuestra.
Shortly after, El Libertario was banned.

124. See, Marta Rojas, "Manifestación de las antorchas por el
centenario de José Martí", in Aldo Isidrón del Valle, Marta Rojas, Arturo
Alape, et al., *Antes del Moncada* (Havana: Editorial Pablo de la Torriente,
1986). pp. 119-126.

125. Daniel James, op. cit., 55.

126. R. Hart Phillips, *The Cuban Dilemma* (New York: Ivan
Obolensky, 1962), p. 18.

127. Mario Llerena, The Unsuspected Revolution, (Ithaca, N. Y.:
Cornell Univ. Press, 1978), Chapter 5, note 7.

128. See, Lee Lockwood, *Castro's Cuba, Cuba's Fidel*, (New York:
Macmillan, 1967), pp. 50, 52, 55.

129. Lee Lockwood, Ibid., p. 57.

130. Paul D. Bethel, *The Losers* (New Rochelle, N.Y.: Arlington
House, 1969), p. 116. Masetti a Peronist in David D. Burks, *Cuba Under
Castro* (New York: Foreign Policy Association, 1964), p. 42. Massetti
had been a member of the Alianza Nacionalista, an organization of
extreme right-wing Peronist thugs. Years later, Massetti left Prensa Latina
and traveled to Bolivia, where he created a small guerrilla group that
planned to invade Argentina. In April 1964 the group had its first armed
encounter with the army, which liquidated most of the guerrillas.
Massetti managed to escape into the jungle and was never heard from
again.

131. Trent Hater, "Danger Signs in Cuba", *The Militant,* April 17,
1961. For a devastating attack on Castroism from a Marxist (or
Trotskyist) perspective, see Bill Vann, "Castroism and the Politics of
Petty-Bourgeois Nationalism", a lecture delivered in Sydney, Australia,
January 7, 1998, at the International Summer School on Marxism
organized by the Australian Socialist Equality Party. http://wsws.org/
exhibits/castro.

132. Testimony of a CIA officer informing Congress that Castro
was not a Communist in *Communist Threat to the U.S. Through the
Caribbean,* 86th Congress, 1st Sess., Part. 3, Nov. 5, 1959, 162-164.

133. Adam B. Ulam, *The Rivals* (New York: Penguin, 1976), p.
315.

134. Paul Seabury, *The Rise and Decline of the Cold War* (New
York: Basic Books, 1967), p. 68.

135. Paul D. Bethel, op. cit., p. 241.

136. Ibid., p. 318.

137. Ibid., p. 388.

138. See, for example, Jean Cau, "Cuba a ses camps de mort", Paris-Match, June 12, 1971, and also Armando Valladares, Contra toda esperanza (Plaza & Janés, Barcelona, 1985).

139. However, some people believe that there was nothing spontaneous about the events, and that everything was planned in advance between Castro and his friends in the U.S. See, Liz Balmaseda, "Exile: 'I Was Mastermind of Mariel'", *The Miami Herald*, July 31, 1989.

140. See, Carlos Alberto Montaner, interview with Manuel Sánchez Pérez, *Diario Las Américas,* April 27, 1986, 5E. See also, Reinaldo Arenas, *Before Night Falls* (New York: Penguin, 1992), pp. 276-285, as well as Alina Fernández, *Castro's Daughter* (New York: St. Martin's Press, 1998), 153-155. In a recent book, Montaner added some gruesome details when describing the actions of Castro's thugs in harassing people who, following Castro's suggestion, tried to leave the island legally. See, Carlos Alberto Montaner, *Journey to the Heart of Cuba: Life as Fidel Castro* (New York: Algora, 2001), pp. 131.

141. A. James Gregor, *The Fascist Persuasion in Radical Politics* (Princeton, N.J.: Princeton University Press, 1974), p. 302.

142. Edwin Tetlow, *Eye on Cuba* (New York: Harcourt, Brace, 1966), p. 132. For several years, one of the posters identifying CDR adorned one of the walls of La Peña, a Communist agitprop center in the Socialist Republic of Berkeley, California.

143. The idea of a "new man"; athletic, virile, capable, laconic, spartan, persevering, willful, full of life; a hero guided by morality rather than material incentives, appears in many of the works of Fascist literature. See, e.g., Aldo Marinelli, quoted in Emilio Gentile, *Le Origini dell' Ideologia Fascista* (Bari: Laterza, 1974), p. 92; D. Begnac, L'Arcangelo sindacalista: Filippo Corridoni (Verona: Mondadori Edizione, 1943); also V. Rastelli, Filippo Corridoni (Rome: Conquiste d'Impero, 1940). However, history has shown that when Fascists take power, as happened in Castro's Cuba, the immediate result has been that the Fascist "new man" becomes a bloodthirsty beast that treats other human beings as if they were animals.

144. For a partial list and description of the prisons and concentration camps in Cuba, see Alexander Torres Mega, *En las puertas del infierno cubano* (Montevideo: Flashes Culturales, 1995), pp. 101-102. See also, "Cuba's Tropical 'Gulags,'" a conversation with Armando Valladares", *The Miami Herald*, December 26, 1982; and Pierre Golendorf, *7 Años en Cuba: 38 meses en las prisiones de Fidel Castro* (Barcelona: Plaza y Janés, 1977). As a curious fact, it was Che Guevara, the beloved idol of the world's leftists, who created the first concentration camp in Castro's Cuba. The camp was on the Guanahacabibes peninsula, an inhospitable, mosquito-infested place near the southern

coast of Pinar del Río province, west of Havana.

145. See, Mark Neocleosus, *Fascism* (Minneapolis: University of Minnesota Press, 1997), p. 13.

146. Ibid.

147. Ibid, p. 23.

148 . Proof of this is that in his speeches Castro always refers to the people of Cuba, never to the Cuban workers or the proletariat. In the same way, Hitler always referred to the German people (volk).

149. See, Ernst Nolte, *Three Faces of Fascism* (New York: Mentor, 1969), p. 269.

150. For a revealing study of the desperate condition of Cuban workers under the Castro regime, see Oscar Espinosa Chepe, "La situación de la clase obrera cubana y sus perspectivas", Revista Desafíos (Havana), http://webstc.com/desafios/perspectivas.htm. For a denuncia-tion by the World Confederation of Labor of the repression of workers in Cuba, see "Represión antisindical en Cuba, denuncia la Confederación Mundial del Trabajo", *Revista Desafíos*, http://webstc.com/desafios/denunciacmt.htm.

151. See, Walter Laqueur, *Fascism: Past, Present, Future* (New York: Oxford University Press, 1996), p. 15.

152. Carl J. Friedrich and Zbigniew K. Brzezinski, *Totalitarianism. Totalitarian Dictatorship and Autocracy* (New York: Praeger, 1964), p. 60.

153. Herman Finer, *Mussolini's Italy*. (New York: 1935), pp. 175-176.

154. John Guerassi, ed. *The Speeches and Writings of Ernesto Che Guevara* (New York: Macmillan, 1968), p. 422. Also at http://guerrilleroheroico.blogspot.com/2010/03/mensaje-los-pueblos-del-mundo.html. Unfortunately, the hatred was forgotten by Che at the moment he needed it most when, upon being captured in Bolivia, instead of fighting to the death like a man, he raised his arms and begged his captors not to kill him, because he was Che Guevara and he was worth more alive than dead. No one listened to him. For Castro, Che was worth more dead than alive.

155. As in the Nazi SS, the admiration of the Spartan-style gay super-macho warrior ideal was present in Castroism. See, Servando Gonzalez, "Sweet Cuban Warriors by Norberto Fuentes: Obra cumbre de la literatura gay castrista", March 29, 2011, http://www.intelinet.org/sg_site/articles/sg_dulces_guerreros.html. For a study of Nazism as a pagan cult, see Louis Pauwels and Jacques Bergier, T*he Morning of the Magicians* (New Yor: Avon, 1968). For a study of Nazism as a gay cult, see Scott Lively and Kevin Abrams, *The Pink Swastika,* [third edition] (Keiser, Oregon: Founders Publishing Corporation, 1997).

156. Unfortunately, the U.S. is well on its way to becoming the fourth Nazi Reich. The total militarization of society and the constant surveillance of citizens indicate that the night of totalitarianism is closing in on the American people.

157. Regis Debray, *The Revolution Within the Revolution* (New York: Monthly Review Press, 1967).

158. Irving Louis Horowitz (ed.), *Introduction to Cuban Communism* (New Jersey: Transaction Books, 1970), p. 18.

159. James A. Gregor *The Fascist Persuasion in Radical Politics* (Princeton, N.J.: Princeton University Press, 1974), p. 310.

160. For a detailed analysis of the Fascist theory of the revolutionary focus, see Gregor, Ibid. pp. 304-310.

161. The capture and death of Che Guevara, as well as the assassinations of Gaitán, Kennedy and Allende, as well as the sabotage of the Cubana de Aviacion plane in Barbados and the shooting down of the Brothers to the Rescue planes, have been among the many Castro-CIA joint operations. For detailed information on these events, see my Psychological Warfare and the New World Order.

162. Fidel Castro, *Palabras a los intelectuales* (Havana: Ediciones del Consejo Nacional de Cultura, 1961). Guillermo Cabrera Infante recounted how, in one of the meetings, Castro gave a concrete expression to the words of Nazi leader Herman Goering, "When I hear talk of culture, I reach for my gun". According to Cabrera Infante, before beginning his speech, Castro took his pistol out of its holster and placed it brusquely on the table before the terrified eyes of his audience. See, Guillermo Cabrera Infante, Mea Cuba (Barcelona: Plaza & Janés, 1992), p. 85.

163. *Revolución*, August 17, 1962.

164. An interesting fact is that the intellectuals of Fidel Castro's "Communist" Cuba have not produced any important Marxist theoretical document. After 60 years of Castroism, still in Cuba the most important book written by a Cuban Marxist is *Los Fundamentos del Socialismo en Cuba*, written by Blas Roca, a leader of the PSP, in the 1940s.

165. The term "amateur anti-Communist" was coined by the deputy director of the U.S. State Department's Bureau of Intelligence and Research in a speech he gave in Minnesota on May 4, 1994. See, W. Rodman, *More Precious Than Peace* (New York: Charles Scribner's Sons, 1994), p. 108.

166. On the collaboration between Castro and the Catholic Church, see Armando Valladares, "El pedido de perdón que no hubo: la colaboración eclesiástica con el comunismo", *Diario Las Américas*, March 22, 2000. Of course, as a militant Catholic, Valladares cannot accept that in reality the ecclesiastical collaboration is not with commu-

nism but with Castro's fascism.

167. On the socialist roots of fascism, see Ze'ev Sternhell, *The Birth of Fascist Ideology* (Princeton, N.J.: Yale University Press, 1994). See also, see Jim Guirard, "'Progressives' in Bed with a Fascist Fidel", Guaracabuya, http://www.amigospais-guaracabuya.org. For a critique of the error of placing Hitler on the right, see Sebastian Haffner, *The Meaning of Hitler* (Cambridge, Mass.: Harvard University Press, 1979), 59-60, 75.

168. Georgie Anne Geyer, *Guerrilla Prince* (Boston: Little, Brown and Company, 1991), p. 391. On the other hand, other scholars have already considered Peronism as a form of left-wing fascism. See, Seymour Martin Lipset, *Political Man*, expanded edition (Baltimore: The Johns Hopkins University Press, 1981) p. 176.

169. Hugh Thomas, "The U.S. and Castro, 1959-1962", *American Heritage*, Vol. 29 No. 6 (October/November 1978), p. 34.

170. Hugh Thomas, Cuba: The Pursuit of Freedom (New York: Harper and Row, 1971), pp. 1490f.

171. *Bohemia*, January 31, 1960.

172. "Amnesty for Fidel Castro and his followers in prison", Speech by Majority Leader Rafael Díaz-Balart to the House of Representatives, Cuba, National Capitol, May 1955. The full speech can be read at http://www.arnoldoaguila.com/diazbalart.html. However, not even a visionary like Díaz-Balart could have imagined that the Fascist tyranny disguised as communism imposed by Fidel Castro in Cuba would not last twenty years, but more than half a century.

173. José Fernández González, *From Socialism to Fascism*. Un español dentro de la revolución cubana, 1980-1996 (Madrid: Ediciones R, 1996).

174. Rogelio Saunders, "Fascism. Apuntes", *Diaspora(s)*, April 14, 1997, reprinted in *La Habana Elegante* (Segunda época), Internet edition, No. 2, Summer 1998.

175. Ronald Reagan, *Remarks at a Cuban Independence Day Celebration in Miami,* Florida, May 20, 1983. May 20, 1983, The American Presidency Project, http://www.presidency.ucsb.edu/ws/index.php?pid=41355#axzz1reg4THVR.

176. Jesus Arboleya, *The Cuban Counterrevolution* (Athens, Ohio: Ohio University Center for International Studies), p. viii.

177. Ibid., p. x.

178. The Nazi Party emerged in the Bratwurstgloeckel, a gay tavern in Munich. See, Scott Lively and Kevin Abrams, *The Pink Swastika*, [third edition] (Keiser, Oregon: Founders Publishing Corporation, 1997), p. 1.

179. See, Angelo Del Boca and Mario Giovana, *Fascism Today*

(New York: Pantheon, 1969), p. 372. The idea of left Fascist regimes also appears in Seymour Martin Lipset, *Political Man: The Social Bases of Politics (*New York: Doubleday, 1960).

180. George Anie Geyer came to the same conclusion. In an article entitled "Fascism reappears under the guise of communism in Central America", El Universal, July 8, 1983, Geyer describes in detail the Castro strategy of camouflaging fascism with a cover of communism.

181 See, Servando Gonzalez, "Dulces guerreros cubanos, obra cumbre de la literatura gay castrista", www.servandogonzalez.org, March 29, 2011,
    http://www.intelinet.org/sg_site/articles/sg_dulces_guerreros.html. On Nazism as a Spartan-style gay cult, see Scott Lively and Kevin Abrams, *The Pink Swastika*, [third edition] (Keiser, Oregon: Founders Publishing Corporation, 1997), p. 19.

182. This fact explains why Celia Sanchez, for many years Castro's personal secretary and one of his most trusted people, never hid her anti-communism and this did not cause her any problems. However, although everyone in Cuba knew that Celia Sánchez was both antiCommunist and lesbian, the fact is only mentioned by Norberto Fuentes, *Dulces guerreros cubanos* (Barcelona: Seix Barral, 1999), p. 138.

183. Herbert Matthews, *Revolution in Cuba: An Essay in Under-standing* (New York: Charles Scribner's Sons, 1975), p. 47-48.

184. See, for example, Robert Rouquette, *Saint Ignace de Loyola* (Paris: Albin Michel, 1944), p. 44,

185. Ibid.

186. H. Boehmer, *Les Jesuites* (Paris: Armand Colin, 1910), p. 192.

187. Ibid., p. 197.

188. See, Manuel David Orrio, "El cuchillo del matarife", *CubaNet* (www.cubanet.org), April 14, 1999, and Pablo Alfonso, "En auge el cuatrerismo pese a drásticas penas", El Nuevo Herald, September 1, 1999.

189. Walter Schellenberg, one of Himmler's closest collaborators, described in considerable detail his boss's fascination with the Jesuits. See, Walter Schellenberg, *The Labyrinth: Memoirs of Walter Schellenberg* (New York: Harper, 1956).

190. For an excellent analysis of the inner workings of Jesuit "democracy", see Malachi Martin, *The Jesuits* (New York: Simon & Schuster, 1987), pp. 228-229.

191. In his controversial book, *Inside the Criminal Mind* (New York: Times Books, 1984), Stanton E. Samenow demonstrates that the cause of their crimes lies with the criminals themselves - not with their

parents, not with their teachers, not with drugs or unemployment. And criminals commit crimes because they want to commit them. According to Samenow, crime resides in the mind of the criminal, and is not caused by social conditions. What a person does is fundamentally determined by what he or she thinks, and criminals think differently than most people. From the time he was a small boy on his parents' farm in Biran, Fidel Castro showed that he thought differently.

192. The true role of the Colegio de Belen Jesuits in the creation of the evil monster must be investigated in detail, and that role must be taken into account when, in a post-Castro Cuba, the Jesuits try to continue their "educational" tasks of creating evil monsters as if nothing had happened.

193. The Castro-Jesuit connection has been ignored by most researchers who have studied the Castro phenomenon.

194. For a detailed study of how the Jesuits transformed themselves from defenders of the Church and the pope into its worst enemies, see Malachi Martin, *The Jesuits* (New York: Simon and Schuster, 1987). In reality, the so-called Jesuit "liberation theology" is more Fascist than Communist.

195. Although it is clear that ideologically Fidel Castro has more affinities with fascism than with communism, it is likely that the real sources of Castro's fascism were not the Nazis but the Jesuits. On Jesuit fascism, see "Communist Barry Davis Obama: 'Who's Your Daddy?'", Vatican Assasins.org, http://www.vaticanassassins.org/2010/01/barry-davis-obama-4/. I have found only one person who shares this idea. Dr. Facundo Lima, a U.S.-based psychiatrist, expressed to Georgie Ane Geyer that Castro "had replaced the learned religious practices of his Jesuit teachers at Bethlehem College with his own brand of Marxism, his new religion". See, Georgie Anne Geyer, "Castro: The 'Knowable' Dictator", in *The Cuban Revolution at Thirty*, texts from a conference sponsored by the Cuban American National Foundation (Washington, D.C., January 10, 1989), p. 46.

Part Three: The Bogotazo

1. False flag operation: an intelligence operation designed in a covert manner so that it cannot be traced to its true originators. Usually, the real executors plant false leads to implicate another organization, group or country, as the executor of the operation.

2. The Hausman Report is mentioned in Gonzalo Sánchez, (ed.), *Great Powers: El 9 de abril y la violencia* (Bogotá: Planeta, 2000), p. 47.

3. Confidential Despatch No. 336, April 26, 1948. American

Embassy, Havana.,http://www.icdc.com/~paulwolf/Gaitán/archives/mallory26april1948.htm.

4. Jules Dubois, *Fidel Castro: Rebel - Liberator or Dictator?* (New York: Bobbs-Merrill, 1959) , p. 18.

5. Far from being a Communist, Betancourt's ideology was apparently closer to that of the Legion of the Caribbean, an organization of non-Communist leftists that included Costa Rican President José Figueres and Cuban Carlos Prío Socarrás. See, Nathaniel Weyl, *Red Star Over Cuba* (New York: Hillman/MacFadden, 1960), p. 69.

6. Alberto Niño H., *Antecedentes y secretos del 9 de abril* (Bogotá: Editorial Pax, 1949), p. 77.

7. Claudia Furiati, *Fidel Castro: La historia me absolverá* (Barcelona: Plaza y Janés, 2003), p. 124.

8. If what the witnesses stated is true, Castro lied. No priest was killed during the Bogotazo.

9. Pawley's statement appears in, *Hearings, Communist Threat to the U.S. Through the Caribbean,* Senate Internal Subcommittee, 86th-87th Congress, Parts 1-12, pp. 725, 756, 806; also in Mario Lazo, *Dagger in the Heart* (New York: Twin Circle, 1968), pp. 144-145.)

10. James Bamford, *Body of Secrets* (New York: Random House, 2001).

11. In 1898, during the height of the Spanish-Cuban War, the U.S. battleship USS Maine was destroyed in Havana Bay by a mysterious explosion. Although Spain immediately denied its involvement in the event, the American yellow press coined the slogan "remember the Maine" to whip up the feelings of the American people and justify a declaration of war against Spain. The ensuing war not only wrested military victory from the hands of the Cuban patriots but opened the door to so-called American imperialism, which in reality is the imperialism of the oil tycoons and Wall Street bankers who have illegally appropriated the American government.

12. They conceived it or simply accepted it, because Operation Northwoods, like other similar aberrations, was most likely conceived in the Harold Pratt House in Manhattan, headquarters of the Council on Foreign Relations.

13. For more on the Preemptive Operations Group (P2OG), see Chris Floyd, "The Pentagon Plan to Provoke Terrorist Attacks", *Counterpunch.com*, November 1, 2002, http://www.counterpunch.org/floyd1101.html; see also, Frank Morales, "The Provocateur State: Is the CIA Behind the Iraqi 'Insurgents' - and Global Terrorism,? *GlobalResearch.com*, May 10, 2005, http://www.globalresearch.ca/index.php?context=va&aid=67.

14. Nathaniel Weyl, *Red Star Over Cuba* (New York: Hillman/

Macfadden, 1961), pp 74-75.

15 . Ibid., p. 75.

16. Richard E. Sharpless, *Gaitán of Colombia: A Political Biography* (Pittsburgh: University of Pittsburgh Press, 1978), p. 173.

17. Dubois, op. cit., p. 19.

18. Arturo Alape, *El Bogotazo: Memorias del olvido* (Havana: Casa de las Américas, 1983).

19. On Castro's photographic memory, see Servando González, *The Secret Fidel Castro: Deconstructing the Symbol* (Oakland, California: Spooks Books, 2001), pp. 164-165.

20. José Martínez Matos (ed.), *Antes del Moncada* (Havana: Editorial Pablo de la Torriente, 1986), p. 50.

21. Mark Falcoff, "How to Think about Cuban-American Relations", in Irving Louis Horowitz, ed., *Cuban Communism, Fifth Edition* (New Brunswick, N.J.: Transaction Books, 1984), p. 547.

22. Mario Lazo, *Dagger in the Heart* (New York: Twin Circle, 1968), p. 182. A more exhaustive study of Fidel Castro as a pathological liar appears in my book *The Secret Fidel Castro*, op. cit., pp. 203-207. For an interesting analysis of the deep roots of lying from an unconventional perspective, see, M. Scott Peck, *People of the Lie* (New York: Simon and Schuster, 1983).

23. Arturo Alape, "Fidel Castro y el Bogotazo", in José Martínez Matos, ed., *Antes del Moncada* (Havana: Editorial Pablo de la Torriente, 1986), p. 52.

24. Ibid., p. 53.

25. Ibid.

26. Ibid., p. 54.

27. Ibid., p. 55.

28. Ibid., p. 57.

29. "Crazy Fidel" is one of the nicknames by which he was known from a very early age. Apparently one of his classmates gave him the nickname at the Colegio de Belen, and the nickname accompanied him to the University of Havana. See, Carlos Franqui, *Vida, aventuras y desastres de un hombre llamado Castro* (Barcelona: Planeta, 1988), p. 35. Due to his lack of personal hygiene, another of the nicknames with which he was known at the University was "bola de churre".

30. The fact that many of his classmates at the Law School accepted without protest that Castro had usurped the position of president of the students' association may have been because they all knew that, like the protagonist of a well-known Mexican ranchera song, Castro always carried a pistol at his belt and gave advice with it.

31. José Martínez Matos, ed., op. cit., p. 61.

32. Ibid.

33.   Despite his photographic memory, Castro forgets that the Ninth Conference was not a meeting of the OAS, but the meeting at which, as a direct result of the riots, Secretary of State Marshall, a secret agent of the conspirators controlling the U.S. government, forced the delegates to create the infamous OAS.

34. José Martínez Matos, ed., op. cit., p. 56.

35. Alape, Op. cit., p. 180.

36. Ibid., p. 181.

See, Peter G. Bourne, *Fidel: A Biography of Fidel Castro* (New York: Dodd, Mead & Company, 1986), p. 46.

38. Ibid., p. 55.

39. John Loftus and Mark Aarons, *The Secret War Against the Jews: How Western Espionage Betrayed the Jewish People* (New York: St. Martin's Press, 1994), p. 110. See also, Ladislas Farago, Aftermath (New York: Avon Books, 1975), and John Cornwell, *Hitler's Pope: the Secret History of Pius XII* (New York: Penguin Putnam,1999).

40. See, Noam Chomsky, *Turning the Tide: U.S. Intervention in Central America and the Struggle for Peace* (Boston, Massachusetts: South End Press, 1985) p. 199.

41. Mark Aarons and John Loftus, *Unholy Trinity: The Vatican, the Nazis, and the Swiss Banks* (New York: St. Martin's Press, 1998), p. 86.

42.   Cushman Cunnigham, *The Secret Empire* (North Ft. Myers, Florida: Restore Sel-Government, n. d.), p. 329. See also, Josh Katz, "On This Day: Aldo Moro Kidnapped by the Italian Red Brigades", http://www.findingdulcinea.com/news/on-this-day/March-April-08/On-this-Day-Aldo-Moro-Kidnapped-by-the-Italian-Red-Brigades.html;and Malcolm Moore, "U.S. envoy admits role in Aldo Moro killing", *The Telegraph,* March 11, 2008, http://www.telegraph.co.uk/news/worldnews/1581425/U.S.-envoy-admits-role-in-Aldo-Moro-killing.html. On the links between the CIA and the Red Brigades, see, Andrew Gavin Marshall, "Operation Gladio: CIA Network of "Stay Behind" Secret Armies: The "Sacrifice" of Aldo Moro", http://www.globalresearch.ca/index.php?context=va&aid=9556.

43. Tad Szulc, *Fidel: A Critical Portrait* (New York: William Morrow, 1986), p. 168.

44. Ibid., p. 70.

45.   The Castro interview was published in English in the Illustrated Weekly of India, and later, translated into Spanish, in the Bogotá newspaper *El Tiempo*. See, Angel Aparicio Laurencio, *Antecedentes desconocidos del nueve de abril* (Madrid: Ediciones Universal, 1973), p. 21.

46.   A few months after his return to Cuba, Castro married Mirtha Díaz-Balart.

47. Niño, op. cit., p. 77.

48. Information on *El Popular* in Aparicio Laurencio, op. cit., p. 39.

49. In CIA parlance, the Mighty Wurlitzer is a disinformative method that consists of inserting a "news item" in a small local newspaper, so that it is eventually discovered by the international press agencies, which then send it to all their subscribers around the world. The original source is soon forgotten, and the information, now assumed to be true, appears the next day in the major newspapers.

50. Jack Davis, "The Bogotazo", *Studies in Intelligence* Vol. 13, (Fall 1969).

51. Gonzalo Sanchez, (ed.), *Grandes Potencia: El 9 de abril y la violencia* (Bogotá: Planeta, 2000) p. 352.

52. The observations of the witnesses are mentioned in a secret report made by the Naval Attaché Col. W. F. Hausman, of the U.S. Office of Naval Intelligence. Cited in Gonzalo Sanchez, (ed.), *Grandes Potencias: El 9 de abril y la violencia* (Bogotá: Planeta, 2000) p. 47.

53. Herbert Braun, *The Assassination of Gaitán: Public Life and Urban Violence in Colombia* (Madison, Wisconsin: The University of Wisconsin Press, 1985), p. 168.

54. This inexplicable behavior of the revoltosos was mentioned in an article that appeared in *El Tiempo* de Bogotá on April 16, 1948.

55. Braun, op. cit., p. 168.

56. Arturo Abella, *Así fue el 9 de abril* (Bogotá: Ediciones Aquí, 1973), pp. 54-55.

57. Rafael Azula Barrera, *De la revolución al orden nuevo: proceso y drama de un pueblo* (Bogotá: Editorial Kelly, 1956), pp. 390-391.

58. See, Sánchez, op. cit., pp. 345-347; Alape, op. cit., p. 269; Laurencio, op. cit. p. 38; and Abella, op. cit.p. 23. The role of the radio stations closely resembles the role that the officialist press has attributed to cell phones and the Internet in the so-called "Arab Spring", also an artificial creation of CIA and CFR conspirators.

59. Abella, op. cit., p. 23.

60. See, for example, Alfonso López Michelsen, *Cuestiones Colombianas* (Mexico City: Impresiones Modernas, 1955), p. 350.

61. Hausman Report cited in Sánchez, op. cit, p. 53.

62. Ibid., p. 348.

63. Ibid., p. 349.

64. Abella, op. cit., p. 36.

65. Ibid., pp. 31-32;

66. To zero in: the process necessary for the sight of a weapon to coincide with the point at which the bullet hits the target. The process, although not very complex, is slow and cumbersome. It requires firing the gun several times while aiming at a target printed with a graduated

target and gradually correcting the sight error.

67. On the role of Communist parties and the Soviet Union in Latin America, see Cole Blasier, *The Giant's Rival: The U.S.S.R. in Latin America* (Pittsburgh: Pittsburgh University Press, 1986).

68. Kennan's memorandum is mentioned in Gonzalo Sanchez, (ed.),*Grandes Potencias: El 9 de abril y la violencia* (Bogotá: Planeta, 2000) p. 50.

69. See, *The Final Act of Bogotá, Foreign relations of the United States* (FRUS), 1948, Volume IX. http://www.icdc.com/~paulwolf/ Gaitán/finalactofbogota.htm. This is further evidence that Operation Bogotazo was based on the Hegelian principle of thesis-antithesis-synthesis: artificially creating a non-existent danger, which seems greater than the real danger planned by the creators of the psyop, so that those affected accept the real danger as a lesser evil.

70. Marshall quoted in Peter H. Smith, *Talons of the Eagle: Dynamics of U.S. - Latin American Relations* (New York: Oxford University Press, 1996), p. 148. This privatization of the sources of financial aid was an old idea of Nelson Rockefeller, one of the main conspirators of the CFR.

71. To understand the difference between information and intelligence, see Appendix.

72. Psychological warfare operations, also called psyops, are operations dedicated to influencing the emotions, motives, reasoning and objectives of foreign populations, as well as modifying the attitudes and behavior of foreign governments, organizations, groups and individuals. The purpose of psychological warfare operations is to induce or reinforce attitudes and behaviors that benefit the originators of the operation.

The U.S. Joint Chiefs of Staff defines psychological warfare operations (psyops) as those that: "include psychological warfare and, in addition, involve political, military, economic and ideological objectives" that lead to influencing the attitudes of foreign groups, whether enemy, neutral or friendly.

However, although by definition psyops are directed at foreign groups, U.S. citizens have been frequent targets of psyops created by conspirators. Two of the private institutions that the CFR conspirators have frequently used to plan their psyops against the American people are the RAND corporation and the Stanford Research Institute.

73. The Bogotazo also served the conspirators to get rid of a man they did not fully trust, CIA Director Admiral Hillenkoeter, and replace him with their secret agent Allen Dulles.

74. See, Jefrey T. Richelson, *A Century of Spies: Intelligence in the Twentieth Century* (New York: Oxford University Press, 1959), p. 217.

75. See, OSS Sabotage Instructions, May 7, 1943, and Simple

Sabotage Interactions, C. 1945. http://www.icdc.com/~paulwolf/oss/ossso.htm#sabotage.

76. For more information on the Morale Operations Branch of the OSS, see, http://www.icdc.com/~paulwolf/oss/ossmo.htm.

77. Black: Said of an operation whose true originator is kept hidden or falsely attributed to another source.

78. Black" propaganda can be both false and true. In psychological warfare operations, the falsity or certainty of the information is irrelevant, what matters is the effect it has on the minds of the people who are the target of the psyop.

79. FBI Office Dismantled, in Secret, No Distribution, Memorandum of March 6, 1947, http://www.icdc.com/~paulwolf/Gaitán/acheson6mar1947.htm.

80. See, Sir Norman Smith, Scotland Yard Report, p. 6, http://www.icdc.com/~paulwolf/Gaitán/scotlandyard.htm.

81. Ibid, p. 7.

82. Ibid., p. 8.

83. Ibid., pp. 13-14.

84. Ibid., p. 4.

85. Ibid., p. 15.

86. Angel Aparicio Laurencio, *Antecedentes desconocidos del nueve de abril* (Madrid: Ediciones Universal, 1973), p. 36.

87. Smith, op. cit., p. 15.

88. Ibid., p. 16.

89. One of the best sources of information on the War Scare is Frank Kofsky's, *Harry S. Truman and the War Scare of 1948* (New York: St. Martin's Press, 1993).

90. Weyl, op. cit., p. 84.

91. Child, op. cit., p. 77.

92. Francisco Fandiño Silva, *La Penetración Soviética en América y el 9 de abril,* (Bogotá: Nuevos Tiempos, 1949), p. 17.

93. Proceso Gaitán (hereinafter cited as PROG), Investiganción Oficial del Asesinato de Jorge Eliécer Gaitán, Casa Museo Jorge Eliécer Gaitán, Bogotá, Colombia, vol. 24A, f. 91 (testimony of Plinio Mendoza Neira).

94. Weyl, op. cit., p. 76. If what the detective stated is true, this conversation between del Pino and Roa Sierra took place only half an hour before the assassination.

95. U.P. report cited in Weyl, op. cit., p. 77.

96. PROG, vol. 1A, f. 5 (testimony of Carlos Alberto Jimenez Diaz).

97. Ibid.

98. Braun, op. cit., pp. 134-135.

99. Arturo Alape, *El Bogotazo: Memorias del olvido* (Havana: Casa de las Américas, 1983), pp. 251-252.

100. Rafael Azula Barrera, *De la revolución al orden nuevo: proceso y drama de un pueblo* (Bogotá: Editorial Kelly, 1956).

101. Azula Barrera, op. cit., pp. 379.

102. Ibid.

103. Ibid., pp. 390-391.

104. Bracker mentioned in Weyl, op. cit., p.84.

105. Willard Beaulac, *Career Ambassador* (New York: Macmillan, 1951), pp. 390-391. Due to the principles of compartmentalization and need-to-know used in all intelligence and espionage operations, the fact that Beaulac was present during Castro's recruitment at Mario Lazo's house does not mean that he was aware of the totality of the secret plans of the CIA and the conspirators controlling the Agency in relation to the Bogotazo operation.

106. Alape, op. cit., p. 226.

107. Ibid., p. 226.

108. Ibid., p. 223.

109. Ibid., p. 223.

110. Ibid., pp. 223-224.

111. ibid. p. 238.

112. Ibid., p. 231.

113. Ibid., p. 232.

114. Ibid., pp. 231-232.

115. Ibid., p. 232.

116. Smith, ScotlandYard Report, p. 11.

117. Alape, op. cit., p. 224.

118. Ibid, p. 226.

119. Ibid., p. 233-234.

120. Ibid., p. 234.

121. Ibid., p. 237.

122. Ibid., pp. 237-238.

123. Ibid., p. 241.

124. Ibid.

125. Ibid., pp. 239-240. 126.

126. Ibid., p. 254.

127. ibid., p. 259.

128. Ibid., p. 257.

129. Ibid., p. 260.

130. Ibid., p. 601.

131. Ibid., pp. 603-604.

132. See, Alape's interview with Castro in José Martínez Matos (ed.), *Antes del Moncada* (Havana: Pablo de la Torriente Publishing

House, 1986), p. 104.

133. See, John Marks, *The Search for the Manchurian Candidate: The CIA and Mind Control (*New York: McGraw-Hill, 1980).

134. In the case of Lee Harvey Oswald, everything indicates that, as in the case of Roa Sierra, the plan entailed his physical elimination once the assassination had been committed. But it appears that Oswald became suspicious at the last minute and fled the scene of the crime. Once apprehended, Jack Ruby, another agent of the conspirators, killed Oswald.

135. Mark Riebling, "Tinker, Tailor, Stoner, Spy", *Osprey Production*, 1944, http://home.di.net/lawserv/leary.html.

136 Ibid.

137 Abela, op. cit., p. 19.

138. Guillermo Tovar, "Nueva visión del crimen de Jorge Eliécer Gaitán que partió en dos la historia del país", *Colombia.com*, April 10, 2006, http://www.colombia.com/entretenimiento/noticias/DetalleNoticia3951.asp.

139. Smith, Op. Cit., p. 8.

140. Proof of how clueless most of the authors who have investigated the Gaitán assassination have been is that none of them have investigated the Gert-Roa relationship in detail. Only recently has Miguel Torres published a novel, El crimen del siglo (Bogotá: Seix Barral, 2006), focusing on the personality of Roa Sierra, in which he gives more details about this strange relationship. Unfortunately, Torres narrates how the idea of assassinating Gaitán came to Roa when one day he saw the leader exercising in the National Park. Yet another example of how fiction never surpasses reality,

141. See, Olga Lopez, "Colombia: 60 years since the murder of Jorge Eliecer Gaitán", *Tiwy.com*, April 9, 2008, http://www.tiwy.com/news.phtml?id=109&mode=print. López mentions the possibility that Umland may have mentally conditioned Roa to commit the crime.

142. See, William Tuner, *The Assassination of Robert Kennedy: The Conspiracy and Coverup* (New York: Thunder's Mouth, 1993).

143. Ibid., p. 196-198.

144. Marks, op. cit., p. 3.

145. Ibid, p. 6.

146. Ibid., p. 4.

147. The purpose of the CIA's code names (cryptograms) is to misinform about the true purpose of the program, and they have no meaning whatsoever. They are now automatically generated by a computer program.

148. All these elements are explained in detail in Marks, op. cit.

149. Smith, op.cit., p. 12.

150. Therefore, I do not think it was naive for Brian Latell, a former CIA officer, to have written that the coincidence of Castro being close to Gaitán during the assassination has given rise to "outlandish rumors" that Castro was involved in the assassination. See, Brian Latell, *After Fidel* (New York: Palgrave Macmillan, 2005), p. 107.

151. Confidential, Memorandum for the Files, January 2, 1958, http://icdc.com/~paulwolf/aitan/gringosintherevolution/topping2jan1958.jpg. What is most interesting about this document is that it reveals that Castro may have had a similar role, as a lookout or prompter, in the assassination of Gaitán.

152. On Castro's psychopathic nature, see Servando Gonzalez, *The Secret Fidel Castro: Deconstructing the Symbol* (Oakland, California: Spooks Books, 2001), pp. 309-315.

153. Francisco Celis Albán, "Así viví el 9 de Abril", interview with Gloria Gaitán, *El Tiempo*, April 8, 2001.

154. The fact that neither the Communists nor any other political party took advantage of or benefited from the Bogotazo is mentioned several times in the Scotland Yard report. See, Smith, op. cit., pp. 5-6.

155. Intelligence Research Project, Intelligence Division, G.S.U.S.A., Project No.4282, 13 May 1948, p. 2 [Classified Secret. Declassified on January 6, 1999.] http://www. project4282.htm.

156. Alape interview in José Martínez Matos (ed.), *Antes del Moncada* (Havana: Editorial Pablo de la Torriente, 1986), pp. 102-103.

157. The principle, formulated by Dr. Locard, is mentioned in Zakaria Erzinclioglu, *Every Contact Leaves a Trace: Scientific Detection in the Twentieth Century* (London: Carlton, 2001), p. 10.

158. Gerardo Reyes and Pablo Alfonso, "Castro hid stimony on Gaitán assassination", *El Nuevo Herald,* October 22, 2000.

159. Information on Spiritto in Daniel Semper Pizano, "La solución al enigma es novelesca, y podría estar cercana", El Tiempo (Bogotá), October 11, 2000; also in "Confesión del agente norteamericano involucrado en el asesinato de Jorge Eliécer Gaitán", August 19, 2000, http://www.vermail.net/justicia/confes/htm.

160. According to Spiritto, Pantomima was the name of the operation created by the CIA to eliminate Gaitán. We do not know if operation Pantomima designated the assassination and riots or just the assassination. On the other hand, in one of his articles Alape mentions the title of the documentary as "Operación Triángulo".

161. See, Gerardo Reyes and Pablo Alfonso, "Castro ocultó testimonio sobre asesinato de Gaitán", *El Nuevo Herald,* October 22, 2000.

162. This version of the Spiritto interview was described by Arturo Alape, "La Confesión del agente Espirito", *El Tiempo*, October 15, 2000, http://www.derechos.net/paulwolf/Gaitán/eltiempo15oct2000.htm.

163. Audio of the Gloria Gaitán interview reproduced in Equipo Desdeabajo, Cali, "Fragmentos de 'Pantomima': Colombia, 9 de abril de 1948", http://www.voltairenet.org/Colombia-9-de-abril-de-1948.

164. Ibid.

165. Gerardo Reyes and Pablo Alfonso, op. cit.

166. Arturo Alap, *El Bogotazo: Memorias del olvido* (Havana: Casa de las Américas, 1983).

167. Arturo Alape, "La confesión del agente Espirito", *El Tiempo*, October 15, 2000, http://www.derechos.net/paulwolf/Gaitán/eltiempo15oct2000.htm.

168. In his article, Alape calls himself a "historian", but his book on the Bogotazo is nothing more than a disorderly collection of unverified testimonies, which he accepted as absolute truth without having made the slightest attempt to verify, analyze or explain them.

169. Daniel Semper Pizano, "Quién mató a Jorge E. Gaitán", *El Tiempo* (Bogotá), October 11, 2000.

170. The American novelist Mark Twain once said that reality always surpasses fiction because fiction has to conform to certain rules, while reality does not follow any rules.

171. Semper Pizano, Ibid.

172. See, H.P. Albarelli, Jr., "William Morgan: Patriot or Traitor?" *WorldNetDaily,* (April 21, 2002), http://www.worldnetdaily.com/news/article.asp?AFRTICLE_ID=27312.

173. García Márquez's anecdote quoted in Juan Carlos Gaitán Villegas, "El misteriosos elegante del 9 de abril", *El Tiempo*, Bogotá, February 26, 2003.

174. *El Tiempo*, April 9, 1973.

175. Testimony of Yesid Castaño quoted in Gaitán Villegas, Ibid.

176. See, Rafael Azula Barrera, *De la revolución al orden nuevo* (Bogotá: Editorial Kelly, 1956), p. 450.

177. Ron Rosenbaum, "The Shadow of the Mole," *Harper's*, October, 1983; Seymour Hersh, "Angleton: The Cult of Counterintelligence", *The New York Times Magazine*, June 25, 1978; Edward Jay Epstein, *Deception: The Invisible War Between the KGB and the CIA* (New York: Simon and Schuster, 1989; David C. Martin, *Wilderness of Mirrors* (New York: Ballantine, 1980); Tom Mangold, *Cold Warrior: James Jesus Angleton: The CIA's Master Spy Hunter* (New York: Simon & Schuster, 1991); William Hood, Mole (New York: Norton, 1982), and David Wise, *Molehunt: The Secret Search for Traitors That Shattered the CIA* (New York: Random House, 1992), just to mention a few of the best known.

178. Aaron Lathan, *Orchids for Mother* (Boston: Litle, Brown, 1977).

179. According to British Prime Minister Winston Churchill, the Soviet Union's foreign policy was "a riddle wrapped in a mystery within a riddle".

180 Martin, op. cit. op. cit. p. 204.

181 Smith, Scotland Yard Report, pp. 9-10.

182. Angleton's physical description appears in Tom Mangold, *Cold Warrior: James Jesus Angleton: The CIA's Master Spy Hunter* (New York: Touchstone, 1991), p. 31.

183 According to his biographer Tom Mangold, Angleton "rarely portrayed himself in public". Mangold, op. cit. p. 31.

184. John Loftus and Mark Aarons, *The Secret War Against the Jews: How Western Espionage Betrayed the Jewish People* (New York: St. Martin's Press, 1994), p. 82.

185. Tom Mangold, Ibid.

186. Ibid., pp. 32, 359.

187. Ibid., pp. 43-44.

188. Ibid., p. 44.

189. Ibid., p. 361.

190. Ibid.

191. See, Allan J. Weberman "The CIA was Into the Assassination of Foreign Leaders From Its Inception", http://ajweberman.com/noduleX3-HISTORY%20OF%20THE%20CIA.htm.

192. For information on the behind-the-scenes struggle between Kennedy and Wall Street bankers, see Donald Gibson, *Battling Wall Street: The Kennedy Presidency* (New York: Sheridan Square Press, 1994).

193. See, for example, Lisa Peace, "This Was One of Those Occassions", *Probe*, July-August, 2000 (Vol. 7, No. 5).

194. Possibly the most comprehensive book on the possibility that Oswald worked for the CIA is John Newman, *Oswald and the CIA* (New York: Carroll and Graf, 1995). For information on how the CIA used Oswald as a scapegoat, see also Joan Mellen, "Who Was Lee Harvey Oswald?", lecture given at the Making Sense of the Sixties symposium at the Wecht Institute, October 5, 2008, http://www.maryferrell.org/wiki/index.php/Essay_-_Who_Was_Lee_Harvey_Oswald.

195. Servando Gonzalez, *The Mother of All Conspiracies: A Novel of Subversive Ideas* (Oakland, California: El Gato Tuerto, 2005), p. 178.

196. Greg Parker, "Bogota Ripples, Was Sierra a 'false assassin'?" *The Education Forum (*Australia), September 30, 2006, http://educationforum.ipbhost.com/index.php?showtopic=8067&mode=threaded&pid=170004.

197. Allan J. Weberman, *Coup D'état in America*, http://www.ajweberman.com.

198. Andrés Rivero, "1948: Fidel Castro en Bogotá ... ¿a las órdenes de la CIA?, http://www.andresrivero.com/informe2.htm.

199. See, Paul Wolf, "Dclassifying Colombia's Greatest Mystery: Notes From a Talk at CITCA Meeting in Chapel Hill, NC", June 13, 2001, http://www.blythe.org/nytransfer-subs/2001-South_America/ Declassifying_Colombia's_Greatest_Mystery.html.

200. In late 1958, Pawley was sent to Havana by President Eisenhower to convince Cuban President Fulgencio Batista to give up power and leave the way clear for Castro. Years later Pawley committed suicide under strange circumstances.

201. The erratic and indecisive behavior of U.S. President George W. Bush in the moments after he was informed of the attack on the twin towers of the World Trade Center indicates that, although he had been informed in advance that something was going to happen that day, he had no clear idea of the scope of the events that followed. One of those who knew for sure what was going to happen was Vice President Dick Cheney but, although both are members of the CFR, the conspirators apparently did not have much confidence in the incapable, vacillating and cowardly George W. Bush.

202. Ramon B Conte, *Hidden History of Fidel Castro's Crimes* (self-published, n.p., 1995), pp. 18-19.

203. The German philosopher Georg Wilhelm Friedrich Hegel (1770-1831) made the concept of change the cornerstone of his philosophical system. According to Hegel, an idea or principle - which he called the thesis - is challenged by its opposite - the antithesis. With the passage of time, out of this conflict emerges a new idea or principle that is but a synthesis of the two.

204. Nehru's commentary was published in *Newsday*, December 12, 1973.

205. It is likely that the alleged failure of the CIA to report the riots in advance was a pretext for getting rid of Hillenkoetter. At the time, the CIA Director had begun an investigation, at Senator McCarthy's urging, into why, when Marshall was Secretary of State, the State Department had granted visas to hundreds of Communists. See, Joseph R. McCarthy, America's Retreat From Victory (Boston: Americanist Library, 1965), pp. 10-11.

206. Willard L. Beaulac, *Career Ambassador (*New York: Macmillan, 1951), p. 236.

207. Portions of these CIA reports were provided by CIA Director Admiral Hillenkoeter to a Congressional investigating committee, and were later published in the press.

208. See, Senate Internal Security Subcommittee, *Communist Threat to the United States Through the Caribbean,* Hearings, Part II,

August 3, 1959, Appendix, "Communist Anti-American Riots - Mob Violence as an Instrument of Red Diplomacy" (staf report), p. 116.

209. This dichotomy, which I have called "the two CIAs", is explained in detail in my book *Psychological Warfare and the New World Order: The Secret War Against the American People* (Oakland, California: Spooks Books, 2010). See in particular pp. 131-144.

210. The Central Intelligencer Agency (CIA) was created in July 1947 in conjunction with the National Security Council. As its name indicates, the CIA's job was to coordinate and centralize the intelligence reports produced by other agencies, such as naval intelligence, military intelligence, etc. It was not until a year later that, illegally, CFR agents in the National Security Council authorized the CIA to conduct covert operations. But up to that point, these operations had been carried out by a remnant group of the Office of Special Services (OSS), which was headed by Wall Street lawyer and CFR agent Frank Wisner from the State Department. Years later Wisner began to have mental problems, was separated from the CIA and then committed suicide (or was "suicided" because he knew too much).

211. See, Senate Internal Security Scommittee, *Communist Threat to the United States Through the Caribbean,* Hearings, Part II, August 3, 1959, Appendix, "Communist Anti-American Riots - Mob Violence as an Instrument of Red Diplomacy" (staf report), p. 116.

212. See, Jack Davis, "The Bogotazo", *Studies in Intelligence* Vol. 13, (Fall 1969).

213. Ibid.

214. See, "Communist Involvement in the Colombian Riots of April 9, 1948", *Office of Intelligence Research (OIR), Report 4696*, U.S. Sate Department, October 14, 1948.

215. Compartmentalization and need-to-know essentially mean that each individual participating in a covert operation only receives information about the specific part of the operation he has to carry out and is unaware of the totality and purpose of the operation as a whole.

216. Francisco Fandiño Silva, *La Penetración Soviética en América y el 9 de abril,* (Bogotá: Nuevos Tiempos, 1949).

217. *U.S. News & World Report,* April 23, 1948, pp. 13-14.

218. Russell Jack Smith *The Unknown CIA: My Three Decades with the Agency* (Washington, D.C.: Pergamon-Brasseys, 1989), p. 38.

219. "Marshall Blames World Communism for Bogota Revolt", *Philadelphia Inquirer,* April 13, 1948.

220. Marshall's statement quoted in Jack Davis, "The Bogotazo", *Studies in Intelligence*, Vol. 13, Fall 1969.

221. *The New York Times,* April 11, 1948, Section 4, p. 10.

222. See, James A. Natham and James K. Oliver, *United States*

Foreign Policy and World Order (Boston: Little, Brown and Company, 1976), p. 58. For a closer look at the reality, which recounts in detail the anti-American activities of the "anti-Communist" George Marshall on behalf of international Communism, see Joseph R. McCarthy, *America's Retreat From Victory: The Story of George Catlett Marshall* (Boston: The Americanist Library, 1965).

223. For an excellent study of how Germany lost the war, but the top Nazis were spared, see Jim Marrs, *The Rise of the Fourth Reich: The Secret Societies That Threatened to Take Over America* (New York: William Morrow, 2008).

224. General George Patton refused to follow Eisenhower's orders, and this cost him his life, when the conspirators ordered their agent William Donovan of the OSS to assassinate Patton. On the Patton assassination see, Servando Gonzalez, *Psychological Warfare and the New World Order* (Oakland, California: Spooks Books, 2010), pp. 103-107; also Robert Wilcox, T*arget Patton: The Plot to Assassinate General George S. Patton* (Washington, D.C.: Regnery, 2008).

225. Earl T. Smith, *The Fourth Floor* (New York: Random House, 1962).

226. Arthur Herman, *Joseph McCarthy: Reexamining the Life and Legacy of America's Most Hated Senator* (New York: The Free Press, 2000); also, M. Stanton Evans, *Blacklisted By History: The Untold Story of Senator Joe McCarthy and His Fight Against America's Enemies* (New York: Crown Forum, 2007).

227. Earl T. Smith, Op. Cit.

228. Secret cables sent by the Soviet embassy in Washington, D.C., intercepted by Operation Venona beginning in 1946, proved that most of those McCarthy accused of treason actually collaborated with the Soviets. What Venona did not prove, however, was that the traitors were spying for the Soviets on orders from their real masters, the CFR conspirators.

229. According to some rumors, in May 1957, while convalescing from an attack of hepatitis at the Naval Hospital in Bethesta, Maryland, McCarthy was assassinated by unknown persons who injected carbon tetrachloride into his veins.

230. See, Carroll Quigley, *Tragedy and Hope: A History of the World in Our Time* (New York: Macmillan, 1966), p. 950.

231. Robert Welch, *The Politician* (Private edition with no place of publication, 1963).

232. Far from being a doctrine whose aim is to liberate the workers from capitalist exploitation, communism is a false ideology conceived by the international bankers and monopoly capitalists to better exploit the workers. If anyone doubts this, investigate the condition of Cuban

workers in pre-1959 Cuba and now under the Castro regime.

233. The operation by which CFR agents infiltrated and took control of the U.S. State Department is described in detail in Lawrence H. Shoup and William Minter, *Imperial Brain Trust: The Council on Foreign Relations & United States Foreign Policy* (New York: Monthly Review Press, 1977), pp. 148-156.

234. Edmond Paris, *The Secret History of the Jesuits* (Chino, California: Chick Publications, 1975), p. 65.

235. H. Boehmer, *Les Jesuits.* (Paris: Armand Collin, 1910), pp. 238-241.

236. Fidel Castro, *History Will Absolve Me* (New York: Center for Cuban Studies, n. d.), p. 62.

237. Hugh Thomas, *Cuba: The Pursuit of Freedom* (New York: Harper & Row, 1971), p. 819.

238. Everything indicates that the capture and assassination of Che Guevara in Bolivia was the result of a joint Castro-CIA operation. The direct result of this operation was that Castro inherited Guevarism, but without the troublesome Che.

239. Carlos Franqui, *Vida, aventuras y desastres de un hombre llamado Castro* (Barcelona: Planeta, 1988), pp. 69-70; see also, Georgie Annie Geyer, Guerrilla Prince (Boston: Little, Brown and Company, 1991), p. 49.

240. See, Jesús Arboleya, *The Cuban Counter-Revolution* (Athens, Ohio: Ohio University Center for International Studies, 2000), p. 12.

241. Thomas, op. cit., p. 812.

242. Mario Lazo, *Dagger in the Heart* (New York: Twin Circle 1968), p. 144; also in Jules Dubois, Fidel Castro (New York: Bobbs-Merrill, 1959), pp. 19-23.

243. Franqui, op. cit., p. 12.

244. Tad Szulc, *Fidel: A Critical Portrait* (New York: William Morrow, 1986), p. 191.

245. José Domingo Cabús, *Castro ante la historia* (Mexico, D.F.: Editores Mexicanos Unidos, 1963), pp. 133-135.

246. Tad Szulc, "Exporting the Cuban Revolution", in John Plank, ed., *Cuba and the United States* (Washington, D.C.: Brookings Institution, 1967), p. 79.

247. See, Mario Lazo, op. cit., p. 195.

248. Geoffrey Warner, "Latin America", in Geoffrey Barraclough, ed., *Survey of International Affairs 1959-1960* (London: Oxford University Press, 1964), pp. 478-479.

249. Castro's words quoted in Andrés Suárez, op. cit., p. 94.

250. See, report by FBI agent William Stevens, File # 105-655, 24 October 1962, quoted in Gus Russo, *Live by the Sword* (Baltimore:

Bancroft Press, 1998), p. 223.

251. See, "Communist Activities in Latin America", *Report of the Subcommittee on Inter-American Affairs,* U. S. House of Representatives Committee on Foreign Affairs (July 1967), p. 7.

252. Paul D. Bethel, *The Losers* (New Rochelle, N.Y.: Arlington House,1969), pp. 424-425.

253. Confidential information from secret sources that surfaced a few years ago seems to confirm what the Castro agents claimed. According to this new information, the notorious terrorist Carlos Ilich Sanchez Ramirez (alias "Carlos" and "El Chacal"), played an active role in the assassination of Somoza. The relationship between Carlos and Castro has been more than proven. When he had his center of operations in Paris, Carlos received logistical and economic support from Cuba. His contact was Armando Perez, a Castro intelligence officer operating under the pseudonym "Archimedes".

254. See, Daryl Lempke, "Cuban Spy Link to Ford, Reagan Death Plot Probed", *The Los Angeles Times*, March 19, 1976.

255. Leo Janos, *The Atlantic*, June 1973.

256. *The Washington Star*, June 25, 1976.

257. *The Washington Post*, July 27, 1975. See also, G. Robert Blakey and Richard N. Billings, *The Plot to Kill the President.* (New York: Times Books, 1981), p. 140.

258. *The Washington Post*, November 25, 1983; also in G. Robert Blakey and Richard N. Billings, op. cit. pp. 137, 176.

259. Anthony Summers, *Conspiracy* (New York: McGraw-Hills, 1980), p. 441.

260. *Human Events*, 24 July, 1979, pp. 13-15.

261. *Alleged Assassination Plots Involving Foreign Leaders, U.S. Senate*, November 20, 1975, 94th Congress, 1st Session, pp. 86-90.

262. Ricardo Rojo, *Mi amigo el Che* (Buenos Aires: Jorge Alvarez,1968), p.130.

263 Ted Sorensen, *Kennedy* (New York: Bantam, 1965), p. 802.

264 Gus Russo, *Live by the Sword* (Baltimore: Bancroft Press, 1998).

265 . Servando Gonzalez, *The Secret Fidel Castro: Deconstructing the Symbol* (Oakland, California: Spooks Books, 2001), pp. 169-186, 212-238.

266. Hermes Benítez, *Las muertes de Allende* (Santiago: RIL editores, 2006).

267. Hugo Guzmán, "El Sacrificio de un ciudadano de América Latina", *La Fogata,* September 11, 2003.

268. Jorge Timossi, "La Moneda, nuestro brutal 11 de septiembre", *La Fogata*, September 11, 2003, http://www.lafogata.org/chile/a5.htm.

269. See, Eduardo Mackenzie, "Cuba Nostra: Fidel Castro's State Secrets", http://www.amazon.ca/Cuba-nostra-Ala.../dp/2259201156.

270. AFP report in *Le Monde*, September 13, 1973.

271. For an interesting study on the GAP, see Cristián Pérez, "Salvador Allende, apuntes sobre su dispositivo de seguridad: El Grupo de Amigos Personales (GAP)", *Estudio Públicos, 79* (Winter 2000).

272. Noam Chomsky, *Turning the Tide* (Boston, Mass, South End Press, 1985), p. 67.

273 . Ponomarev quoted in Leon Gouré and Morris Rothenburg, *Soviet Penetration in Latin America* (Coral Gables: Univ. of Miami Press, 1975), p. 111. It is very likely that Ponomarev, like Suslov, Andropov and, of course, Gorbachev, were secret CFR agents infiltrating the CPSU.

274. Robert S. Leiken, "Fantasies and Facts: The Soviet Union and Nicaragua", *Current History*, (October 1984), p. 315.

276. See, Javier Ortega, "El viaje que saboteó a Allende", *La Tercera*, October 28, 2001.

276. Gloria Gaitán, "Declaración de amor a Fidel Castro", http:// gloriGaitán.blogspot.com/; also reproduced in *Revista Mariátegui* 01/02/ 07, http://www.nodo50.org/mariategui/index.htm.

277. See, "La colombiana Gloria Gaitán revela que fue la amante del presidente Allende", *line.es,* May 15, 2007, http://www.lne.es/galeria/ 1638/colombiana-gloria-Gaitán-revela-amante-presidente-allende/ 520667.html.

278 Sun Tzu, *The Art of War* - translation by Samuel B. Griffin (London: Oxford University Press, 1963). Sun Tzu is a Chinese general who lived 2,300 years ago. His book *The Art of War* is considered a kind of Bible of intelligence and espionage.

Appendix

1. Cited in Michael Warner, "Wanted: A Definition of 'Intelligence.' Understanding Our Craft". CIA's Center for the Study of Intelligence, https://www.cia.gov/library/center-for-the-study-of-intelligence/csi-publications/csi-studies/studies/ vol46no3/article02.html.

2. Quoted in Allen Dulles, *The Craft of Intelligence* (New York: Signet, 1963), p. 11.

3. Sun Tzu, *The Art of War* - translated by Samuel B. Griffin (London: Oxford University Press, 1963), p. 144.

4. Actually, the Democratic Party and the Republican Party are two sides of the same coin which I call the Repucratic Party.

5. See, e.g., David Wise, *The Politics of Lying* (New York: Random House, 1973).

6. The case of WTC 7, a 47-story skyscraper that was unaffected by the plane crashes and mysteriously collapsed on its own footprint, is so difficult to explain even with a far-fetched theory that it is not even mentioned in the *Report* of the commission that studied the events. As might be expected, most of the members of the commission were secret CFR agents.

Index